Imaging in Advertising

Southampton

The dominance of advertising in everyday life carries potent cultural meaning. As a major force in the rise of "image based culture," advertising spreads images that shape how people live their lives. While scholarship on visual images has advanced our understanding of the role of advertising in society, for example in revealing how images of extremely thin female models and athletic heroes shape ideals and aspirations, images circulated through language codes—or "verbal images"—in advertising have received less attention.

Imaging in Advertising, explores how verbal and visual images work together to build a discourse of advertising that speaks to audiences and has the power to move them to particular thoughts and actions. In this book, Fern L. Johnson presents a series of case studies exploring important advertising images—racial connotations in cigarette advertising, representations of cultural diversity in teen television commercials, metaphors of the face appearing in ads for skin care products, language borrowed from technology to sell non-technology products, and the illusion of personal choice that is promoted in many Internet web sites. Johnson argues that examining the interplay of verbal and visual images as a structured whole exposes the invasive role of advertising in shaping culture in twenty-first-century America.

Fern L. Johnson is Professor of English and faculty member in the Communication and Culture Program at Clark University. She is author of *Speaking Culturally: Language Diversity in the United States*.

Imaging in Advertising

Verbal and visual codes of commerce

Fern L. Johnson

Routledge
Taylor & Francis Group

NEW YORK AND LONDON

First published 2008
by Routledge
270 Madison Ave, New York, NY 10016

Simultaneously published in the UK
by Routledge
2 Park Square, Milton Park, Abingdon, Oxon OX14 4RN

*Routledge is an imprint of the Taylor & Francis Group,
an informa business*

© 2008 Taylor & Francis

Typeset in Perpetua by
RefineCatch Limited, Bungay, Suffolk
Printed and bound in the United States of America on
acid-free paper by
Edwards Brothers, Inc., Lillington, NC

Library of Congress Cataloging in Publication Data
Johnson, Fern L.
   Imaging in advertising : verbal and visual codes of commerce /
Fern L. Johnson.
      p. cm.
   Includes bibliographical references and index.
   1. Advertising—Social aspects.   2. Symbolism in advertising.
3. Culture.   I. Title.
   HF5821.J64 2008
   659.1'042—dc22   2007028440

ISBN 10: 0–415–97881–5 (hbk)
ISBN 10: 0–415–97882–3 (pbk)
ISBN 10: 0–203–92864–4 (ebk)

ISBN 13: 978–0–415–97881–1 (hbk)
ISBN 13: 978–0–415–97882–8 (pbk)
ISBN 13: 978–0–203–92864–6 (ebk)

For Will and Julius—who long ago gave me a good reason to pay close attention to advertising.

Table of Contents

List of Figures

List of Tables and Transcripts

List of Tables

List of Transcripts

Acknowledgements

My interest in advertising language over the years has been primed, challenged, and sharpened by many people. I began to pay serious attention to the language of advertising in the late 1990s when I was teaching the foundation course for the Communication and Culture Program at Clark University. What began as a small unit on advertising and culture grew into a major section of the course, and finally into a separate upper-level course. Students were understandably eager to study advertising and culture, and I had discovered a new direction for my long-standing work in understanding language and culture. I began more and more to pay close attention to the advertising that I saw in magazines and on television, point-of-purchase displays and billboards. I also began to listen carefully to the voices I was hearing in commercials on both television and radio. I often joked with my students that they might some day hear that I had been in a car accident because I was making notes about a billboard or jotting down something from a radio commercial I heard while approaching the university on Interstate 290.

Many people help bring a project to fruition—sometimes in small but important ways and sometimes in substantial ways. A number of students and colleagues were especially helpful as my interest in the discourse of advertising deepened and the project that is now this book began to take shape. I am grateful to the many students who have taken my "Cultural Discourses of Advertising" class. Our class discussions yielded many insights and often took productive directions that I could never have planned. The group projects always provided new ways of thinking about advertising discourse in its cultural context, and many of the papers and term projects presented incisive analyses of advertising texts and discourse innovations. I especially value what I have learned from a number of students whose projects and independent research provided opportunities for many wonderful conversations about advertising—Deepali Sarin, Jeff Johnson, Karren Young, Jen Clark, Yoichiro Fujii, Erica Ciporen, Alex Kelly, Rory Ruane, Meg O'Connell, and Bei Zhang.

Good colleagues are a treasured resource, and I have been fortunate to have many interesting colleagues who are always willing to take up the spirit of intellectual community to talk about work-in-progress. To those who went "above and beyond" by offering supportive and constructively helpful readings of portions of the manuscript, I am especially appreciative. Thanks to Marlene Fine, Don Rubin, Gail Dines, Tess Pierce, and Vonda Powell for giving time to my project. I was also greatly encouraged by my friend and colleague Parminder Bhachu who kept me thinking about the "30 minutes" plan, even when I didn't hold to it. There are also the people who are always there in a supportive way. My friend Carolyn Anderson seems to know just when to ask about progress and when to keep silent. My sister Mary Ho is endlessly supportive of my work and makes it a point to ask across the miles how I am doing.

The Alice Coonley Higgins School of Humanities at Clark University provided funding for expenses associated with part of the project, and I feel fortunate to be in a university where this type of support for the humanities faculty is possible. I presented early versions of parts of this project at various conferences and events, including the Clark Women's Studies Research Conference, Michael Bamberg's Psychology seminar, the English Department Colloquium series, and the Popular Culture Association Conference. Each of these experiences afforded the opportunity for me to develop and test my ideas. Questions and comments by so many colleagues helped me to see, to hear, and to think about that which I would not otherwise have considered.

Many people at Clark University helped this project along the way. SunHee Gertz and Virginia Vaughan have both been supportive department chairs. Edie Mathis, Terri Rutkiewicz, and Shirley Riopel Nelson in the English department office are endlessly helpful, good-humored people. I appreciate the support and intellectual stimulation of my colleagues in Clark's interdisciplinary Communication and Culture Program. Something interesting always happens at our meetings. Thanks especially to Matt Malsky (program director), Parminder Bhachu, Marcia Butzel, Sarah Michaels, and Ben Korstvedt for their intellectual companionship. Anthony Helm in the IT department not only answered all the pesky questions I had about scanning magazine advertisements, but also helped me decipher some of the technological codes in ads.

Matthew Byrnie, my editor at Routledge, has been very encouraging throughout the process of completing the book, and he deserves an award for his patience. The final stages of writing were not as smooth as I had hoped, but Matt stayed with me—more agreeably than I sometimes deserved. I am grateful for Matt's interest and support of the project. He "got" the idea from the beginning and helped me frame what would be the final project. I also appreciate the careful assistance provided by Stan Spring at Routledge in New York.

For bringing the completed manuscript to its final book form, thanks go to Stewart Pether, Production Editor for Taylor and Francis, and to the production services of RefineCatch in Suffolk, England—especially Bob Banbury who coordinated everything.

A special thanks to my sons, Julius and Will, both of whom were summoned a number of times to decipher a television commercial or to give their interpretation of something in an ad that I didn't understand. Their helpfulness was especially important when I was working on the chapters on technology discourse in advertising and on cultural diversity in teen advertising.

Finally, I thank Marlene Fine for much more than reading chapters. She helped me work when I needed to do that, offered to chat about whatever was on my mind about the book, lived with stacks of magazines and video tapes strewn about the house, tolerated my displacing social events so that I could work, and—as always—was my toughest and most helpful critic.

Chapter 1

Advertising images and discourse

We are long past a time when advertising was considered to be just one of many influences on culture—pushing its messages into the cultural mix, interrupting cultural spaces, distracting citizens from more worthy pursuits but yet not part and parcel with culture. Advertising today *is* part of the cultural environment, weaving in and out of our lives on a daily basis. Advertising, as such, speaks as one of the prominent discourses of our time. James Twitchell (2003) skillfully expresses the almost mythic qualities of advertising in today's consumer culture when he says that, "advertising is the folklore of a commodity culture" (p. 187). While long-standing concerns about the influence of advertising on commodity consumption (that is, with its impact in leading consumers to purchase and use certain goods and services and to view consumption as a critical cultural practice) continue to be an important research interest (see Scott and Batra, 2003), another significant concern about advertising implicates its role in culture more broadly. Advertising as ever-present in the cultural environment circulates images of cultural importance by contributing to socialization and honing attitudes and behavior. "Advertising is not just a business expenditure undertaken in the hope of moving some merchandise off the store shelves, but is rather an integral part of modern culture . . . [I]ts unsurpassed communicative powers recycle cultural models and references back through the networks of social interactions" (Leiss et al., 2005, p. 5). Some of these images are drawn from outside advertising while others are shaped in significant ways through advertising itself.

Advertising has gained cultural prominence because it is the engine of consumer culture. Consumer culture places extraordinary emphasis on goods as signifiers of worth and social identities, with product proliferation at its very core. In an essay recapping scholarship related to consumer culture since the 1980s, Eric Arnould and Craig Thompson (2005) point to its force when they say that, "consumer culture—and the marketplace ideology it conveys—frames consumers' horizons of conceivable action, feeling, and thought, making certain

patterns of behavior and sense-making interpretations more likely than others"
(p. 869). There are other forces to be sure, and individuals do make choices
from options they perceive as viable. Nonetheless, it is hard in this day and age
to fathom identity outside the context of consumer culture.

Academic interest in advertising and culture has been heavily dominated by
enchantment with the visual image and its primacy in the structuring of meaning. "Visual culture" has been a prominent concept in media studies for some
time, which is not surprising given the rapid rise of visual media such as
television and video recording in the twentieth century. The visual appeal of
advertising cannot be ignored, but I believe conceptualizing advertising as
steeped in "discourse culture" opens the lens wider on ways in which advertising works as cultural text. My interest in writing this book lies first in a
desire to explore the types of discourse images presented in advertising, especially the role of verbal codes in the imaging process. Second, I am interested in
focusing on advertising as a circulator of evolving ideological codes. In this
regard, advertising figures as part of our experiences as cultural beings quite
apart from the particular products that are being sold. How does the advertisement circulate its visual and verbal images within larger societal discourses,
and what images are circulated? Katherine Frith in "Undressing the ad: Reading
culture in advertising" (1997) makes the point that:

> [T]he background of the advertisement is as important as the foreground
> because it creates the context without which there can be no meaning.
> Analyzing the cultural content of an advertisement involves interpreting
> both verbal and visual aspects of the advertising text to determine not only
> the primary sales message but also additional secondary social and cultural
> messages. (Frith, 1997, p. 4)

The secondary aspects to which Frith refers are more than secondary in today's
barrage of advertising across media—print, television, Internet, mobile phone,
Personal Digital Assistants.

Advertising as an enterprise is centered on establishing the "commodity-as-
sign." The verbal and visual images featured in advertising draw from a know-
able world but then rework, magnify, simplify, contort or otherwise reshape
and sharpen the salient signifiers. The logic of advertising relies heavily on
ellipsis and inference, or the omission of items necessary to complete the text.
The ellipsis draws into the ad unstated, complex sign systems that are meaningful in a cultural, ideologically coded context and left unarticulated, and must be
inferred by the cultural reader. As Robert Goldman (1992) states it:

> The commodity-as-sign operates when images are allied to particular

products and product images are then deployed as signifiers of particular relations or experiences . . . [The] image is then arbitrarily attached to a product which has *itself* been detached from the customary relations of usage formerly associated with it. In this process, the product becomes equivalent to the discrete image . . . and begins to function as a sign of that image, so that when we think of the product we think of the image and when we think of the image we think of the product. (p. 18)

Guy Cook (2001) uses the term "fusion" to characterize the relationship of the signs in an advertisement to their more expansive, cultural sphere.

Advertising is a purveyor of ideological codes and cultural patterns through the arrangement of discourse elements that are calculated to establish certain images. An ad has "meaning" by virtue of the verbal and visual imaging of its text, as interpreted by a spectator. The chapters in this book address specific instances of imaging in advertising. As case studies, each chapter analyzes a different way in which imaging draws on language, and each focuses on issues that have larger social and ideological characteristics and consequences. In some cases, the analysis closely examines the relation of verbal and visual codes, and in others, a broader analysis of the communicative form and potential of the ads is at issue. The type of analysis presented in this book features critical interpretative examination of advertising in relation to culture, especially to the linkages of advertising and codes of meaning that are the building blocks for ideology. As context for these chapters, I first address the concept of imaging in advertising and then provide a brief review of the type of work that has been focused on language (and discourse more broadly) in advertising.

Imaging in advertising

My approach to understanding the verbal and visual elements in advertising is part of a broader interest in what I term "discourse imaging" in advertising. In the chapters that follow, I am working with the idea that images and the processes of imaging engage verbal as well as visual codes. Most people tend to think of images as activated by vision—literally through the eyes or even the lens of the camera. But we also know that language evokes the visual when there is no eye to see or lens to capture a picture. The visual is typically seen as the quintessence of advertising culture, and the term "image-based culture" has come to mean visual dominance in culture. Most people do, in fact, describe their consumption of advertising as *looking*. We say that we "look" at ads, not that we "read" them (unless, of course, the person uttering the statement is a cultural critic who uses the notion of "text" to mean any presentation of connected signs). Sut Jhally (2003), for example, characterizes the image-system of advertising, and other visual media, as having two basic characteristics: "reliance on visual modes of representation and the increasing speed and rapidity of the images that constitute it [the visual representation]" (p. 255). Robert Goldman and Steven Papson (1996), in an excellent treatment of the signification process in advertising, discuss the "floating signifiers" that recombine in ways that disjoint expected signifier–signified relationships as leading to "image banks"—where image means the visual repository of signs—photos, logos, graphic design—put to the ends of selling and product or service promotion.

Yet, almost any advertising image we can think of takes its meaning at least in part from language. Even in ads that carry no verbal elements in addition to product name, that product name as a verbal element is central in the creation of the ad's meaning. The composition of perfume and cologne ads, for example, often consists of three elements: a visual image of the product in its bottle; a visual image of a person in some pose designed to evoke particular meanings; and the product name, which has been selected for its connotations, such as "Euphoria," "Trésor," "Armani Code," "Clinique Happy," "Ralph Lauren Hot," "Ralph Lauren Polo Blue," "Guess Man," "Phat Farm Spirit of Man." Even if "Happy" and "Hot" smelled exactly the same, their meanings would differ because of the connotations evoked by their names. The linguistic elements circulate with the visual images in and out of the larger cultural discourses from which they are drawn and that they impact. The verbal elements are all the more prominent in Internet advertising, where new, extended formats of brand extensions are popping up with greater and greater frequency. Some of the more elaborate Internet advertising provides the viewer with "talking pictures" that unfold in narrative form using multiple resources of language.

In considering the totality of advertising in the context of consumer culture and as a major vehicle of ideology, language, then, must be seen as integral to the images that flow from advertising. Language has the capacity to frame, either sharply or more diffusely, an idea or disposition. Indeed, the entry for *image* in *The Bedford Glossary of Critical and Literary Terms* (Murfin and Ray, 2003) notes that, "At its extreme, *image* may be used to mean 'idea' " (p. 210). Applied to advertising, we might say that consumers make sense of advertising by interpreting the interplay of verbal and visual representation within a meaningful cultural context to form some type of meaningful impression.

Advertising moved some time ago from product demonstrations and information to image-based displays that are often only marginally related to the products themselves, or that so substantially abbreviate product information that interpretation rests on the viewer/reader bringing to the ad a cultural discourse more fully developed than appears in the ad's presentation. We are rarely presented with extensive product information, except where required by law or where the product itself would not be accepted without verbal elaboration (for example, advertisements for pharmaceutical products). Some technology products are also advertised with extensive text, as are a few ads for cars. What we are presented with in most cases is an imaging process using carefully selected words and visual symbols. Although fixed within the print ad, commercial, or Internet segment, the moment of any advertisement is a process through which the elements constituting the images that are perceived are in relationship to the ongoing accumulation of cultural meanings and personal experiences of the advertising audience.

Why is it important to understand verbal and visual discourse images in advertising? Richard Dyer (1993) in his book, *The Matter of Images*, discusses representation in a way that helps us think about image.

> . . . [R]epresentations are presentations, always and necessarily entailing the use of the codes and conventions of the available cultural forms of presentation. Such forms restrict and shape what can be said by and/or about any aspect of reality in a given place in a given society at a given time, but if that seems like a limitation on saying, it is also what makes saying possible at all. Cultural forms set the wider terms of limitation and possibility for the (re)presentation of particularities and we have to understand how the latter are caught in the former in order to understand why such-and-such gets (re)presented in the way it does. Without understanding the way images function in terms of, say narrative, genre or spectacle, we don't really understand why they turn out the way they do. (p. 2)

The point here is that the meaning of any image is always embedded in other patterns of cultural representation.

In media studies, the nature and significance of representation is associated most directly with the work of Stuart Hall. In what is considered a landmark essay on race and ideology, Hall (1981) identifies language as the central resource for elaborating ideological resources, and major media forms and institutions as a primary source for defining ideology. The role of media in circulating ideology—both by reiterating and transforming its themes—is especially central, says Hall, because media produce "representations of the social world, images, descriptions, explanations and frames for understanding how the world is and why it works as it is said and shown to work" (p. 31). This proposition about ideology and media can be applied to the specific medium of advertising. Through language and visual images, advertising packages discourse codes that grind out representations of the social world but can also disrupt, redirect and accelerate how the social world is conceptually configured. To take a prominent example, advertising in the US has for some time been a central force in the abundance of discourse codes that represent thinness as the ideal female body image and as central to the conception of (White) female beauty. The avalanche of fashion ads on the one hand and ads for diets, diet aids, exercise programs, and body alteration on the other keeps this image system alive despite the growth of critiques of this negative system of representation. The analysis in Chapter 4 demonstrates how advertising is more recently cementing the image of a wrinkle-free face as normative—not just aspirational—for middle-aged and older women. More and more, the message is that women should and must deal with their facial aging. Advertising also repetitively reaffirms racial polarities, especially the polarity of Black and White, even if new elements of racial configurations appear from time to time. Advertising does not act alone in these ideological trajectories, but it is central because of its day-to-day prominence in the cultural environment. Advertising presents a broad range of "public symbols" that have the potential to guide individuals "in their daily work of identity development and maintenance" (Richards et al., 2000, pp. 2–3). Who we are—individually, as members of groups and categories, as a society—is intimately tied to the image system communicated through advertising.

Defining discourse

The emphasis I am placing on verbal imaging in advertising is not intended to minimize the larger pool of discourse imaging elements. Rather, this emphasis serves to bring the significance of language to the forefront of our understanding of advertising as a cultural process. Advertising, taken as a whole, is itself a discourse, meaning both that it is articulated with conventions of practice and that it uses particular discourse elements to structure its meaning potential. To examine what the discourse of advertising entails, we need specific concepts and terms to guide our work. For this purpose, a working definition of discourse and several key features of discourse are presented here as a way of introducing the case studies that follow.

The most significant move in claiming the importance and not just the techniques of discourse, specifically language, in advertising was Judith Williamson's 1978 *Decoding Advertisements: Ideology and Meaning in Advertising*. Williamson argued, "advertisements . . . provide a structure which is capable of transforming the language of objects to that of people, and vice versa" (p. 12). Working within a semiotics perspective, she skillfully unraveled what she called "correlation," or the way in which advertising links two things "not by the line of an argument or a narrative but by their place in a picture, by its *formal structure*" (p. 19). Her work stands as a landmark in the study of discourse and advertising and, without question, represents the most sophisticated semiotic analysis available.

Discourse can be defined in a number of different ways. Linguistically, discourse is distinguished from isolated words and sentences, which are elements of discourse but not discourse itself. Discourse occurs when there is a meaningful stretch of speech or written text. Linguistically, discourse is unfolding, for example, when people exchange greetings, engage in conversation, or participate together in a meeting. Specialists in discourse analysis refer to these as examples of "language-in-use." Discourse could also refer to a written text, such as a "discourse on immigration reform" or even a love letter.

Another perspective on discourse comes from the field of sociolinguistics and is centered more on the resources used to communicate and how those resources function and have impact in their social context. This definition of discourse draws both on language and on systems for nonverbal communication and visual representation. When patterns of discourse are developed sufficiently so that they are well recognized in a society or group, they can serve important ideological functions. There are always a number of different and quite specific patterns of discourse functioning at any one time in a culture. Jim Gee (1992) provides a sociolinguistic explanation of discourses that shows the complexity of language in its cultural context:

> Each Discourse involves ways of talking, acting, interacting, valuing, and believing, as well as the spaces and material "props" the group uses to carry out its social practices. Discourses integrate words, acts, values, beliefs, attitudes, social identities, as well as gestures, glances, body positions, and clothes . . . Discourses are always ways of displaying . . . membership in a particular social group or social world. (p. 107)

Discourses also build up to create social knowledge and to regulate social behavior—a perspective on discourse developed extensively by Michel Foucault. In this usage of *discourse*, language and all that goes with it create meaning but also limit meaning. Discourse construed in this manner is the central defining system for culture, into which the individual is subsumed and socialized.

An approach called *Critical Discourse Analysis* (CDA) has been developed in recent years to decipher and explain how discourse works in society, especially to establish and maintain power relations. CDA is not, thus, limited to analysis of discourse but rather extends to *critical* analysis of the interlacing of discourse with political, economic, and social conditions. Norman Fairclough (1995) has provided a detailed treatment of how the CDA perspective can be applied to media. The analysis of discourse, says Fairclough, involves working with two interrelated domains: (1) communicative events and (2) the order of discourse. Communicative events are specific discourse moments that are enacted in the context of three facets of discourse (in this case, the reference is to language) that work together to create social meaning and impact: (1) *text*, including vocabulary, semantics, grammar, sentence organization, structure; (2) *discourse practice*, which refers to types of discourse and how text is produced, distributed and consumed; and (3) *social practice*, or how the discourse relates to particular patterns of social organization and communication. Text and social practice are brought together through the intermediary dimension of discourse practice. In his discussion of media discourse, Fairclough (1995) pointed out that discourse practice operates in two different ways. Conventional discourse practice is characterized by "normative use of discourse types" (all the perfume ads are pretty much alike in their structure), while creative discourse practice breaks these patterns, often combining discourse elements in creative ways or using new discourse elements where an older one might be expected (for example, when an ad presents text in the language of Instant Messaging, or presents cows on pogo sticks to signify the unconventional nature of a financial services company).

In periods of rapid social change, media discourse will be more creative, meaning that it will reveal heterogeneous and hybridic elements. We live in such a period of rapid change: political events are reported instantaneously, new products come to market every day, and information technologies facilitate access to other people, to the newest breakthroughs, and to the "newest news" in every conceivable category. Fairclough is quick to caution that discursive creativity in this context does not mean individual creativity but, rather, "is an effect of social conditions" (p. 61). What Fairclough calls the "order of discourse" provides the context in which any communicative event(s) can be critically analyzed. The order of discourse refers to the more general practices and properties of the discourse frame in which specific events occur. In the case of advertising, any particular ad would be a communicative event to be understood as a product of the organization of advertising as an enterprise. The order of advertising discourse includes business practices (for example, lodging the production of advertising in advertising agencies rather than in the business entities that need advertising to promote their products), conventions (for example, how ads are packaged, placed, and priced), as well as values (for example, creativity and the semblance of veracity). In the case of advertising, many communication events that are recognized as advertising appear familiar, with only the particulars changing from ad to ad (for example, ads for cars, shampoo and cereals). We also, however, see innovations, especially in the larger context of postmodern practices in which fragmentation, pastiche, appearance and destabilized meaning are prevalent. By its very nature, the order of advertising discourse will be susceptible to changes more so than, say, the order of religious discourse, which changes but not quickly, or the order of judicial discourse, which is stubbornly entrenched.

By expanding the reach of the discourse concept to nonverbal and well as verbal means of communication, the CDA approach offers a way to give insight to the relationship of any particular advertisements first to the enterprise of advertising and then to the wider cultural context in which both operate. There are legions of discourse moments of advertising, and many of these are interesting in and of themselves, sometimes because of their creative composition and sometimes because they skillfully redirect attention and meanings.

A 1997 Mercedes Benz magazine ad is a good illustration of different trajectories of interest depending on whether the examination is of only the specific moment or its position in a complex of social practices. The ad features a close-up of Marilyn Monroe's face against a red background. She wears sparkly blue earrings, and looks directly out at the spectator with her carefully made-up eyes slightly closed and her bright red lips parted. The word "Glamour" is positioned at the bottom right of the ad. The creative twist on the classic Monroe glamour portrait is the substitution of a small Mercedes Benz icon for the characteristic black mole on the left side of Monroe's face, slightly up and to the left of her mouth. Having pointed out some interesting semiotic features, we could stop the analysis at this point. As an advertising moment in 1997, however, there is much more to say once we engage the social context and prevailing social practices surrounding the ad. Monroe's glamour image is a skillful juxtaposition to Mercedes' stodgy image, and it is well timed to coincide with baby-boomers and their immediate predecessors who have come of financial age and have discretionary income available for luxury purchases. This is a time when expensive cars are in fashion, appearance and consumer culture are booming, and Mercedes is stuck with the image of a car driven by old, wealthy people in conservative clothes. The verbal element "Glamour" (presented in a font identical with the title of *Glamour* magazine) and the visual elements work together to facilitate a new connotation for Mercedes Benz. It's useful to remember that all of this creativity is channeled toward luring consumers to spend a lot of money to purchase a luxury car. Other examples of advertising at the same time would likely confirm a pattern in creative representations of products as a way of reconfiguring signs to attract an affluent consumer sector.

Exploited discourse elements in advertising

Several specific discourse elements have special importance in the circulation of images through advertising. Here I call attention to seven discourse features: ellipsis, connotation, paralanguage, tropes, point of view, person and narrative.

Advertising depends on ellipsis of varying types. Language *ellipsis* leaves out elements that are recoverable by the reader. Because ads are time and space constrained, ellipsis is a valuable element as long as what is omitted is easily recoverable by the intended audience. McShane (2005) presents a complex set of cases to show how ellipsis functions. In advertising, most ellipsis (with the Ø symbol used to mark where the elided content begins and ends) is either syntactic by omitting a grammatical chunk ("ØIt is/you areØ *A little bit older* ØIt is/you areØ *A whole lot bolder*"), or semantic by leaving out content that must be supplied for the statement to make sense ("*In just 5 minutes* Øwhich is how long you leave the lotion on your face before peeling it offØ, Øyou will experinceØ *the power* Øof ReNovisteØ *to restructure your skin*"). *Intertextual ellipsis* leaves out elements of the ad that are external to the ad but are signifi- cant for giving meaning to the ad. When an ad for a Sport Utility Vehicle places "SIZE DOES MATTER" in large letters, the full meaning of the text depends on knowing about a discourse outside the text related to the size of a man's penis or a woman's breasts. Similarly, an ad for a notebook computer that uses the tagline, "Less is more," is literally presenting an oxymoronic idea. If, how- ever, the reader can relate this tagline to a broader theme of downsizing and its relationship to quality, which is missing from the text in the ad, the message takes on a different meaning. Fairclough (1995) discusses intertextuality in advertis- ing, although not explicitly in relation to ellipsis. His comments are instructive:

> Intertextual analysis focuses on the borderline between text and discourse practice in the analytical framework. Intertextual analysis is looking at text from the perspective of discourse practice, looking at the traces of the dis- course practice in the text. Intertextual analysis aims to unravel the various genres and discourse—often, in creative discourse practice, a highly com- plex mixture—which are articulated together in the text. The question one is asking is, what genres and discourses were drawn upon in producing the text, and what traces of them are there in the text? (p. 61)

It is the trace elements that key the reader or viewer to retrieve what is missing and to fill in the ellipsis with material from discourses outside the ad.

Connotation is the suggestive meaning of a word or string of words. Connota- tions can be private and idiosyncratic or be shared broadly within a social or cultural group. To understand fully how connotation works, it is useful to begin by defining the denotative meaning of a word, and then moving to the suggested meanings that are in wide circulation within a particular cultural context. Colors, for example, have connotations, but these connotations are not universal. To describe a product such as the color of lipstick, for which temperature is not a salient property, as "hot" requires that we know some- thing through the usage of the denotation of "hot," meaning "high temperature, giving off heat."

In linguistics, *paralanguage* is the term used for aspects of voice and diction that shape and give meaning to verbal elements. Paralanguage includes pitch, stress patterns, intonation, volume, prosodic patterning in how the language is uttered and also facial expression, body position, spatial configurations, touch, and so forth. Paralanguage is also relevant to written text through choices such as font style and size, layout of the text on the page or screen, and color.

Tropes, which are also called figurative language and figures of speech, are commonly used in advertising to liken products to something else that can be relied on as meaningful within a cultural context. Many tropes provide needed shortcuts for advertising discourse because they invite a range of meanings that do not have to be stated. In this regard, tropes share something with ellipsis in that the missing elements must be recovered by the reader or viewer in order for the meaning to be supplied. Because modern advertising is steeped in the creation of appearances and semblances, metaphors are especially prominent in advertising discourse. If an ad uses the phrase, "a battle with the expanding waistline," or "battle of the sexes," the meanings called upon are of combat, aggression, and fighting with strategy and weapons. Likewise, when Chevrolet advertises with the tagline of "An American Revolution," the metaphor of revolution is used to create meanings associated with an overthrow of the past through powerful resources determined to succeed. The use of tropes in advertising has been the subject of several extensive analyses (Leigh, 1994; McQuarrie and Mick, 1996, 2003).

Advertising discourse always displays choices that have been made about *point of view*, which is established by the ad's creators selecting who tells the story or gives the message. Point of view positions who is speaking in the ad on behalf of the product or service and, by implication, what position the reader or viewer takes when presented with the ad. Barbara Stern's (1991) analysis of how the story in an ad gets told explains how literary theory can inform pre-sentational style in advertising. Stern lays out three different points of view that are used in ads: first person, third person, and dramatic characters. The first person narrative is in the form of testimonies or interviews using "I" statements and sponsor/firm statements that use "we" to refer to the entity. Consider these examples.

- Cleveland Clinic recently advertised using a picture of an empty leather chair, above which was written, " 'I'll be checking e-mail right up to my aneurysm operation. And a few days later I'll be discharged. If anyone's been sitting in my new Italian leather chair, they can forget their bonus. I'll see you on Monday, bright and early,'—signed Laurel."
- Toyota's Texas style print ad announces that, "They say thing are bigger in Texas. Just look at the trucks we build there."

The third person narrative is named as such because references to characters in the story or ad are made in the third person. Sleep medications often use this format, picturing a sleeping person with a voice-over uttering a statement such as, "Mr Matthews has discovered the secret to a good night's sleep." The perspective of dramatic characters uses mini-drama to speak for the product. This form of advertising language works essentially like a vignette performed for the audience, which is placed in the position of drawing a conclusion from what she or he witnesses the characters to be doing and saying. The caveman series of ads (and previously its gecko series) from Geico auto insurance is in this form. Although the mini-drama that unfolds has nothing to do with insurance, it provides a transition to the tagline, "GEICO: so easy a caveman could do it." Each point of view has strengths and weaknesses, which advertisers likely weigh carefully when constructing their advertising strategies.

Related to but not identical with the point of view is the *grammatical person* of the advertisement's statements that address the reader or viewer. Is the viewer directly called into the ad, or does the viewer have to position him- or herself as implied by the ad? Many ads use the formulation of second person "you": "you'll see . . .; "You can find out more by signing on to . . .". When this pattern is used, the discourse structure is usually in a pseudo-advice or lecture form in which the speaker in the ad or behind the ad is addressing the viewer or reader directly. The other option is to position the viewer as observer and/or listener.

Narratives can be effective discourse styles for presenting products and the lifestyles associated with them. Television commercials often use narratives to tell stories about their products, either by using the point of view of dramatic characters or by having a voice-over tell the story of the product in relation to its users. Print ads can also present narratives. On occasion, a print ad will use visual layout to show stages of a story. For example, an ad for Physicians' Formula Multi-colored Face Powders pictures a distressed looking young woman who is making statements represented in thought bubbles: "I look dull/ Almost fake/Great, I'm a mannequin/A dull, plastic mannequin/Oh look! It's a bird/it's a plane/it's plastic mannequin girl." Print ads can also imply narratives for the reader to enter into. The ads in the MasterCard campaign (both print and television versions) that present the various components of a particular pleasant experience with their price tags and the experience or some aspect of it as "priceless" invite readers and viewers to engage in similar narratives. They too will get their priceless experience if they follow the story's dictate that, "For everything else there's MasterCard."

Overview of chapters

The five chapters that follow examine trends in the way processes of cultural coding appear in the verbal and visual images of advertising. Each chapter stands alone as a case study, but they are related by a focus on significant discourse configurations and an analysis of how advertising discourse contributes to ideological codes prominent in twenty-first-century America. Chapters 2 and 3 both address discourse processes in advertising that are related to race (Chapter 2) and diversity representations (Chapter 3). Chapter 2 ("Smoke and mirrors —Circulating racial images in cigarette advertising") demonstrates how specific verbal images used in print advertising for cigarettes (especially menthol varieties) engage connotations related to race. The examples used in the chapter illuminate how verbal text, when paired with particular visual images, recirculates stereotypes of Blacks and African Americans. The analysis presented in Chapter 3 ("Keeping race in place—Multicultural visions and voices in teen advertising") addresses how cultural diversity is represented in television advertising placed in teen programs. Using a variety of capsule profiles of programs that are popular with teens, the advertising is examined in the context of the accompanying discourse of the program in which it is embedded. The analysis suggests that racial and cultural diversity continue to be relatively minimal in ads directed at teens, with some exceptions for programs that feature Black performers. In programs with largely White casts and (presumably) White audiences, commercials displaying Black situations tend to cement particular conceptions of Black youth culture. Chapter 4 ("Different tropes for different folks—Advertising and face-fixing) profiles a particular preoccupation, primarily for girls and women, with facial perfection as that preoccupation is fueled by advertising discourse. I coin the term "face-fixing" to designate the goal underlying a range of advertising discourses across the life-span that are directed at management of the physical face. The chapter draws attention to the use of different tropes for different age groups, and also addresses how advertisements for face-fixing products position the faces of women of color and men.

In Chapter 5 ("Madison Avenue meets Silicon Valley—Technology imprints on advertising") a new form of discourse, which I term "technographic," is explicated to show how the restricted language (argot) of a culturally prominent domain makes its way into advertising discourse. The concept of "community of practice" is applied to understanding the intelligibility of technographic discourse, and different types of technographic discourse that appear in ads for non-technological products are described.

The book concludes with Chapter 6 ("From Barbie to BudTV—Advertising in the Fifth Frame"). In this chapter, I consider the growth of Internet Brand Extensions through advertising that exploits narrative to develop an advertising frame fashioned to place the spotlight on individual identity and to suggest that the consumer is in charge of accessing advertising. Focused on narrative options catering to self-absorption, issues are raised about the potential displacement of community, social contact, and social responsibility when Internet advertising offers extensive soft advertising in the hybrid form of *advertainment*.

By nature, advertising is always changing, and we should expect some of its prominent discourse to be evolving as cultural interests and priorities evolve. I have provided a number of examples in each chapter to demonstrate the discourse features being highlighted. In most cases, the examples of advertising provided in the chapters are documented with a specific source in order to convey who is likely to be exposed to the advertising example and to assist the reader who would like to access the advertisement directly. Some of the examples may turn out to be durable, and others will already be a matter of history by the time this book is read. In either case, the examples as communicative events accumulate to point to discourse practices that are embedded in broader social practice and that circulate orders of meaning of substantial cultural importance. As a major public discourse of our time, advertising carries codes that are potent with cultural meaning and ideological implications.

Chapter 2

Smoke and mirrors

Circulating racial images in cigarette advertising

Cigarette smoking and advertising are linked in controversy. For a public skeptical about "truth in advertising," the exposure of the tobacco industry during the 1990s' litigation leading up to the $206 billion Master Tobacco Settlement Agreement (MTSA) gave the best evidence to date of deception. In that Agreement with 46 states, Puerto Rico, the US Virgin Islands, American Samoa, the Northern Mariana Islands, Guam, and the District of Columbia, the five largest tobacco manufacturers were ordered to pay damages for the costs incurred by states because of health problems caused by smoking (Wilson, 1999). The public learned in news story after news story about the tobacco industry's disregard for the known negative health consequences of smoking. We also learned about the tactics used to target potential smokers and to garner brand preferences. Another major accomplishment of the settlement forced the tobacco companies to curb their advertising to youth. Overall, the MTSA struck a major legal and financial blow to the tobacco industry and put that industry in a vulnerable, suspect position with the public. Venues and types of advertising became points of regulation, and increasing numbers of watchdog groups and researchers cast their eyes toward the tobacco industry.

Post-MTSA, the tobacco industry actually increased its expenditures on advertising. The Federal Trade Commission (2001) reported that while cigarette sales fell by 10.3 percent from 1998 to 1999, advertising and promotional expenditures rose in the same year by 22.3 percent to reach $8.24 billion. Prohibited by the settlement from advertising on billboards, other outdoor venues, and in public transit venues, the tobacco companies have more than compensated for these forced advertising reductions by stepped up placements in newspapers, magazines, promotional displays and events, and—more recently—on the Internet. By 2001, cigarette advertising expenditures had risen to $11.2 billion (Federal Trade Commission, 2007), representing an increase of over 35 percent; "incentives-to-merchants and retail-value-added categories [of advertising] comprised more than 80 percent of total expenditures" (Pierce and Gilpin, 2004). Advertising and promotion expenditures continued to rise, peaking in 2003 at $15.5 billion. Data available through 2005 show some decline since 2003, likely the result of financial strain throughout the industry (see Table 2.1 for data covering 1998–2005). Even with this decline, the increase in expenditures for advertising and promotion from 1998 to 2003 was a staggering 125 percent.

While attention in the years since the MTSA has been focused on enforcement of the bans on youth advertising, restrictions on advertising venues, and on the process for allocation to and use of funds by the states, the industry has pushed forward with its need to recruit new smokers to replace those who die and those who quit. The challenge is monumental considering that the overall prevalence of smoking has declined ever since the health impacts became known and anti-tobacco educational programs were launched. From 1965 to 1995 the incidence of adult smoking in the population dropped from 42.4 percent to 22.5 percent (Centers for Disease Control, 2004). By 2005, the percent had decreased to 20.9 (Centers for Disease Control, 2006c)—a triumph of sorts resulting from anti-smoking education, dissemination of health information related to smoking, and exposure of the tobacco industry's assault on the public. Like any producer of a product, the tobacco industry needs to find strategies for successful marketing, even in the face of massive public information against smoking. Targeted marketing has been central to this effort. For example, cigarettes were marketed specifically to women because women smoked less than men. The introduction of Virginia Slims in 1968 came just a few years after the prevalence of smoking among women started to decline (Centers for Disease Control and Prevention, 1996). Of great concern throughout the 1990s' litigation process was the targeting of cigarette advertising and particular brands to youth (Arnette, 2001), who are the best prospects

Table 2.1 Tobacco industry expenditures on advertising and promotions: 1998–2005

Year	Expenditures in $billions	% change from prior year
1998	6.73	—
1999	8.24	+22.4
2000	9.50	+16.4
2001	11.22	+17.0
2002	12.47	+11.1
2003	15.15	+21.5
2004	14.15	−6.6
2005	13.11	−7.3

Source: Federal Trade Commission (2007).

for replacing smokers who quit or die. Race too figured as an important component of targeted marketing and advertising of cigarettes.

Although not directly related to marketing and advertising, the tobacco industry's struggle to keep smokers addicted once they start smoking also shows up in changes in the cigarettes that are sold. A recent study by Harvard University researchers from the School of Public Health confirmed the presence of increased levels of nicotine in cigarettes and more puffs per cigarette industry-wide from 1998 to 2004 (Smith, 2007).

The focus of this chapter is on the way in which race is verbally imaged in cigarette advertising. More specifically, the analysis presented here addresses verbal imaging in cigarette advertising that engages the Black–White polarity of race and features Black/African American people. Such imaging is of concern both (1) because of the way it targets Blacks and (2) because of its role in circulating racialized images through the larger culture. The first concern is central to what advertising is all about, that is, focused marketing and promotional strategies aimed at boosting sales. The second concern adds an important dimension of social and cultural significance because of the ways in which advertising—and in this case cigarette advertising—is part of the larger system of cultural meaning in discourse that instantiates race in particular ways. Although the tobacco industry claims to be an equal opportunity solicitor of adult smokers and potential smokers, the advertisements examined in this chapter reveal the smoke and mirrors nature of that assertion. Norman Fairclough's (1995) argument for scrutinizing discourse in the media captures the concerns of this chapter: "a useful working assumption is that any part of any text . . . will be simultaneously representing, setting up identities, and setting up relations [with the audience]" (p. 5). Using this perspective, cigarette advertising, when it engages race, represents a particular cultural map through which identities are created verbally as well as visually. The relationship of the racial identities represented in the ads to potential audiences is yet another iteration of race polarities and, as will be demonstrated, racism. Central to the analysis presented here is a consideration of how racial connotations may be ignited by the combination of verbal and visual imaging present in many cigarette advertisements. Connotations range from those unique to particular persons to those that are widely shared. "A connotation may be perceived and understood by almost everyone if it is a product of or reflects broad cultural associations" (Murfin and Ray, 2003, p. 73). In the case of race in the United States, certain images reliably evoke certain connotations related to race.

The chapter begins with background information on race and cigarettes, including the demographics of cigarette smoking, the marketing of menthol cigarettes to Blacks, and the health and economic impact of tobacco use for Blacks in the US. The second section reviews research focused on the ways in which African Americans have been and continue to be targeted in cigarette advertising. The third section provides a number of examples of how cigarette advertising draws on long-standing cultural connotations about race in both its visual and verbal imaging. The fourth section examines several cases of cigarette advertising where the verbal elements contrast sharply in association with visual representation of Black and White people who are pictured in the ads. The examples in this section are intended to implicate cigarette advertising as a racialized text that positions the Black smoker/potential smoker in the larger cultural ideology of race by drawing on connotations carrying racial meanings. The chapter concludes with several observations about racial texts in advertising as part of the cultural environment.

Race and cigarettes

Demographics

The demographics of cigarette smoking reveal differences among major race and ethnic groups and between men and women. A National Health Interview Survey administered in 2005 (Centers for Disease Control, 2006c) reveals a great deal of variability underneath the overall smoking rate statistics (see Table 2.2). The 2005 estimates place the rate of smoking for non-Hispanic Whites in the US at 21.9 percent: 20.0 percent for White women and 24.0 percent of White men. The prevalence of smoking among non-Hispanic Blacks was similar overall to Whites at 21.5 percent of the Black population; the gender pattern, however, was more skewed with Black males smoking at higher rates than Black females (26.7 percent and 17.3 percent, respectively).

During the 1990s, the prevalence of smoking among Black high school students increased 80 percent, but—fortunately—that trend reversed between 1997 and 2003 with a decline of 33 percent, from 22.7 percent of Black high school students to 15.1 percent (reported by the American Lung Association, 2004). Data for 2005 reported by the Centers for Disease Control and Prevention (2006a) estimate that among high school students, approximately 13 percent of Black students smoke compared to higher rates among teenage Whites (26 percent) and Hispanics (22 percent). The same report also includes data on smoking by middle school youth pointing to similar smoking rates among Whites, Blacks, and Hispanics (9 percent, 10 percent and 8 percent, respectively) but a substantially lower rate of 3 percent among Asian Americans.

As context for these data on the prevalence of cigarette smoking among Blacks in the US, substantially fewer Asians in the US smoke, with an overall prevalence of 13.3 percent, which is approximately a 1 percent increase from 2001. The differential rate of smoking for Asian-ancestry men and women is

Table 2.2 Percentage of adult smokers for selected groups in the United States: 2005 (based on National Health Interview Survey)

Group	Men	Women	TOTAL
Total Population	23.9	18.1	20.9
Race/Ethnicity			
White*	24.0	20.0	21.9
Black*	26.7	17.3	21.5
Hispanic	21.1	11.1	16.2
American Indian/Alaskan Native*	37.5	26.8	32.0
Asian*	20.6	6.1	13.3
Education Level			
GED diploma	47.5	38.8	43.2
High School graduate	28.8	20.7	24.6
Undergraduate degree	11.9	9.6	10.7
Graduate degree	6.9	7.4	7.1
Poverty Status			
At or above	23.7	17.6	20.6
Below	34.3	26.9	29.9
Unknown	23.9	18.1	20.9

*non-Hispanic.

Source: Centers for Disease Control and Prevention (2006c).

extreme, with the male rate at 20.6 percent and the female rate at only 6.1 percent. Hispanics overall smoked somewhat less in 2005 than non-Hispanics: their overall prevalence was 16.2 percent, skewed heavily toward men at 21.1 percent compared to women at 11.1 percent. Of the ethnic groups that have been tracked, the highest incidence of smoking occurs among American Indians and Alaskan Natives, with a 32.0 percent smoking rate (37.5 percent men and 26.8 percent women).

Educational attainment is also implicated in the demographics of smoking. The more education one has, the less likely that person is to be a smoker (Centers for Disease Control, 2006c). The 2005 data show a huge range, with 43.2 percent smokers among those who have attained only a GED diploma compared to 7.1 percent smokers for those who have attained a graduate degree.

The case of Black/African American positioning in cigarette advertising is significant for several reasons related to the sale of cigarettes: this racial group represents easily segmented market potential, has a strong preference for menthol, and experiences steep health consequences from smoking.

Market and menthol preference

First, in the overall context of declining rates of cigarette smoking, the overall percentage of adult, non-Hispanic Blacks who smoke is, as noted above, somewhat lower than that for White non-Hispanics who smoke. The gender spread, however, is greater. More Black men smoke, making them a vulnerable target for advertising efforts to sustain as well as increase their smoking. Fewer Black women smoke, also making them a clear target for efforts to recruit new smokers. Both sides of this gender equation fuel the industry's need to make smoking viable to Black youth. Second, Black smokers prefer menthol cigarettes.

The differential in menthol preference between Blacks and Whites is huge, with three-quarters of Blacks preferring menthol cigarettes compared to one-quarter of Whites (Centers for Disease Control, 2003). Advertising and "public relations" efforts by the tobacco industry skillfully created this differential. Philip Gardiner (2004) explains:

> Through the use of television and other advertising media, coupled with culturally tailored images and messages, the tobacco industry "African Americanized" menthol cigarettes. The tobacco industry successfully positioned mentholated products, especially Kool, as young, hip, new, and healthy. During the time that menthols were gaining a large market share in the African American community, the tobacco industry donated funds to African American organizations hoping to blunt the attack on their products. (p. S55)

Data from the 2001 National Household Survey on Drug Abuse (2003) documented the particular brands preferred, with Black smokers in recent years overwhelmingly preferring Newport (45.2 percent) followed by Kool (10.7 percent). The same national study found that Whites and Hispanics prefer Marlboro cigarettes (44.5 percent and 59.5 percent, respectively). Within these broad preference groups, several more specific profiles are significant: there is greater preference for menthol cigarettes by women compared to men, middle school aged youth compared to adults, and some Asian ancestry groups (likely Filipinos) compared to Whites (Sutton and Robinson, 2004). These preference profiles raise the question of why preference matters. In the case of African Americans, preference matters in one very important way. According to the American Cancer Society (2004), the additional adverse effect of menthol cigarettes is that "people who smoke menthol cigarettes can inhale deeper and hold the smoke inside longer than smokers of nonmenthol cigarettes."

Health effects

The health consequences of smoking for African Americans are more severe compared to the White population (Health disparities, 2005). The preference for menthol cigarettes is a broad, causal umbrella for a range of specific health effects of smoking. Information compiled by the Centers for Disease Control (2003) points to a number of serious health issues related to cigarette smoking that have an especially adverse impact on Blacks: (1) Blacks have higher rates of lung cancer, with Black men over 50 percent more likely than White men to develop lung cancer; (2) cerebro-vascular disease and stroke—both elevated by smoking—are twice as high for Black women and men than for their White counterparts; and (3) controlling for the number of cigarettes smoked, Black smokers have higher levels of serum cotinine, which is metabolized nicotine, than do White smokers. Added to these adverse factors, African American smokers are more likely to smoke brands with higher nicotine levels than are White smokers (American Lung Association, 2003).

Economic consequences

In addition to the health consequences, smoking has disproportionate economic consequences for Blacks compared to Whites. Blacks in aggregate earn less than Whites, and cigarettes are increasingly a costly habit. The median income in 2005 for Black households was $30,858 compared to $50,784 for White households (US Census Bureau News, 2006). It is difficult to gauge a true average for how much it costs to smoke cigarettes because of variation from state to state. However, for the purpose of illustration, we can use the CDC estimate that in 2004, an average pack of cigarettes cost $3.90 in the US, excluding state and local taxes, which vary greatly (State cigarette excise tax rates and rankings, 2004). If a hypothetical smoker smokes five packs of cigarettes each week with an average price of $4.00 per pack, she or he spends in excess of $1,000 annually on this dangerous habit. Like any fixed-price consumer good, the real cost to the consumer increases as income decreases. Translation: the cost of cigarettes on average is dramatically larger as a percent of income for those in Black households than for those in White households. Health care costs add to the economic impact of smoking.

Tobacco industry targeting of African Americans

Evidence that the tobacco industry specifically targets African Americans comes from a variety of sources. One line of research has investigated explicit racial components in cigarette advertising. Research focused on cigarette ads

in *Ebony* and *Life* magazines that were published in the 1950s and 1960s documented the almost exclusive use of Black models (especially athletes) in *Ebony*
while at the same time no Black models appear in ads placed in *Life* (Pollay
et al., 1992). Another study (Cummings et al.,1987) found both quantitative
differences and cigarette type differences in ads placed in magazines with wide
circulation among Black readers (*Jet, Ebony* and *Essence*) compared to those
placed in magazines with predominantly White readership (*Newsweek, Time,
People* and *Mademoiselle*): the magazines targeted at Blacks contained both more
cigarette ads and more ads overall for menthol brand cigarettes than did the
magazines targeted at Whites.

One of the best-documented cases focuses on RJ Reynolds (RJR), which is
best known for the Camel and Salem brands. RJR documents that were made
public as part of the MTSA contain specific content showing the intent of the
company to use particular strategies to entice Black smokers (Balbach et al.,
2003). The most blatant tactic was the development of a cigarette named
"Uptown" in 1989/90. RJR designed this cigarette specifically for the African
American market niche. The brand was ready for marketing and sales when
RJR met with substantial resistance headed by a Philadelphia group that took
the name "Uptown Coalition." Protest derailed "Uptown," but the company
was not deterred from its efforts to woo African Americans.

RJR has pitched mentholated cigarettes to African Americans for many
years. Subsequent to the tobacco settlement in 1998, RJR stepped up advertising in magazines read by African Americans. Balbach et al. (2003) analyzed the
content of RJR cigarette ads placed in *Jet, Ebony*, and *Essence*—three magazines
oriented to Blacks—compared to the RJR ads placed in *People*. For the years
1999–2000, the themes in the ads placed in the Black-oriented magazines
compared to *People* were significantly more likely to emphasize "escape and
fantasy" and "expensive objects" and somewhat more likely to feature "nightlife." The difference between Black-oriented magazines and *People* in the incidence of ads for menthol cigarettes left no doubt about whom RJR sought for
their minty brands: 98 percent of the 43 RJR ads placed in the Black-oriented
magazines promoted menthol cigarettes, but not even one ad for menthol
cigarettes appeared in *People*.

RJR's reach expanded in 2004 when the company merged with Brown and
Williamson (the makers of Kool and Lucky Strike). The new parent company, Reynolds American, Inc., has three companies: (1) RJ Reynolds, maker
of Camel, Winston, Kool, Salem, and Doral; (2) Santa Fe Natural Tobacco
Company, maker of Natural American Spirit; and (3) Lane Limited, maker of
Dunhill products and various other tobacco products (Reynolds American,
n.d.). What is especially relevant about this merger for the case of advertising
to African Americans is that RJR now oversees a larger slice of the menthol

market. (The top selling menthol cigarette is Newport, produced by P. Loril-lard; see National Household Survey on Drug Abuse, 2003.) The advertising campaign for Kool that targeted Black youth with hip-hop style is a clear case of the attempts to lure more African American youth to their brand (more will be said about the ads in this campaign later in the chapter). After substantial protest, the new RJR agreed to curtail advertising using the hip-hop theme and to pay $1.46 million toward youth smoking prevention programs (Herman, 2004).

The cultural text of racialized ads

The polarity of race in the United States as a Black–White concept shows up not only in the particular ways that advertisers cultivate smokers but also in the racialized discourse from which advertisers draw when constructing their compact sales messages. The alluring strategies that have been used to target the African American population for cigarettes in general and menthol products in particular contribute to circulating a racialized signification system marked by the ideology of race in the United States. These two axes—advertising strategy on the one hand and cultural text on the other—intersect to create a semiology of race that is displayed in ads not just in the visual images that highlight racial categories and in the choice of advertising venues, but also within the verbal element structure of cigarette advertisements. Through the case examples described below, we shall see how this semiology of race as a Black–White polarity is evident in the interplay of verbal and visual images found in cigarette ads. The verbal images work in conjunction with the visual images because they draw on and reinforce a broad cultural ideology of race. This process will be demonstrated through a number of illustrations from cigarette advertising, including detailed case examples from advertising campaigns for Benson & Hedges, Salem and Kool. These examples demonstrate how race is textualized to create ongoing stories about Blacks and Whites.

First a word about "Joe Camel" . . .

The case of "Joe Camel"—now retired as the king of cigarette advertising—is notorious. "Old Joe," who appeared on the scene as a cartoon character in 1978, appealed to youth through his portrayal as a guy who enjoyed fun and mischief. The ads featured Joe in a number of different scenes, included Joe riding a motorcycle, drinking with friends, playing pool, riding in a convertible and just hanging out with friends; he was seen as a pilot with a blond "girl" in the background, in Hollywood with the same blond in the background, doing a radio show, and in many other situations. RJR added the verbal image of "smooth character" to Joe, rounding out the discourse of fun on the cool and wild side.

Once the tobacco industry was in the throes of litigation, the suspected link between this tobacco icon and the appeal of cigarette smoking among young audiences received massive media coverage and research attention. The Federal Trade Commission reopened an earlier investigation of the link between Joe's appeal and youth advertising in May of 1997, and the RJ Reynolds Tobacco Company announced its decision to "retire" Joe in July of 1997 (Slade, 1999).

The story of Joe Camel as a cultural icon holds special interest because he made his debut long after the 1971 ban on cigarette advertising on television. The life of Joe Camel was portrayed in magazines, point-of-sale displays, events carrying Camel sponsorship, and on large, attention-grabbing billboards. Joe's face and identity seemed to be everywhere. I recall the huge billboard of Joe Camel looming over Harvard Square as I drove into Cambridge. Early in the Joe Camel campaign, the impact of this cigarette icon became clear. In 1991, the *Journal of the American Medical Association* (Fischer et al., 1991) reported on research that found that 91 percent of 6-year-olds and 30 percent of 3-year-olds could recognize Joe Camel as a symbol for Camel cigarettes. For the 6-year-olds, recognition of Joe matched that for Mickey Mouse as the icon for Disney. Another study showed that after Joe Camel was introduced, Camel's share of the underage, teen market increased from 0.5 percent to 32.8 percent (DiFranza et al., 1991): a whopping 656 percent increase!

As the important allegations and discoveries about Joe Camel's appeal to youth took center stage, another socially significant marketing aspect received little if any notice: in some of the later ads, Joe's visage was presented in a racialized manner. Magazine ads for Camel Menthol Lights introduced in January and February of 1997—just a short time before Joe's "retirement" was announced in July 1997—presented the camel as a cool dude sporting a Black, shortly clipped, stylized flat-top hairstyle (see Figure 2.1 taken from *Ebony*, February 1997). All three of the camel guys in the ad in Figure 2.1 are shown with cigarettes: one holds a cigarette in his hand, with the cigarette jutting forward in large distorted size, while the other two dangle cigarettes from their mouths, with one of them thrusting an open pack of Camels forward to the would-be smoker. The word MENTHOL appears in extra-large capital letters at the top of the ad. This *Ebony* ad for Camel Menthols is especially conspicuous because it covers two pages, positioned vertically so that the magazine reader has to stop and attend to the ad by rotating the magazine 90 degrees; the ad is also set up to be pulled out for poster display. In the context of *Ebony* magazine, it is difficult to miss the racialization of the visual images of Black-like camels combined with the large display verbal image announcing "MENTHOL." It appears that RJR was making one final effort

Figure 2.1 **Camel** Menthol Lights "Joe and Friends" (*Ebony*, February 1997).

Figure 2.2 **Camel** Lights "Joe and Friends" (*Ebony*, July 1997).

before Joe's retirement to push Camels to the Black audience by giving the well-known Joe campaign a racialized, menthol signification.

Yet another ad placed in Ebony during the same period of time (July 1997) depicts three camels just hangin' out together on a fire escape of a brick building, likely intended to represent an urban apartment building (see Figure 2.2).

Although not advertising menthols, a close examination of the camels makes clear that for the two who are not wearing a cap, the hair is short and black. Again, all three of these camel guys are shown with cigarettes.

Prominent themes of racialized verbal imaging in cigarette advertising

Newport pleasure

One prominent theme that the tobacco industry uses to target African Americans is the association of *escape and fantasy* with cigarette smoking (Balbach et al., 2003). This theme emerges repeatedly as an appeal to hedonism through the verbal image of *pleasure*.

Ads for Lorillard's Newport cigarettes—the number one brand preference among African Americans—have long used the verbal image of *pleasure* as the major verbal image and branding element. Beginning in 1972, the Newport "pleasure" branding endures to this day. The ads all focus on either a couple or a small group of lively young adults enjoying themselves in some sort of fun activity. The initial ad campaign, which proclaimed Newport to be "Alive with pleasure!" featured White smokers, but this theme transferred effectively to the Black audience when that shift was made in the late 1980s. The reasoning for the shift was simple: as cigarette sales and the number of smokers in the US declined as a consequence of effective publicity about the negative health effects of smoking, new markets and refined marketing became increasingly important to tobacco companies. In 1979, the sales of Newport equaled 9.8 billion cigarettes, placing this brand eighteenth in the ranking for cigarettes sold (Borio, 1997). Lorillard's campaign to sell Newports to African Americans paid off for the company, as shown in the sales figures for 1990, when Newport rose to fifth place, at 24 billion cigarettes (Borio, 1997). Although the verbal image of pleasure linked Whites as well as Blacks to Lorillard's menthol brand, the rise of this image in association with Black smokers was conspicuous. Unlike many ads using Black models, the Newport ads typically featured dark-skinned models. The words "Alive with pleasure!" provided the verbal frame for visuals of the good life filled with smiles, romance and friendships.

Newport later changed "Alive with pleasure!" to "Newport pleasure!" One 1999 ad in *Ebony* and elsewhere (see Figure 2.3) shows three attractive, young African American adults—a male in the center flanked by two females—in bathing suits, engaged in an active pose suggestive of beach volleyball. The three are flashing bright white teeth through their big smiles in a scene labeled "Newport pleasure!" One of the women is holding a cigarette in her hand. The connotations of "pleasure" with the visual representation of the three young,

Figure 2.3 **Newport** Pleasure! (*Ebony*, August 1999).

Black adults is intriguing because of the lack of background for the scene. The only clues to the signification of a beach scene are the bathing suits and ball-like object on the man's head. That one of the women has a cigarette in her hand seems utterly bizarre in the context of playing beach volleyball. Other ads have featured visual images such as a Black couple ice skating, a Black woman hugging her man who is playing an electric guitar, a Black man with two Black women on a Ferris wheel, and a Black couple leaning against some type of chain-link fence (see Figure 2.4 from *Essence*, June 2004).

A few Newport ads represent friendly activity between Blacks and Whites; for example, a December 2002 ad (in *Jet, Cosmopolitan* and elsewhere) pictured two African American couples and one White couple in a holiday scene, proclaiming a seasonal message of "Holiday pleasure!" The year 2002 was also when Newport ads first included the slogan, "Fire It Up!"—a verbal image easily read in relation to marijuana smoking. Two ads from *Ebony* connect this potentially marijuana-related connotation to Black social life. In one, we see a Black couple dancing at a club, and in another we see two Black men and one Black woman playing cards.

In 2004, the text of the Newport ads expanded to include "Finest Quality Menthol!" Three examples of these ads (*Essence* and elsewhere) show the connection of pleasure *enjoyed by Black people* and quality lifestyle with Newport; the idea of the discourse is to give Newport cigarettes the connotations of *Blackness and enjoyment*. In one (see Figure 2.4), a handsome young African American couple in casual attire is shown next to a fence that might be around a sports area. They are flashing toothy white smiles as they engage in their pleasure. His hair is fashionably braided and hers is long and in loose curls. In a second ad (*Essence*, April 2004), three handsome young African Americans (a woman and two men, one of whom appears to be the same male model as in the first ad) appear to be at a table in a nightclub. The drink on the table is suggestive of either white wine or a wine spritzer, and the woman's wrist is adorned with a chunky amethyst bracelet. The third ad (*Essence*, October 2004) pictures two handsome Black couples, with one of the men lining up his pool shot while the other three watch. Again, these are handsome, very dark-skinned, well-dressed people, who smile expressively in their moment of "Newport pleasure!" Because a tobacco company cannot expose itself to the charge of rigid racial targeting, ads appear with White models engaged in pleasurable situations as well, but the dominant connotation sets Newport pleasure as united first and foremost for Black smokers.

Circulating images of the mysterious Black

A second prominent theme in cigarette ads related to race presents a contrast of Black and White by imaging Black people as mysterious or exotic in contrast to White people. This theme was present in the Virginia Slims' "Find Your Own Voice" campaign, which ran mainly in women's magazines from 1999 to 2001. The ads in this $40 million campaign featured colorful close-up

Figure 2.4 **Newport** Pleasure! (*Essence*, June 2004).

photographs of attractive women from different cultural backgrounds, and were typically run as multi-page ad spreads. For example, the November 1999 issue of *Elle* and the December 1999 issue of *Self* magazine included a six-page ad spread, with one page featuring an Asian woman (probably Korean), one page a

Black woman (probably African American), one page a blonde blue-eyed woman (of Euro/White background), and one page a darker-haired ethnic-looking woman (probably Hispanic). The photographs are gorgeous and the font attractively formatted and displayed. The contrast in the verbal images of the ads picturing the Black woman and the White woman engages the mind–body dichotomy along with the long-standing stereotype of black-skinned people as strange, mysterious, and exotic. The one-liner for the White woman is, "I look temptation right in the eye and then I make my own decision." This verbal element creates the image of independence and mental control: "I make *my own decision*" (emphasis added) is an image of mind. The one-liner for the Black woman is, "The mysterious power of my voice endures" (see Figure 2.5). This verbal element not only associates mystery with blackness but also strengthens the idea that mystery is a universal, enduring attribute of Black people.

Philip Morris pulled the ad campaign in 2000 (Fairclough, 2000) as a result of pressure from various groups about both the transparent targeting of minority woman and youth and the use of "voice" to entice smokers when, in fact, cigarette smoking had been linked to cancer of the larynx (voice box) (Centers for Disease Control, 2006b). The ads themselves, like so many high-end ads, became collector's items—on display in various places for new audiences to see their artistic beauty and read their racial text. Some have even been for sale on eBay.

The cool allure of Kool

The advertising campaigns for Kool cigarettes have stood out for their racialized themes. Two examples will be discussed here to demonstrate how the verbal and visual images used to advertise Kool cigarettes circulate long-standing cultural notions about Black people. The first example of racialized verbal and visual imaging is taken from the Kool ad campaign launched in 2004 for its specialized line called "Smooth Fusions" offered as part of "The House of Menthol." (The house concept was established in 2000 as part of Kool's advertising.) A limited-edition cigarette collection, Brown and Williamson offered four varieties of "Smooth Fusions," each with a verbal image made up of a name plus an attribute. In the stiff fold-out magazine advertisements that were published at the beginning of the launch, each name was given a more elaborate description (shown below underneath the names), and the smoker/potential smoker was invited to "TASTE THE UNEXPECTED."

MOCHA TABOO—ENTICING
"Inviting and surprising. MOCHA TABOO will entice you with its sweet indulgence."

Figure 2.5 **Virginia Slims** Find Your Voice (*Elle*, November 1999).

CARIBBEAN CHILL—ALLURING

"Let the alluring charm of CARIBBEAN CHILL take you on a cruise to the islands."

MINTRIGUE—TANTALIZING

"Tantalizing MINTRIGUE leaves you guessing as to the secret of its intriguing refreshment."

MIDNIGHT BERRY—ENCHANTING
> "Deep and velvety, MIDNIGHT BERRY surrounds you with the enchantment of the darkest night."

This ad campaign was steeped in controversy—but not because of its racial imagery. The issue that drew understandable national attention was the appeal of these flavored cigarettes to the youth audience. Yet, the racial images in the text combined with the verbal images evoke the ideological themes of mystery, exotic intrigue, and darkness long associated in America with racial coding. Consider the example shown in Figure 2.6, which is taken from the right panel of the fold-out advertisement (*Vanity Fair*, June 2004). Here we see a Black woman placed in a background of green tones; the caption, which is placed over her buttocks, offers an enticing verbal image: ". . . with a charming island accent . . .". To her right is a display of the Caribbean Chill pack with some additional text. The mystery connotations continue in the text on the panel placed below the woman and next to a display of the Mintrigue pack: ". . . a question. An answer. And an enigma. All at the same time." In the text throughout this fold-out ad, ellipsis marks are used to signify the unstated, which is suggestive of mystery. One of the panels repeats the image of the woman seen in Figure 2.6, using a visual rhyme in which the text is deleted, the image is dimmed, and swirling lines are superimposed over the image of the woman. Directly below the woman is a panel showing an image of a Black man's face—also dimly displayed.

The image shows about two-thirds of the face in close-up vertically, such that only one eye is visible. The man is broad-nosed and large-lipped, and he is peering out at the viewer of the ad with the white of one of his eyes clearly contrasted to the black, green and blue tones of the ad. His face is juxtaposed on the left with a woman wearing stiletto heels and lace hose: we see only her legs and feet positioned in a sexually suggestive manner. The imagery of Black mystery and sexuality is simply too blatant to miss.

Verbal and visual imaging in black and white

In this section, I present three case examples of how verbal imaging works as part of broad cultural/social discourses. These cases demonstrate contrasts in the verbal images and connotations that accompany visual images of Black and White. In these cases of cigarette advertising, the verbal imaging is not just about selling cigarettes to particular markets, but also about cultural meanings beyond the ads themselves that precede the ad and that the ad substantiates or creates. The ads featured in this analysis are for menthol cigarettes sold as

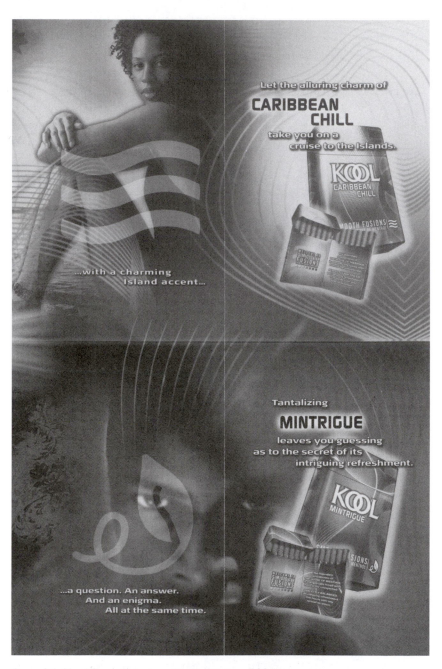

Figure 2.6 **Kool** Smooth Fusions (*Vanity Fair*, June 2004).

competitors to Newport, which—as noted earlier—is the brand of preference for African Americans.

Benson & Hedges Menthol (1999)

I focus in this case on two particular advertisements that appeared widely in 1999 in popular, mass-audience magazines including *TV Guide*, *Entertainment Weekly* and *Cosmopolitan* but also in Black-oriented magazines such as *Ebony*, *Jet* and *Black Elegance*. These ads were created as part of a larger series of ads done in dark tones—black, gray, foggy green, with soft, blurred edges and slightly out-of-focus people.

All of the ads in the series launched in 1999 feature people, and the two ads that I am focusing on provide a racial contrast in the people pictured: one with a group of White women and men and the other with a single, Black adult female. Apart from the green tones, the impression is of "black and white" visual representation. The green tones against this black and white core are indexical of menthol—no ambiguity involved here. Both ads show a cigarette pack in the bottom left and the name, Benson & Hedges Menthol, displayed vertically along the right side border in block capitals, perpendicular to the pack of cigarettes. Both ads carry the same verbal text on the bottom right side:

IT'S A SMOOTHER PLACE TO BE.

The "smoother place" construction sets the context for possible interpretations of the ad in two important ways. The first important signification is to narrow the meaning of menthol to "smooth" (likely to be distinguished from "harsh") rather than to open the meaning to other associations such as "crisp," "clean," or "refreshing." The second important signification metaphorically anchors "smoothness" to a place—and a place to dwell. Appropriating the metaphor of "place" for the experience of smoking draws on the usage in American English of "place" as a metaphor for one's position or circumstance in life, as in the expressions, "This relationship is just not the place where I want to be" or "He is in a better place now," where the reference is not to a location but to a condition, say, prior to breaking up with a romantic partner or after a person gets control of his/her depression.

The caption, "smoother place to be," engages a dominant discourse within cigarette advertising. The most obvious association is found in Camel cigarette advertising, where "smooth taste" as a signature verbal element was made especially powerful in the personified "Joe Camel." Joe Camel was presented verbally as a "smooth character" who promised smooth character-ness to Camel smokers. Of interest, Camels and Benson & Hedges are produced by different companies (RJ Reynolds producing Camels and Philip Morris producing Benson & Hedges), making the "smooth" connection more intriguing as an example of an intertextual sign for cigarettes. There is, thus, a discursive connection between this particular ad and another prominent cigarette product.

We come next to the elements in the Benson & Hedges ads that engage larger discourses of race in US society. One of the ads will be designated "Table for Five" and the other "Woman Smoking." These two ads engage the verbal image of "smoother place" quite differently and in ways that take advantage of racialized meanings circulating in the larger culture.

In "Table for Five", we see three women and two men, well dressed and likely in their mid to late 20s, sitting closely together at a round table covered with a light-colored tablecloth and set with stemmed glasses (filled perhaps with ice water), salt and pepper shakers, and a few indistinguishable food items (see Figure 2.7). The two men have dark, stylishly cut hair, and one is clearly wearing a necktie. Two of the women are blondes, and the third has dark hair.

All three women appear to be in dress-up dinner attire, showing bare shoulders covered only by spaghetti straps. All five adults are smiling, with their gazes focused—mainly toward one of the blonde-haired women. These are beautiful, alert and happy White people enjoying an elegant evening. Two of the couples appear to be together because of their placement in the ad, with the dark-haired woman seated at the far right in the grouping. The table at which the group is seated sits behind a dark green, slightly out-of-focus, softly draped curtain of luxurious-looking fabric, pulled into a triangle frame with tied swags on both sides. The curtain frames the table to create the impression that we are looking in on this happy "Table for Five." One of the blonde women in this group (placed second from the left) has her arm on the table and is resting her head in her hand, which is holding a cigarette from which smoke rises above the group. The rest of the setting is sufficiently blurred as to be only suggestive: behind the table there appears to be a blurry light or moon, and—perhaps—a distorted, wide-angle series of French doors with a billowy fabric above them; in front of and close to the top of the left side tied-back curtain is an image that might be either blurred lights or a pole. All of these elements together portray the "smoother place" referred to at the bottom right as a setting—an elegant-looking restaurant table complete with crystal goblets and linen tablecloth. The "smoother place" is one of refinement, and the diners are situated in the scene. At the upper left, larger than the statement at the bottom right, we read:

THE MOOD IS MENTHOL.

The scene and the verbal image of menthol as a mood add a pleasurable meaning to the situated location.

Figure 2.7 **Benson & Hedges** "Table for Five" (*Ebony*, August 1999).

Another ad in the series contrasts sharply with "Table for Five." In what I have named "Woman Smoking," we see a dark-skinned woman, almost certainly African American, in large profile, with eyes closed and hair pulled off the face and up in the back; she is gently exhaling smoke from her laxly parted

Figure 2.8 **Benson & Hedges** "Woman Smoking" (*Black Elegance*, October 1999).

lips—the smoke rising as if free-flowing from her mouth in slow, relaxed exhalation (see Figure 2.8). We see a bare shoulder, and a hand holding a long (recently lit) cigarette that is starkly white against the gray-green and black coloration of the rest of the advertisement. The cigarette is placed to the right and above center of the advertisement, extending vertically from the woman's chin up to the bottom eyelid.

Vaguely visible in the back left, we see a man with arms raised as though he is dancing. He is a background figure, facing forward, with about one-third of his body cut off by the left-hand border that frames the visual structure of the ad. The man's dark-colored, long-sleeved shirt is open, revealing a white undershirt. At the upper left, larger than the statement at the bottom right, we read:

MENTHOL AFTER DARK

This verbal image offers a striking contrast to "The Mood is Menthol" language of the "Table for Five" ad. Contrasting with the association of the mood of a happy evening among five happy friends engaged with one another and anchored socially in a situated location, the verbal image of "Menthol After Dark" engages a semiotic domain of darkness and mystery. The woman might be in a nightclub, but nothing places her concretely in this "after dark" location. Although this woman is shown smoking a cigarette that we as viewers of the ad are to assume comes from the Benson & Hedges box below it, her pose with eyes closed and smoke softly billowing from her mouth looks suggestively drug-related. The dislocated visual image framed by the verbal images of "smoother place" juxtaposed to darkness stands in sharp contrast to the con- crete dinner scene where *smooth is a place* and *menthol a mood* that can be achieved in that place. We might even ponder the possible reading of the verbal–visual image display as suggestive of a "lady of the night" where the indeterminate man with no particular face is the backdrop to her evening.

Looking at the two ads together, the discourse of race and its long-standing associations of blackness with both darkness and mystery positions the "Woman Smoking" as a powerful symbol for a broad range of racialized associations. Discursively, the "smoother place" has no locale—except for its association with night—its place left for us to imagine against the visual display of a Black woman with her eyes closed. She is gazing nowhere, the place is nowhere specific, and the reader of this ad must speculate about this mysterious set of signs, which is not so much the case in the "Table for Five" where the White partygoers are clearly in view and in focus in a situated place. Menthol as the cigarette additive that can create a mood compared to menthol placed in a time "after dark" replicates the idea that Blacks are associated with mystery and escape. Add to this the images of the White smokers as alert and the Black smoker as in some type of trance or personal reverie, and the significance of polarized race intensifies. The "Woman Smoking" also connotes sensuality and even sexuality—both clearly related to pleasure disassociated from grounded location.

Salem, "One world. Two sensations"

The second set of ads is from a Salem campaign named "Stir the Senses." The ads in this series suggest quite different images than did earlier Salem ads. The earlier ads used verbal images to establish a sign relationship between Salem cigarettes and refreshing taste: Salem "the refreshest"; "Salem Spirit"; and the enjoinder to "Refresh yourself." These earlier ads pictured lush scenes, crisp green colors, and beautiful waterfalls. The newer campaign, according to RJ Reynolds, "highlights the fact that Salem is the first menthol cigarette brand to actively market two unique taste signatures within its product line" (Salem launches, 2003, p.16). The ad campaign—launched in 2003—features two types of Salem menthol cigarettes: one named BLACK LABEL and the other GREEN LABEL. (A third variety, SILVER LABEL, was also launched at the same time and is described in the section on "Product Varieties.") The ads appear in several different forms. At the opening of the campaign, the higher-end version of the advertising appeared in a glossy, stiff paper format as an "open-me" type magazine insert inviting the reader to open at the fold (similar to the "sniff" cologne ads where the consumer can open up the ad for a whiff of the fragrance). "**welcome to a world of sensation**" is positioned in the center-right position, and once opened, the fold-out shows the two versions—side by side—of the menthol "world." The standard version of the ad consists of two facing pages bound into the magazine as regular pages—essentially the same as the inside of the "open-me" version but somewhat larger (8 inches by 10½ inches compared to the 7 inches by 10½ inches insert).

The ads present bold, geometric images in green, white, and black tones. There are no people in the first group of ads that was released in 2003, only two cigarette packs each for BLACK LABEL and GREEN LABEL with the word SALEM shown in bold white with the appropriate "label" below in capital letters (people were added to later ads). The left-hand page shows BLACK LABEL in two package forms—one for LIGHTS packaged in a flip-top box and the other for FULL FLAVOR packaged in a slide box (see Figure 2.9). The FULL FLAVOR version of BLACK LABEL shows a section of a cigarette box pulled out to expose three cigarette tips in the background. The FULL FLAVOR pack is angled toward the center-right (as though leaning toward the facing page) and is positioned more in the foreground than the LIGHTS pack. The right-hand page shows GREEN LABEL in the same two package forms, with the FULL FLAVOR flip-top box open to expose the cigarette tips (see Figure 2.10).

Again the FULL FLAVOR pack is more in the foreground than the LIGHTS pack, and it is positioned facing toward the opposing page. The visual effect is of the two labels occupying separate space but acknowledging each other through their "posture." The placement clearly positions the FULL FLAVOR as

Figure 2.9 **Salem** Black Label (*People*, April 14, 2003).

visually dominant. All of the cigarette boxes display an icon developed for the campaign: a sphere-shaped object ("the orb") that looks like the yin–yang symbol, which Salem's advertisers used in earlier campaigns. The separation of the two parts of the sphere are images of complementary halves—one dark, almost black-green and the other lighter, bright green; the bulbous part of the

Figure 2.10 **Salem** Green Label (*People*, April 14, 2003).

left side is in lower position showing the dark version, and the bulbous part of the right side is in upper position showing the lighter version. Like the yin–yang symbol, there are small circles within each half, but these reflect shiny light against the object rather than conveying the presence of the other half as in the yin–yang symbol. The green color of the GREEN LABEL package is vibrant, resembling the peel of a lime. The green color of the BLACK LABEL package is close to black with a few lighter tones around the globe and in the package label area.

The text in the ads is minimal, yet it clearly establishes its sign relation to the broader discourses of race, thus creating distinctively racialized verbal images. The contrasts serve as verbal images for the two varieties.

BLACK LABEL
Mysteriously rich. Deliciously intense.

vs.

GREEN LABEL
Intriguingly smooth. Refreshingly spirited.

In addition, the information on tar and nicotine for all four varieties is contained at the bottom of the BLACK LABEL page, with the Surgeon General's Warning placed at the top right of the GREEN LABEL page.

The verbal images in the ad propel racialized codes of meaning in at least two ways: (1) through the names of the product varieties (BLACK, GREEN); and (2) through the textual images that are used to describe these varieties.

Variety names

An argument could be made that the contrast of black with green is not intended or does not function as racial code, because the contrast is not black–white. I argue, however, that the contrast is racialized because *green is associated with menthol and is, thus, the unmarked linguistic element, with black then standing as a marked element to contrast it with the generic green menthol.* In other words, we would expect a menthol cigarette ad to emphasize green, which makes it the default color of the ad. To blacken the cigarette makes it more menthol because now it's *dark menthol*. To blacken the cigarette rather than making it dark green is to heighten its association with the Black consumer—especially the Black male.

In the product information for both varieties of the Salem menthol cigarettes that is placed at the bottom of the page on which the BLACK LABEL is displayed, there also appears the statement, "Black Label may not be available in all areas." Through this statement, BLACK LABEL as a marked product name is positioned as a "minority" menthol cigarette—a meaning that could be understood within the larger cultural discourses in which these ads circulate. Black signifies "minority" (among other things), and the limited availability makes this label at least a numerical minority cigarette, but perhaps also a special cigarette targeted at the Black minority (recall the failed Uptown cigarette). And indeed, this seems to be the case.

A phone number is included in the product information on the ad. Calling that number will tell the interested party where the BLACK LABEL variety can be purchased. Its availability at the time the ad was released, per the recorded message from RJ Reynolds, was in 29 states plus three cities. Placement of the product by RJR would have been determined based on marketing information corresponding to the demographic profiles of smokers and potential smokers. Striking in the list of locations is the overlap with high population areas for Blacks in the U.S. Population estimates compiled in July, 2002, by the U.S. Census Bureau (2003) for the population of "Blacks or African Americans Alone or in Combination" show 17 states with one million or more Blacks (of the 38 million total). The availability of the BLACK LABEL variety in 2003 was limited to 15 states, all of which matched the list of 17: Alabama, Florida, Georgia, Illinois, Louisiana, Maryland, Michigan, Mississippi, New Jersey, New York, North Carolina, Ohio, Pennsylvania, South Carolina and Virginia. The only missing states from the list of 17 are California and Texas: in both of these states, BLACK LABEL was available in one city: Oakland and Houston, respectively—cities with high Black population numbers. The two additional cities where BLACK LABEL was said to be available are St Louis, Missouri, and Washington, DC—both high density Black population cities. These target selling locations for the BLACK LABEL variety strongly point to a positioning of this "minority" brand in areas where Blacks are more heavily represented in the population. We might say that what is going on here is a sociolinguistic product positioning through the verbal images embedded in the product name: Black Label is a special cigarette for the Black population in the United States.

Variety descriptions

The two varieties advertised as a pair are part of "one world" of Salems—the world of menthol cigarettes. But they are also "two sensations" in that "one world." BLACK LABEL is: "Mysteriously rich. Deliciously intense." GREEN LABEL is "Intriguingly smooth. Refreshingly spirited." The "one world" shows a clear division into Black and White.

The verbal image of associating black with mystery makes blatant what the earlier Benson & Hedges MENTHOL AFTER DARK ad suggested: darkness signifies mystery, and that which is black is mysterious. Moreover, the mystery is "rich." The pack itself proclaims RICH FLAVORFUL MENTHOL, and the message at the other end of the 800-number characterized this label as the one with "more flavor." The magazine ad does not use the word "flavor," but this characteristic is implied in the phrase, "Deliciously intense." In recent years, "flavor" has circulated as a term associated with marked ethnicity and race—as in the doll line called "Flavas." Geneva Smitherman (1994) includes the word "flavor" in her dictionary, *Black Talk*, defining it as "attractiveness" and "style" (p. 111), and urbandictionary.com lists the same meaning. Verbally connecting the smoking of BLACK LABELS with an experience that is "deliciously intense" focuses the image on the senses directly. The smoker wants something intense, something immediate—immediate gratification comes to mind in the larger discourse of racism where certain people—African Americans—are stereo-typed as more sensual, more moved to seek pleasure, more untamed. The verbal image carries the connotations leading to an ideology of race in which Black people have historically been reduced to sensory beings.

The description of GREEN LABEL as INTRIGUINGLY SMOOTH. REFRESHINGLY SPIRITED establishes a verbal image that is more generic, and again that is verbally unmarked. "Smooth" is a generic sign for cigarettes—an attribute crossing brands and varieties within brands (recall the Benson & Hedges ads). The pack itself proclaims SMOOTH REFRESHING MENTHOL. For the cigarette to be intriguing moves it to a more cerebral plane compared to the evocative signs of mystery given to the Black Label. REFRESHINGLY SPIRITED as a verbal image elevates the cigarette experience to the outside. Refreshment renews as it brings in something from the outside. Refreshment can be uplifting and rejuvenating. The image is of advances in the way in which the old cigarette—whoever might have smoked it—has been brought into a new state of taste.

A third product line, called SILVER LABEL, was also launched in 2003, but it was advertised separately as a limited edition, of "limited quantities." Ads for this line proclaimed it as a cigarette "Breaking the mold." Packaged in an elegant "exclusive Silver Slide Box," the smoker or potential smoker was warned to "Look for it before it's gone." And, indeed, it is now gone from the market. The verbal imaging for this line associates it with exclusivity and status. The contents in the SILVER LABEL boxes presented "A premium col-lection of four unique menthol taste sensations" available "at select retailers." In the initial two-page ad spread for SILVER LABEL, this variety bore the descrip-tion of "The new menthology"—a term suggestive of cerebral appeal through the analysis of premium menthol options. The four designer boxes presented in the September 2003 issue of *Ebony* and elsewhere were color-coded to their "taste sensations":

DARK CURRENTS—A luscious menthol sensation with a touch of berry. A deeply rich experience. [the box colors are cranberry and silver]
DEEP FREEZE—Intensely cool menthol with a streak of spearmint for a deep minty chill. [the box colors are dark green and silver]

COOL MYST—Soft, sweet with a hint of creamy vanilla. A subtly fresh
menthol sensation. [the box colors are teal/blue-green and silver]
FIRE & ICE—A lively mix of fiery spices and cooling menthol. [the box
color is silver]

The appropriation of verbal signs that invite racial interpretations are clear:
"*dark* currents"; "*deep* freeze"; "*cool* myst"; and "*fire*" cooled by "*ice*" all evoke the
deep, dark imagery of African Americans (emphasis added).

Two ads in the "Stir the Senses" series are especially provocative in their
racial images and carry significant cultural messages, because each ran for many
weeks not only in Black-oriented magazines but also in general circulation
titles such as *Newsweek*. In one of these ads, the scene is dark to suggest night,
with stars glowing green against the black background. The whole ad is in green
tones, as though lit with green lamps. The ad shows a Black woman floating on
her back in water—perhaps a lake but possibly a large pool (see Figure 2.11).
A number of lit candles are floating in the water, and the woman is posed with
eyes closed, head somewhat back as though on a pillow, arms and one knee
showing above the water. The fingers of her right hand are lightly touching the
water, making a small ripple effect. The caption is simply, "stir the senses."

The other ad is also set at night, and the background scene depicts a large
multi-story building that is lit up to suggest an urban location (see Figure 2.12).
Close up in the front right side of the ad appears a Black man who looks as
though green light is shining on him. He is leaning down slightly as though to
light the cigarette which is between his lips and held between two fingers. His
eyelids are almost closed. We also see a series of bright globes of light—
perhaps to suggest the headlights of cars moving fast on an urban highway.
Again, the caption is simply, "stir the senses." What catches the eye in this ad is
that the cigarette is extended into the front globe of light—almost as though
the man is reaching for the light and is in a state whose connotation might
engage images of drug use. Both of these ads explicitly associate Salem cigarettes with images of Black representation. Both place the characters in scenes
that are quasi-realistic but include elements that break the "reality" of the scene.
Both show isolated individual Black people, without the sociality of others. And
both visually present images of stillness, closed or nearly closed eyes, large lips.
There are ads in the "Stir the Senses" campaign that picture White people, but
none that I have seen look anything like this. Two frequently published ads in
which a White person was shown depict these individuals looking straight at the
spectator with eyes wide open. They look alert compared to the representations of Blacks in this advertising series. The contrast is yet another reification
of the Black–White polarity in which Whites seem not only more in control but
also more anchored in reality. These are powerful racialized images.

Figure 2.11 **Salem** Stir the Senses "Woman in Water" (*Essence*, October 2004).

Figure 2.12 **Salem** Stir the Senses "Man Lighting Cigarette" (*Newsweek*, June 28, 2004).

BE TRUE. with Kool

In June 2005, Kool debuted a new race-linked advertising campaign dubbed **BE TRUE.** This campaign was part of RJ Reynolds' decision to give marketing major priority to its Camel and Kool brands, with lesser attention to Winston and Salem (Louis, 2005). The ads circulated in a number of different magazines (e.g. *Newsweek, Time, Dub, Sports Illustrated* and *Vogue*), with the basic visual layout similar for each different ad. The layout includes a background in blues and greens to create an aquamarine effect design, in front of which is superimposed a character placed on the left side of the page, angled toward the right, and shown (in most cases) from head to mid-leg. Two ads were circulated at the beginning of the series. One features a Black man who is represented as a musician. He wears a purple suit jacket with navy blue tie and shirt—open at the neck and tie loose. His hair is in dreadlocks and he has a mustache and short chin beard. He is also wearing black-rimmed glasses and a gold index-finger ring on the hand that holds a trumpet and cigarette (see Figure 2.13). The other ad features a Black female who has long curly hair and is dressed in blue jeans and shimmering green tube top. She wears large gold hoop earrings and a stack of gold bangle bracelets. Her right arm is bent at the elbow such that her hand, which is holding a cigarette, rests against her upper chest. She is learning forward slightly, with more weight placed on her left foot than her right (see Figure 2.14). Both figures are smiling, have conspicuously white teeth, and are shown with their eyes closed. The rising smoke in each picture is conspicuously shown in swirls.

The verbal text for the ads in this campaign consists of two elements. At the bottom right of the page, **KOOL** (in white letters, with green borders and interlocking Os) is placed over interlocking rings that are the signifiers for this brand. The imperative statement, **BE TRUE.** is positioned beneath the second "O" in "KOOL" in smaller font and yellow lettering. In the center right of the page, a simple two-word imperative statement in the form of **BE [+ adjective]** is placed in yellow letters and font size to match the "be true" statement.

The text for these two ads in the imperative **BE [+ adjective]** statements provides verbal images to accompany the visual images of Black models, both of whom are in some state of pleasure but in no particular scene. The adjective for the male model is AUTHENTIC, and the adjective for the female model is SMOOTH. For the Black male model positioned as a musician, Kool cigarettes are associated with being "authentic"—perhaps a reference to the authenticity of Black maleness combined with jazz musicianship. For the Black female model, no identity is signified in the ad apart from her Blackness, femaleness, and sensuality/sexuality. "Smooth" in this context is a verbal element joining the cigarette to the experience of the woman—perhaps both her experience in smoking and the spectator's experience of her. The positioning of the woman's

Figure 2.13 **Kool** Be True "Man with Trumpet" (*Sports Illustrated*, August 8, 2005).

Figure 2.14 **Kool** Be True "Shimmering Woman" (*Sports Illustrated*, October 10, 2006).

hand and angle of her body add to the connotations of "smooth" to suggest a sensual abandon and bodily identity that engages what Collins (2004) describes as constituting the modern jezebel image of "Black women's sexuality [as] grounded in sensuality and desire" (p. 72). There is clearly a racial text operating in these ads: a recognizable role for a Black man is that of jazz musician, and for a Black woman that of a sensual, sexualized body.

Several other ads in the "Be True" series serve as context for the racialized verbal images associated with the Black man and woman models. A glossy eight-page booklet insert that included both Black and White models was placed in a number of different magazines. One of the two White models was represented as a musician but had no adjective written next to his picture. A second White model—a woman who appears to be singing in a recording studio—is shown with the verbal text, "It's about old world CLASS and new world STYLE." The third White model—also a woman—is singing and playing the piano, with the accompanying text, "It's about being AUTHENTIC and ORIGINAL." Each of these White models is placed in a specific context with a clearly delineated background. The advertising image of the Black man described above is positioned on the last page of the booklet with only the "Be True" text. One page, which is visually on the left of the center fold, pictures a Black woman in profile who appears to be dancing—but possibly sitting at a counter with her arms outstretched. She is wearing a white dress with spaghetti straps and sequins. Her eyes are closed and her lips parted. The verbal text below her breast reads, **IT'S ABOUT UPTOWN ATTITUDE**. Opposite her is a page in which an Asian-looking man is shown sitting on a stool in a music studio with his guitar balanced in one hand, a cigarette in the other, and an ashtray full of butts next to him. The verbal text positioned at the bottom of the page is **MIXED WITH DOWNTOWN VIBE**. The font size of ATTITUDE and VIBE is larger than the rest of the text, with "attitude" printed in white against a black background and "vibe" printed in bright blue against a parquet tile floor. The Black woman, again, is marked as sensual, with her body as the primary signifier in the ad. The uptown–downtown contrast is also significant in view of the two people of color on these facing pages. "Uptown" might connote high status but was also the name of the cigarette that RJ Reynolds designed and unsuccessfully tried to introduce especially for Blacks in the late 1980s. "Downtown" has many connotations, which include being alone, heroin and oral sex.

Kool's 2006 entry into the BE TRUE. campaign features a new line of cigarettes called **XL**—a metaphorical appropriation of the X-tra Large concept for a wider cigarette. The ads released in late 2006 and early 2007 for XL differ from the initial group of BE TRUE. ads in several ways. The first ads in this series were formatted as glossy bi-fold inserts. What is seen in all of the ads is a realistic photo-type picture of a well-dressed Black man with closely cropped hair. Figure 2.15, which is the front cover of the bi-fold insert, shows this Black man with a dark-haired woman whose race is not clear. While retaining a Black person as the central figure, the ads place the models in specific scenes rather than against sceneless backgrounds, use a greenish black-and-white color scheme and sometimes include models in addition to the featured Black man. Three adjectives are used to brand this cigarette: **SMOOTHER. WIDER. DIFFERENT**. In the bi-fold version of the ad, these adjectives are positioned on the back cover, above a picture of a box of Kool XLs. The body of the male model shown in these ads appears fit and trim and probably rather tall, yet there is nothing that pushes the interpretation of his physical size as extreme.

Figure 2.15 **Kool** XL (*Rolling Stone*, November 16, 2006).

He may, indeed, wear XL size shirts, but in this ad, the connotations for XL are linked to the verbal images of "smoother, wider, different"—adjectives suggestive of the lingering equation of Black man with penis. If the bi-fold is removed from the magazine and flattened out, the SMOOTHER. WIDER. DIFFERENT characterization appears directly across from the head of the Black male model. With this ad for the new XL line of cigarettes, Kool has rounded out its sexualization of Blacks by circulating a representation of Black men to complement the representation of Black women as sexualized bodies consistent with long-standing ideological codes for race in America.

The role of race in event sponsorship and Internet ads

The Salem "Stir the Senses" advertising campaign has been developed far beyond the basic presentation in magazines and point-of-sale displays. After the launch of the differentiated menthol products, Salem followed with both rap music events in selected cities and an elaborate Internet display of the brands, as well as short stories about the nightlife of Salem smokers.

Salem and event sponsorship

In 2004, Salem sponsored both an auction and three music tours, which were verbally imaged on their web page, salemaccess.com, as 3 DIFFERENT TOURS. 3 UNIQUE SENSATIONS. Magazine and point-of-sale ads promoted the web site. The entire presentation shows strongly racialized themes through the discursive elements that make up its particular text and visual presentation.

The general theme of the event sponsorship revolves around rap music and artists. The auction, using "Pack Codes" was called BACKSTAGE ACCESS. The prize: "the ONE AND ONLY Cadillac Escalade ESV® customized by FUNK-MASTER FLEX." In the ads that I saw, this auction promotion included product information for the BLACK LABEL FULL FLAVOR variety only (see Figure 2.16). Thus, we see an explicit reference to a Black rapper, to the SUV associated with Black rappers, and to the Black Label of Salem. These are the combined defining features of the 2004 Stir the Senses tour series. The discursive equation might be expressed as:

senses + rap + Escalade = Black.

The equation is explicitly stereotypical, reducing Blacks to a sensorium focused on rap style.

The salemaccess.com website, restricted to those 21 years of age or older, has in the past offered a variety of entertainment options, again strategically

Figure 2.16 **Salem** Access Tour Series (*Jane*, November 2004).

focused on the African American population. One major event option was the Tour Series, with three different tours covering 14 cities. Each tour was given a distinctive name: **VIBE**, **FLOW**, and **GROOVE**—all verbal images associated with pleasure and physical sensation. Each of these series carried a name that extends the Salem "Stir the Senses" campaign by picking up on the word "sense":

- Sense of SOUND, June 2004
- Sense of EXPRESSION, August 2004
- Sense of STYLE, October and November 2004

Although Black rap as one of the most popular musical forms is by no means restricted to the African American audience, the concert locations convey the strong linkage between Salem (and menthol more generally) and the Black consumer of popular culture and his or her priorities. Each of the 14 concert locations for the Tour Series was a city with a sizeable Black population in comparison to the overall Black population of the US. The tour locations and percent of Black and African American population in those locations (US Census Bureau, 2001) show the pattern: Philadelphia (44 percent), Pittsburgh (28 percent), Cleveland (52 percent), Columbus (26 percent), Detroit (83 percent), Milwaukee (39 percent), Chicago (37 percent), Indianapolis (26 percent), St Louis (52 percent), Memphis (62 percent), Houston (26 percent), Atlanta (62 percent), Miami (24 percent) and Baltimore (65 percent). These percentages range from more than twice to more than five times the percentage of Blacks in the US population (12.3 percent in 2000). This distribution of tour locations serves a marketing function by targeting the African American young adult smoker or potential smoker (and the teen audience because of the ready availability of magazines such as *Essence, Jet* and *Vibe* as well as point-of-sale promotions). The locations also circulate images and associations of Blacks with a particular popular culture movement (rap) and with the world of sensation.

At the time when the concerts were advertised, the web page for Salem offered more options to the visitor than descriptions of the brands and the concert venues. Through a series of clicks, the web site visitor could link to entertainment options organized around themes that changed from time to time. In 2005, the web site featured narrative stories of the nightlife of Salem smokers. Called "Salem Stories," several different options presented from the point of view of dramatic characters (Stern, 1991) included mixed-race casts. For example:

3 FRIENDS, 1 NIGHT
AND A WORLD OF SENSATION
FOLLOW THEIR NIGHT OUT ON THE TOWN SALEM-STYLE

The three friends are Eric (who is Black), Dylan (who is White with dark hair), and Miranda (who is also White with dark hair and a dark complexion). The plot line tells a story about these friends, the obstacles they face in getting together for a social occasion, and their choices of Salem varieties. Although the friends plan to take the same subway to a club, obstacles arise—a missed train (Eric), distraction by a beautiful woman (Dylan), and an intriguing man (Miranda). The web site visitor is offered two episodes of the story, with links to a segment for each friend in each of the two episodes. Because this is a "Salem-style" story and a "Salem-style" night on the town, each character is identified with a brand. Both Dylan and Miranda (the White characters) select their brand because of the person of the opposite sex who they meet: Dylan's beautiful woman passes him a Black Label pack with her phone number written in lipstick; and Miranda's new-found man offers her a Silver Label "Deep Freeze." Eric—the Black man in the narrative—is the only one who has his brand from the beginning of the story—Green Label. This is not the Black Label that one would expect because of the verbal image. Yet, on the web site, Green Label is described differently than in the magazine ads: Green Label is still "intriguingly smooth and refreshingly spirited" but in addition, the web site describes this variety as "a lighter, *more menthol*, less tobacco taste available in seven styles—in the Green Label Box." The verbal imaging of Green connects the one Black character in the story with the variety of cigarette that has *more menthol*. The first statement that describes Black Label announces "a bolder, more tobacco, less menthol taste." The semiotic linkage joins the White smoker with less menthol and the Black smoker with more menthol. Strategically, this switch of labels helps RJ Reynolds avoid the accusation of racial targeting, but the accompanying switch of verbal elements unites the Green label with Black smokers by emphasizing its menthol intensity. This is a complex case of racial targeting behind the smoke and mirrors of surface changes in the ads. The cultural placement of Blacks and Whites is only minimally disturbed, if at all, in this rendering of racial imagery.

Kool and event sponsorship

Kool cigarettes were associated for a number of years with music events clearly targeted to young Black adults (and other youth who want to be associated with Black music culture). DJ battles, co-sponsored by *Vibe* magazine, have been one of the featured events. An ad early in 2004 (e.g. *Details*, April 2004) under the branding of **KOOL MIXX**, proclaimed Kool's recognition of DJs "as the center of Hip Hop". Two Black DJs (male) are pictured in central positions in the ad, and two young Black women are shown separately in the periphery, each dancing. Potential spectators were lured with the message, "In its sixth year, this fierce coast-to-coast battle of the hottest rising DJs is the ultimate way for you to . . . EXPERIENCE THE SOUNDTRACK TO THE STREETS." Interested persons are directed not to a generic website for Kool, but to houseofmenthol.com. And just in case Internet access is not available— which certainly might be the case in inner city areas—a toll-free number is provided. In 2004 Kool also sponsored "The Kool Nu Jazz Festival" in Chicago, Philadelphia, Atlanta and Detroit—all cities with a substantial Black popula-tion. The festival was billed as a celebration of "the music that's the foundation of today's urban culture" (*Essence*, October 2004). The connotations of "urban culture" give jazz a youthful image. Kool continued to sponsor events with the controversial New Jazz Philosophy Tour of 2005. John Polito (2005), founder of whyquit.com, wrote a biting satire of this RJ Reynolds' initiative. He begins by asking how—if you were RJR—you might "replace your share of the 440,000 U.S. nicotine addicts who annually smoke themselves to death . . .? How would you trap and enslave their replacements?" The answer he gives is The New Jazz Philosophy Tour featuring Black artists such as Floetry, John Legend, Common, DeLa Soul, Busta Rhymes, and Miri Ben-Ari (specific artists at specific venues subject, of course, to change). The advertising so clearly positions Black culture that the link to a potential Black audience is certain. Yet, White teens and young adults love the music too, and what they get from the advertising images is not just the juice-flowing-feeling of being able to hear one of these artists or groups, or envying those who will, but yet another mass circulated image of what Blackness means in our society—music, rap, hip-hop, mainly tough Black men, and urban cool—this time fueled by Kool.

Conclusions and implications

The illustrations and case studies analyzed here provide a glimpse at the ways in which the verbal and visual images comprising an advertising text engage particular racialized representations. Surely, not every person will interpret the racialized text as such, but the elements for the larger cultural semiotic are made up of specific instances of images—verbal and visual—as they circulate in cultural forms. It is not only that these ads are advertising moments targeted at African Americans, because their placement is much wider than magazines directed at African Americans. These ads also contribute to a more general ideological discourse in which Blacks and Whites are verbally positioned through a kind of fast-text imaging. In this case, the fast-text imaging dips deeply into the ideological pool of race in America.

Advertising, as many have observed, draws on signs already well established as the elements for compact, image-driven promotions (Fowles, 1996; Frith, 1997; Goldman, 1992). We may be vexed or perplexed, delighted or disgusted with what we see and hear, but our responses should not end there. Advertising speaks, respeaks, and newly speaks our culture just as much as do the conversations we have, the books and the magazines we read, and the television programs and movies we watch (and hear). Writing as an anthropologist making sense of advertising in a cultural context quite different from that of the United States—that of advertising in Bombay—William Mazzarella (2003) addresses the reality that advertising language belongs to the culture in which it appears:

> I would suggest that we owe it to advertising to do what nowadays it least expects us to: to take it seriously. Just as we should not placidly accede the fiction that advertising simply responds to consumers' desires, so we should not peremptorily dismiss it as fraudulent. Its languages—whether we like it or not—are our languages, it spaces are our spaces. What we need to do is to examine how and why advertising intervenes in these languages and spaces. (p. 62)

The racialized and racist images circulating in the cigarette advertisements examined in this chapter (as well as others for these particular cigarettes and other brands whose advertising take up racialized images) clearly serve the interests of the tobacco companies whose advertising agencies produce and place the ads. The verbal images and more encompassing discourses contained in these ads are the smoking gun exposing the tobacco industry's racist ideology. The creators of the ads may or may not be aware of the powerful contrast in the imaging of Black and White through textual choices, but when the textual choices are combined with the visual images, it is hard to imagine that a visually and verbally literate person who is responsible for producing the advertisements is unaware of the racialized contrasts. At a broader, cultural level, this type of advertising contributes in subtler ways to the perpetuation of practices that most people believe are history. Not so.

The analysis developed in this chapter focuses attention on an aspect of advertising too seldom at the center of attention: the verbal codes of advertising. As advertising has expanded in print, television, and more recently the Internet, the verbal codes that are used are increasingly part of our cultural environment and our language. They cannot be dismissed as trivial or as "take it or leave it." Because advertising must rely on minimal verbal elements to make its points, every choice contributes something to the overall semiotic of the ad. Characteristically telegraphic and elliptical, the language used in advertisements functions much like the "sound bites" of political discourse. The "verbal bites" of ads are designed to grab attention and to be memorable. They can be playful, inventive, and representative of the latest trends in language use, but they can also circulate disturbing images that are part of the signification system beyond the product or service being advertised. The tobacco companies responsible for the cigarette advertisements analyzed in this chapter continue to engage in unethical practices in their targeting of African Americans. At a broader societal level, the potency of the messages offered by these companies reiterates that we live in a country divided by race and coded with racism.

In the recirculation of images, advertisers face the challenge of both tapping into culturally familiar meaning and creating contexts for those meanings that compel attention. Jib Fowles (1996) phrases the challenge in terms of its societal-psychological connectedness:

> The symbols [in advertising] must be comprehensible by the many, since the advertising strategy strives to enlist multitudes, and so must be composed of familiar elements that articulate commonalities within the society. Yet by the same token, the symbols must not be so overly familiar, so banal, that they elicit indifference or even rejection from consumers. The work of the advertising industry is to scratch away at the psyche of the public, to uncover deeper veins of sentiment, and to produce fresher symbols with improved chances of striking newer chords with consumers. (p. 167)

This mix of familiarity and the challenge of fresher symbols is precisely what operates in the cigarette advertisements examined here. The racist codes may not be so apparent when contrasts such as black–green occur as significant signs for cigarette varieties, but on closer examination, the verbal images in concert with the visual signs expose what is behind and beneath the smoke and mirrors, giving evidence for the positioning of racialized discourse.

Writing about American literature and, more broadly, American culture, Tony Morrison (1992) engages the idea of race as metaphorically part of our culture:

> Race has become metaphorical—a way of referring to and disguising forces, events, classes, and expressions of social decay and economic division far more threatening to the body politic than biological "race" ever was. . . . It [racism] has a utility far beyond economy, beyond the sequestering of classes from one another, and has assumed a metaphorical life so completely embedded in daily discourse that it is perhaps more necessary and more on display than ever before. (p. 63)

It is entirely possible that race may not be immediately "read" in the advertisements considered here, but their meaning as cultural discourse cannot be understood without recourse to an elaborate system of signs mapping an ideology of race. Apart from the aim of cigarette advertising to recruit and retain new smokers and to influence brand choice, people of every race and ethnic background witness a parade of verbal and visual images in these ads that promote particular ideologies of race. The process of imaging Black people and White people in particular ways draws deeply from the wells of cultural connotation. Robert Ferguson (1998), in his analysis of race and the media, reminds us that when we consider race and racist discourse in the media, "similar discourses circulate in everyday life" (pp. 55–6). For the White spectator who engages with the types of ads I have discussed, the images they see cement a familiar racial "otherness" that diminishes Black people by representing them through images reminiscent of old and debilitating stereotypes. For the Black spectator of ads, the images they see recirculate oppressive meanings about selfhood—images with the potential to undermine social progress and self-respect. As Patricia Hill Collins (2004) states it, Black gender ideology, unless broken down and rebuilt, "instruct[s] Black people how they should *feel* within their own bodies. This ideology severs mind, soul, and body from one another and helps structure oppression" (p. 282).

Chapter 3

Keeping race in place

Multicultural visions and voices in teen advertising

While working on a project in the late 1990s related to gender and discourse in television advertisements directed at young children (Johnson and Young, 2002), my colleague and I noticed the conspicuous near-absence of children of color in the ads and the particular absence of children of color with speaking lines in the ads. The representation overall depicted a society mainly composed of White faces and voices, with only the occasional child of color. When children of color did appear in ads, they were almost always seen with White children—often placed to the side or in the background. In the hundreds of ads that we watched, only one featured an African American boy by himself who had a speaking role in the ad. The ad, which aired in 1999, was for Reese's Puffs cereal. In the center of the screen was an African American boy about 10 years old who was visually and verbally represented as a hip-hopper. He promoted the product in a language style scripted to signify African American vernacular English, a style which you couldn't miss as "sounding Black."

What struck me about this ad was not just that it was the only ad to feature a solo African American boy but that, as the only ad featuring an African American boy, the representation was hip-hop and urban ghetto in style. Encountering this ad led me to think back to an ad I had seen earlier that year for Sleeping Beauty Barbie in which a White girl and an Asian girl (probably Chinese) were featured. The Asian girl in this ad stands aside but slightly behind the White girl as both behold the White sleeping beauty Barbie doll, which is lying on a beautiful bed with her eyes closed. The Asian girl looks at the White girl and says, "Her eyes really close"—as if to register astonishment in comparison to the White girl's sanguine attitude. Prince Ken, who of course is White, arrives to awaken Sleeping Beauty, and the final quick shot is of the two girls standing by Barbie, while the White girl is the one to touch the doll. The effect is to show the Asian girl as less knowledgeable about the doll, as an outsider astonished by Barbie's eyes (which may be a subtle code to represent Asian envy of non-Asian eyes) and less directly engaged in agentive behavior with the doll.

These two ads together might be said to be culturally significant simply because they represent non-White children, yet each portrayal is troubling because of the social position into which the non-White child is placed—hip-hop, vernacular-speaking African American boy and sweet, marginalized Asian girl who is fascinated with Barbie's eyes. In both cases the ads call upon stereotypes to create the images that we see and hear, but they also go further by propelling those stereotypes to fill in the specifics of what it means to live in a multiracial, multiethnic society. In this sense, they have an ideological function in the way they circulate codes of meaning associated with race.

I have often thought back to those advertising images of the African American boy and the Asian girl as signifiers of race in the advertising environment that is part of young children's lives. As television programs have proliferated for the youth market, so too have the opportunities to represent cultural models in advertising. In this chapter, I explore how television advertising incorporates the reality of our multicultural society into the scenes and narratives that are used to promote products within programming directed at "tweens" and teenagers. This age cohort is significant within consumer culture for two main reasons. First, spending by tweens and teens has been on the increase. Second, this cohort is just around the age corner from independent adulthood, less externally controlled spending, and greater access to credit cards. Advertisers are, thus, cultivating the practices of spending that are the foundation of today's out-of-control consumer economy—an economy in which adult savings are now in the "red." The US Commerce Department reported on January 29, 2007 that the annual American savings rate, for the first time since the Great Depression of 1932 and 1933, fell "into negative territory at minus 0.5 percent, meaning that Americans not only spent all of their after-tax income [in 2006] but had to dip into previous savings or increase borrowing" (MSNBC, January 30, 2007). In a culture of spending, product proliferation and promotion drive these startling patterns of American consumption, with advertising providing the fuel.

As many adults know first-hand, teens are big spenders, especially in comparison to their parents when they were teenagers. In 2003, teen spending was reported to be $175 billion, with estimated 2006 spending at $190 billion (Mintel, 2006). Many teens earn money through jobs after school and on the weekends, and parents and other family members contribute to their spending as well. In a 2005 telephone survey, International Communications Research (2005) found that teenage girls spend about $47 per week, compared to boys who spend about $45 per week. The teen market, then, is prime territory for advertising. And with advertising comes a barrage of images and narratives about experiences and lifestyles associated with the ever-expanding array of products.

The cultivation of consumerism begins at a young age. Young children are bombarded with television advertisements for toys, snacks, and entertainment, and their influence on purchases by their parents through the "I want . . ." avalanche of requests is legendary. As the proclivity, inclination, and means to create identities through consumer goods increase in the "tween" and teen years, advertising catering to this market is ever present. Certain products are designed for and explicitly pitched to tweens and teens, while other products more suitable for the adult consumer are made visible—likely as a way to continue the pattern of youth influence on adult purchases and, even more important, as a way to develop tastes for the products that are potentially available in the future, such as cars, boats and expensive jewelry, and the attitude that credit cards provide quick access to these products.

With exposure to advertising in its many forms and in a range of media, teens are presented not only with products but also with images of society and lifestyles. There is no escaping the substantial role played by advertising in the larger environment of everyday life. Advertising offers, then, not just products but also images—both visual and verbal—serve as representations and recipes for living. These images circulate ideological codes for everything from how to look and smell to how to hang and be cool to whom to be seen with and what technology devices to use in the various venues of teen activity. The ideological coding addressed in this chapter is that which relates to multicultural society. More specifically, I am interested in the representations of racial and ethnic diversity appearing in TV commercials aired during tween and teen programming. Several general questions have guided my examination of the racial and ethnic diversity in commercials:

- How are characters in ads marked for race and ethnicity?
- What relationships between people of color and Euro/Whites are seen and heard in commercials?
- What representations of multicultural society exist in advertising directed at teens? What cultural models of cultural diversity prevail because of the ways in which racial and ethnically marked persons appear in ads placed in programs for teenagers?
- How do representations of diversity promote particular ideas about multicultural society and how might these representations contribute to the circulation of ideological codes?

In addressing these questions, my intent is to bring focus to the juxtaposition of the likely audience for a television program and the presence (or absence) of multicultural text in advertising.

The chapter is organized into four sections. The first section presents a brief discussion of the ideological nature of advertising, conceptualizes the teen advertising audience, and describes the approach I took to analyze critically the discourse of ads in their larger context. Next, I provide an overview of the demographic context for addressing issues related to cultural diversity and teen advertising. Information about both the increasing cultural multiplicity of the United States and youth demographics within this cultural multiplicity are presented. The third deals with representation and the ways in which the representations of people of color in teen advertising contribute to what West and Fenstermaker (1995) have termed "the doing of diversity." In this section I review research focused on the presence of people of color in advertising. Section four consists of (1) a series of examples of how race and ethnicity show up in the advertising placed in programs watched by teenagers and (2) a close examination of two ads to illustrate how people of color are represented in commercials placed in programs written mainly as White narratives that likely appeal to White audiences; here I analyze ads for Boost Mobile and for a public service campaign sponsored by Above the Influence.

Ideological codes and diversity

Teenagers present a ready audience for ads that depict diversity and a multi-cultural society because they have been widely exposed to a range of multicultural ideas through personal experiences, school curriculum, and popular culture. The tweens and teens of today were preschoolers in the 1990s—a time when both the idea and the presence of a multicultural society was clearly evident in the US. Many teens today have lived their daily lives in communities where they regularly see and interact with people from different cultural groups. Others live in metropolitan areas that are racially and ethnic-ally segregated. Still others are more isolated in small towns and rural areas but still experience a vast popular culture environment that displays representa-tions of cultural identities, albeit limited ones.

The media products directed at and consumed by tweens and teens offer a range of recipes for lifestyles and templates for social relationships. This is no less the case for advertising than for program content into which commercials are inserted on television or ads inserted among the content items appearing in magazines.

Ideology codes in advertising

As noted in the introductory chapter, advertising is a major circulator of ideo-logical codes. Although there are many different perspectives on ideology, for the purposes of media analysis, Grossberg et al.'s (1998) characterization is helpful. The media, these authors contend, have come to play a powerful role in shaping prevailing ideology: "In the contemporary world, the media are involved in the production of ideology all the time. After all, they are . . . perhaps the most important producers of meaning and the codes of meaning in contemporary society. Furthermore, they are often a central and important part of people's everyday lives" (p. 182). These authors draw on Louis Althusser (1970), who emphasized that ideology is a system of representation, which is a kind of symbolic stand-in for "reality" but also a stand-in that is likely to be perceived as reality itself. It is the system of representations that guides the day-to-day experiences of people living their lives. Althusser's (1971/2001) now-famous idea was that ideology works by " 'constituting' concrete individuals as subjects" (p. 116). In a process that he referred to as "interpellation," individuals are brought ("hailed" as Althusser puts it) into ideology and become subjects to meaning systems that precede them. This idea of the relationship between ideology and interpellation is helpful in understanding how advertising often works to bring its viewers and listeners into the abbreviated worlds associated with the product and communicated through careful selection of signifiers. Ideological coding may be inconspicuous in the sense that its presence becomes quite ordinary and, thus, does not call attention to itself. A person who grew up in a nuclear family might not, for example, think to examine the repetitive representation of the nuclear family in media fare or the implications of instantiating this type of family structure as "natural" because this person is easily brought into the world of the ad. Another person may see the ad as strange or irrelevant because there is nothing in it that looks familiar. Yet another person, similarly situated as one who does not see him- or herself in the family representation of the ad, may nonetheless be brought into the ad by being subject to its ideological codes; for this person, there may be a desire to be in the nuclear family constellation or simply to be associated with attributes of this type of family and their product environment. Similarly, the association in our society of nurturing with mothering may make it quite easy for an ad portraying a mother in a nurturing relationship to her children to set off no mental neon light, signifying that ideological coding continues to reinforce traditional sex roles. Although not always presented in the context of ideology, many content analysis studies of advertising serve to document the very patterns of stereotyping and representation that cement particular ideological themes. Presenting Asian Americans in ads as highly educated, affluent, and associated with technology, for example, codes this racially identifiable US group in relation to socioeconomic status (see Paek and Shah, 2003).

Critical approach

To uncover how ideological codes operate in the discourse of cultural diversity in teen advertising, I have approached my general questions through a qualitative, critical analysis of the specific placement of ads in television programming. I watched numerous television programs broadcast between 2005 and early 2007 that are either explicitly designed for the tween and teen audiences or directed at this group as a major part of the audience. Because youngsters often tend to "watch up" in the age portrayals in television programs, the younger, "tween"-age group (made up of children roughly nine to 13 years old) is conceptualized here as part of the audience for teen-oriented television programming. The term "tween" carries richer meaning than the more conventional "preteen" because it captures a mentality and lifestyle that bridges childhood and the teen years. A *Newsweek* article in 1999 (Kantrowitz and Wingert, 1999) characterized this age group as "stuck on fast forward, children in a fearsome hurry to grow up" (p. 62). The notion of conceptualizing the potential audience for certain television programming and the ads contained within that programming is important because of the reciprocity of the advertising environment with, in the case of cultural representations, the ways in which a pivotal age group in society is given the opportunity for interpellations into ideologically coded worlds.

To gain an understanding of teen television programs and advertising contained within them, I immersed myself in a broad range of programs that are popular with teen audiences. My viewing was concentrated in October and November of 2005; March, May and June of 2006; and January of 2007. The programs I watched included "That's So Raven" (Disney), "Sister Sister" (Disney), "Veronica Mars" (CW), "Degrassi" (The N), "One on One" (The N), "Sabrina the Witch" (The N), "Beyond the Break" (The N), "Smallville" (Fox), "Malcolm in the Middle" (Fox), "The OC" (Fox), "Ugly Betty" (ABC), "Grounded for Life" (ABC Family), "Falcon Beach" (ABC Family), "One Tree Hill" (WB), "The Bedford Diaries" (CW), "106 & Park" (BET), "Wayans Brothers" (BET), "Total Request Live" (MTV), and "Friday Night Lights" (NBC). These widely watched programs—some long-standing and others new—include comedy, drama, and music/variety. I made notes on hundreds of commercials and charted more carefully all of the commercials in 20 programs to identify (1) the presence of any multicultural representations, including the presence of physically distinct racial or ethnic minorities and audible varieties of English that would be considered "marked," that is, not typical of any varieties of mainstream US English, (2) the physical and cultural characteristics of persons of color (for example, light or dark skinned; thin or heavy; unmarked speech versus marked dialect), and (3) whether persons of color speak and, if so, what variety of language and communicative function is performed in the speaking lines.

To focus on the way ideological codes move through the ads, I attended closely to the total program "package" that is made up of the actual program content (including the story or events and characters) plus all of the commercials that run during the program. The main questions related to the program package ask to what degree and how cultural diversity is represented in the commercials that are shown and how the package provides context for the commercial. As texts, each ad is potentially an ideological snapshot, and the work here is oriented to showing how these advertising texts position cultural diversity. Following Norman Fairclough's framing of the critical discourse analysis of media (1995), the project is "an attempt to show systematic links between texts, discourse practices, and sociocultural practices" (pp. 16–17).

Teen demographics and cultural diversity

The main data source for information about the presence of teens in the US population is the US Census Bureau, which collects information on self-reported race and Hispanic origin. These statistics always lag behind, but they still provide a solid overall profile of the population. The decennial census of the population is based on questionnaires delivered to every address in the country, with canvassing added as an extra measure to increase the participation rate—especially in areas in which responses to the census questionnaire lag behind. The aim of the Census Bureau in its decennial survey is to have every possible person accounted for so that the statistics approximate the total population as closely as possible. The data are not perfect nor are they complete, but they do provide reasonably valid snapshots of the population and its defining features. Between the 10-year intervals of the population census, surveys of samples of the population are conducted to ascertain how the population is changing.

The census data for 2000 were based on a US population of close to 281.5 million people. Today that number exceeds 300 million, so the numbers presented in the paragraphs that follow will have increased. Yet, the proportionality will give a good idea of the composition of the teen population. The census data are broken down into several main groupings for race and ethnicity. Data from a 2005 update of the US population (US Census Bureau, 2006) showed the racial breakdown for the entire population as approximately 67.4 percent non-Hispanic White, 13.4 percent Black and/or African American, 4.8 percent Asian and Pacific Islander, and 1.5 percent American Indian or Alaskan Native. The Hispanic population comprised 14.1 percent of the population, which includes Hispanics in any self-designated racial category. The specific data are presented in Table 3.1. Recently, the Department of Homeland Security has estimated that an additional 10.5 million unauthorized immigrants were living in the US in 2005 (Hoefer et al., 2006).

The Census Bureau presents the age of the population in groupings. For our purposes, two age groups are important: 10 to 14 years and 15 to 19 years. Together, these groups cover the tween and teen years, including the first post-high school year. The Census Bureau's 2005 estimate puts a total of close to 42 million individuals in these two age cohorts, broken down as follows (US Census Bureau, 2006):

10 to 14 years	20,857,743
15 to 19 years	21,038,989
TOTAL	41,896,732

Tweens and teens constitute approximately 14 percent of the entire US population. Like the population in general, this youth group is characterized by racial and ethnic diversity (see Table 3.2).[1] The majority of tweens and teens are still

Table 3.1. Population of the United States by race and ethnicity: 2005

Race and Ethnicity	Number	Percent
TOTAL Population	**296,410,404**	**100.0**
White only/non-Hispanic	198,366,437	66.9
White Hispanic	39,488,517	13.2
White in combination with other race	241,806,816	81.6
Black only/non-Hispanic	36,324,593	12.2
Black Hispanic	1,584,748	0.53
Black in combination with other race	39,724,136	13.4
Asian only/non-Hispanic	12,420,514	4.2
Asian in combination with other race	14,376,658	4.9
American Indian & Alaskan only/non-Hispanic	2,863,001	1.0
American Indian & Alaskan in combination with other race	4,453,660	1.5
Native Hawaiian & Pacific Islander/non-Hispanic	405,019	0.14
Native Hawaiian & PI in combination with other race	989,673	0.33
Hispanic or Latino origin	42,687,224	14.4

Source: US Census Bureau (2006). National Sex, Age, Race and Hispanic Origin: 2000–2005.

1   Information on ethnicity is limited to Hispanic and non-Hispanic because of the method used by the Census Bureau. Two separate questions are asked: (1) one about race, which has several choices plus the option of indicating a combination, and (2) one about ethnicity, which is simply a choice between Hispanic or non-Hispanic. Some scholars advocate abandoning the term "race" and using the term "ethnicity" to cover all of these arbitrary categories. Hecht et al. (1993) define ethnicity as "shared heritage" (p. 2). There are advantages to this type of definition because it bypasses the culturally steeped notions associated with

Table 3.2. Teen population of the United States by race and ethnicity: 2005

Race or Ethnic Group	Ages 10–14	Ages 15–19
TOTAL	**20,857,743**	**21,038,989**
White only/non-Hispanic	12,379,142	13,031,784
White only including Hispanic	15,897,506	16,192,543
Total: White and White with other race (inc. Hispanic)	16,371,990	16,590,680
Black only	3,330,715	3,279,954
Total: Black only and Black with other race	3,579,255	3,460,715
Asian only	792,275	800,284
Total: Asian only and Asian with other race	989,073	973,543
American Indian/Alaskan only	259,477	268,811
Total: American Indian/Alaskan only and AIA with other race	402,084	417,668
Native Hawaiian only	45,375	44,264
Total: Native Hawaiian only and Nat. Haw. with other race	95,868	91,814
Hispanic origin	3,859,218	3,460,936

Source: US Census Bureau (2006). National Sex, Age, Race and Hispanic Origin: 2000–2005.

White and of non-Hispanic origin, but there is diversity present of sizeable proportions. Approximately 17.5 percent are Hispanic or Latino/a, which is a higher percentage than for the population as a whole. The group identified as Black only (without another race) is approximately 15.8 percent—also higher in proportion than is the case in the overall population. While the Asian group is still relatively small in absolute numbers, the rate of growth over past years is reflected in the percentage of the tween and teen population in this group: 3.8 percent and 4.7 percent respectively for the category of Asian in combination with another race.

Overall, the White only group has been shrinking over the years, which is most dramatically revealed by the fact that 40 percent of the group ages 10 to 14 and 38 percent of the group ages 15 to 19 are made up of those who are classified in one or another of the racial minority groups and/or as Hispanic. The teen population is, without question, culturally and racially diverse.

Research by the PEW Foundation provides interesting information on the use of various forms of media by tweens and teens (Rainie, 2006). They use the term "millennials" to describe the group of 8- to 18-year-olds and to distinguish them from earlier age groups in the population. One characteristic of millennials is their immersion in a world of media and gadgets. Television

artificial categories for both race and ethnicity. On the other hand, it is precisely the culturally steeped categories that most people orient to and which carry the ideological force of "naturalness."

remains a large part of the daily environment for millennials, averaging 3 hours and 51 minutes of viewing per day, and some form of computer use averages 1 hour and 2 minutes per day.

The picture, then, is of an age cohort of tweens and teens—what PEW terms *millennials*—who are racially and culturally diverse, who are media saturated, and who watch television while at the same time increasing their use of the Internet, iPods and other such devices, mobile phones, and all manner of variations and interconnections among these.

Representation and "doing diversity" in advertising

In examining the way advertising represents multicultural society, the first issue to confront is what any such representations of diversity might signify about the arrangements of race and ethnicity in US society. Unquestionably, the saturation of our lives with mediated communication has changed the very nature of cultural meaning and the means for becoming and re-becoming cultural beings. Television, radio, film, and the Internet all provide the venues for cultural material and then shape the practices that we engage in as cultural beings. Every time we watch something on television (even if only for a moment), open a magazine, and use the Internet, we enter into a complex world of re-presentation steeped with the codes of ideology. Media culture circulates ideological codes that shape not only attitudes and practices but even the terms through which those codes might be contested and opposed. The media environment is so pervasive that it is not only through direct, engaged participation that we are flooded with its meaning systems. We are also brought into this media environment through discourses about mediated representations: conversations, intertextual references, and commodities that are drawn from mediated texts. Advertising is one substantial element in the environment of media culture, and our interest for this chapter is in how advertising gives meaning to the cultural make-up of society through the representations that are circulated. Both the general nature of mediated representation and the specific patterns of representing cultural diversity are important for understanding the complexity of verbal and visual images circulated through advertising.

"Advertising moments" and re-presentation

As we consider themes and variations in advertising that reference cultural diversity, it is important to focus not only on the specific ad but also on the more complex ways in which a range of ads stand in relation to one another. Advertising is a cultural practice, and cultural practices are made up of moments of their articulation. Lilie Chouliaraki and Norman Fairclough in their book *Discourse in Late Modernity* (1999), describe the process of how practices are related to other practices:

> Each practice is located within a network of practices . . . Practices are shiftingly articulated together to constitute networks of which they themselves become moments in ways which transform them . . .
>
> Networks of practices are held in place by social relations of power, and shifting articulations of practices within and across networks are linked to the shifting dynamics of power and struggles over power. (pp. 23–4)

Every ad is an *advertising moment*. By an *advertising moment*, I mean a particular ad in its immediate context. An advertising moment is the combination of the ad itself and what Cook (2001) refers to as the "accompanying discourse," or the discourse in which the ad is embedded but to which the ad makes no direct reference. For example, ads for L'Oréal's Vive for Men Daily Thickening Shampoo have appeared in a number of magazines, including *Rolling Stone* as well as in *Sports Illustrated*. Depending both on the focus of the magazine and the specific contents of the issue in which the ad appears, the context frames the ad differently. The cover of *Rolling Stone* for August 11, 2005 shows a large picture of Jimi Hendrix, legendary Black rock star with his unshaped, "natural" hair, and the headline reads, "The Legend of Jimi Hendrix." Encountering the Vive ad a few pages into the issue might be met with laughter in relation to this and other stories in the issue ("I guess Jimi didn't need this!") and to *Rolling Stone* itself, or possibly as a product worth a try for guys who would like to have a thicker hair look. The same ad in a *Sports Illustrated* issue will be seen by many older men—many of whom will be thinking of their disappearing hair—and by many more working-class men. The advertising moment, then, is the ad plus the accompanying discourse in a specific historical moment for the viewer/ consumer. Such moments have the potential to comment on cultural practices, practices related to broad patterns of consumption, specific products as cultural practices, but also images of social actors and their doings.

Advertising moments highlight particular ways in which *representation* works. When representations are repeated, they become what Stuart Hall (1997) terms "repertoires of representation and representational practices" (p. 239). Possibilities for the representation of racial and ethnic diversification in ads range from integration to separation—the comingling of races and ethnicities to the presentation of racial and ethnic groups separated from one another.

There are four main possibilities. In *advertising moments of integration*, the representation will show various racial and ethnic groups as equals, with similar interests and preferences, and with no conspicuous domination of one group by another, except possibly by one group's representations numerically outnumbering those of other groups (the early "United Colors of *Benetton*" campaign did this by presenting models of different racial and regional origins wearing Benetton clothes, and later has done this in some of its advertising by presenting juxtapositions of models who look racially and/or ethnically different from one another in a context that emphasizes their universal qualities).

Advertising moments of pluralism also represent various racial and ethnic groups but do so in a manner designed to preserve the distinctive cultural integrity of the groups that are represented (Virginia Slims' now infamous "Find Your Own Voice" campaign featured gorgeous pictures of women from different racial and ethnic groups wearing clothing to accentuate their distinctiveness).

In *advertising moments of tokenism*, the peopled scene will add some marker of non-Euro/White diversity to create a potential signification of multiculturalism without going the next step to represent a complex, diverse society. For example, one Tommy Hilfiger ad for classic men's clothing places a Black teenage boy in a portrait scene with two adult Whites (one male and one female who appear to be a couple), one White teenage boy, and a dog; the representation of the Black teenage boy is ambiguous and could be interpreted as the son of the White man and woman or as a friend of the White boy, who is the son of the White couple.

In *advertising moments of segregation*, the peopled scene separates one race or ethnic group from others. In fact, most ads that we encounter through mass media are moments of segregation, because most ads show only Euro/White people, but there is also racial and ethnic segregation in ads, especially when placed in media outlets targeted to specific groups such as *Ebony* magazine or *Latina* magazine. Segregation also exists in the language we hear in televised or Internet commercials simply because the speakers who we also see are Euro/White, and they, along with the many voice-overs, speak a variety of mainstream US American English. Rarely do we hear a version of English associated with a particular immigrant group or with the English spoken in other countries; when we do hear "difference," it's commonly British or, for women's cosmetics especially, French. In these different advertising moments, the people who are marked as "different" (more recently, I have often heard the term "diverse" people) can be represented as the "other."

Representation has in recent years received considerable attention in the field of cultural studies. One way to think of representation is to conceptualize it as an edited "re-issue," rather than a simple repeat of the "real" thing. When something or someone is re-presented, the object of representation is revised to highlight certain aspects and to diminish or to make disappear other aspects of that which is represented. Another way to think about representation is through the concept of *framing*, which takes the picture frame as its metaphor; when a picture is framed, certain things are excluded, certain things are included, and emphasis is a matter of how the boundaries give emphasis to the subject. This metaphor can be updated further by adding the metaphor of "Photoshopping": just as we can change, add, and subtract elements through easy photoediting processes, so too does representation change, add, and subtract elements of its object. Some years ago, Erving Goffman (1974) characterized the frame as answering the question, "What is it that's going on here?" Frames, he said, are made up of "strips" of activity: "any arbitrary slice or cut from the stream of ongoing activity, including here sequences of happenings, real or fictive, as seen from the perspective of those subjectively involved in sustaining an interest in them" (p. 10). In mediated contexts, the media producers are representing strips of activity, sometimes in freeze frames, sometimes in strips of isolated action, sometimes in mini-narratives that are intended to tell a particular story. These frames, to use Tucker's (1998) characterization, are made up of "a common stock of key words, phrases, images, sources, and themes [that] highlight and promote specific facts, interpretations and judgments, making them more salient" (p. 143).

Patterns of imagery associated with "difference" at any specific historical moment constitute what Hall (1997) terms a "regime of representation" (p. 232). When a regime of representation is operating, images are read in the context of one another, that is, they are always interpreted *intertextually* once a representation reaches the status of a regime. Returning to Grossberg et al.'s (1998) conceptualization of ideology, it is the recurring representations that provide the codes that underlie ideology. In the context of media, regimes of representation are significant for their role in constructing versions of "reality." Applying this idea to our consideration here of advertising that is directed at tweens and teens, we are interested in the particular types of recurring representations of cultural diversity as well as what breaks from those representations might mean in their contexts of articulation. Myra Macdonald (2003), in her book *Exploring Media Discourse*, puts it this way:

> The construction of what "race", or "femininity", or "Islam", or "media violence" might mean becomes an important feature of the media's productive work. The notion of construction [of reality by the media] implies neither an intention to deceive, nor an ability on the part of the media to determine our thinking. Instead, it suggests a vital interaction between the media's role in forming the "frames of understanding" we construct in our heads . . . and the actuality of our behaviour and attitudes . . . . [I]t is useful to refer to the media as *helping to construct* versions of reality. (p. 14)

If we substitute the word "advertising" for "media" in the above quotation, the point is that advertising has the power *because of its role in representation* to contribute through its production of representations to the frames of understanding for important social issues such as race, ethnicity, and cultural diversity more generally.

Representation bears a close relationship to *stereotyping*, but the two concepts are not synonymous. Representation re-presents and re-visions experiences by designating some things and not others and by framing that which is designated in particular ways. "Race" provides a clear example of representation. There is no definitive biological determination that corresponds to racial divisions, yet race in an American context has been designated a salient concept and is, thus, framed in particular ways, usually in four categories of representation that are labeled White, Black, Asian and Native American. These categories have historical standing relating to spurious theories of race that arose in centuries past. One influential theory came from the German physiologist, Johan Friedrich Blumenbach, who lived from 1752 to 1840. Based on his study of skulls, he classified humans into five race groups: Caucasians, Ethiopians (later termed Negroids), Mongolians (later termed Asians), Aboriginal New World people (later called Native Americans) and Malayans. He had various theories about the geographic origins for each group that are largely discredited today. Today, few people know the history of particular racial concepts, but we still carry those concepts as representational "realities" not only related to skin color but to a range of ideas about racial meaning, including notions of mixture, as in "mixed race."

Stereotypes are forms of representation, but they are specific in certain ways. Again, Hall (1997) is helpful in clarifying the distinction: stereotyping "classifies people according to a norm and constructs the excluded as 'other' " (p. 259). To Hall's characterization, I would add that stereotyping functions through reductionistic framing through which limited and recurring representations draw on a set of characteristics to signify the stereotyped object. For example, Native Americans are frequently stereotyped as slow, overweight and lazy. Such a stereotype is oblivious to both spiritual beliefs and historic circumstances that have shaped the experience of native peoples since the European conquest of the Americas. Once a stereotype is established as a representation for Native Americans, this regime of representation contextualizes how any given Native American is perceived as "other." Should the individual person or representation be perceived as not fitting the stereotype, that person will be considered an "exception." The dynamic in this case takes the "other" and reassigns that other to the category of "normal" by marking her or him as "exceptional" and not like all the "others."

"Doing diversity" in advertising

Emphasis on social roles and cultural identities easily leads to seeing people as objects and their actions as characteristics of their status as objects. Being able to identify roles and cultural identities can be helpful in understanding how historical patterns of media representation, especially societal discrimination and power inequities, influence current cultural practices. The drawback to restricting the consideration of cultural diversity to calibration of the roles that are re-presented for people of color is that the agency behind the re-presentation can take a backseat. One way of moving the agency behind the ads to the front seat is to think of diversity as a "doing." Here I draw on the work of sociologists Candace West and Sarah Fenstermaker (1995), whose discussion of socially marked "difference" is based on earlier work by West and Zimmerman (1987). West and Zimmerman discussed gender as an on going accomplishment, that is, *gender as a verb rather than a noun*: they theorized gender as "fundamentally interactional and institutional in character" (p. 137). West and Fenstermaker expand this idea to conceptualize race and class similarly as a way of thinking through the simultaneous enactments of gender, race and class by social players. Their contribution to our understanding of diversity is to situate it not only as created and reinforced through what people do and say, but also as created continuously in relation to the doing of gender and class. (Although these authors did not consider "age," this feature of social life could be similarly construed.) "The accomplishment of race," they said, "consists of creating differences among members of different race categories . . . Once created, these differences are used to maintain the 'essential' distinctiveness of 'racial identities' " (West and Fenstermaker, 1995, pp. 25–6.)

We can think about the ways in which cultural diversity is represented in advertisements as a doing—both by those who create the ads and then by the very representations circulating within the ads. The creators of ads are doing diversity when they place markers in the ads to signify culturally meaningful categories: the placement of people of color in particular ways, the appearance of people in ways that distinguish them as particular types of racial or ethnic actors, and so forth. But the ad is not just a frozen script of visual and verbal pieces fabricated into some type of whole "thing." Once placed in its accompanying discourse, the ad *does* something with the relationships of its elements, both visual and verbal. When the ad contains moving parts and audible voices, the doing of diversity becomes further multidimensional. Advertising in this way is part of the institutional processes through which difference, otherness, and diversity are created and presented as meaningful and relatively stable fixtures of the social environment. The doing of difference and diversity provides pathways for interpolating audiences into the ads and for—the advertisers hope—propelling their own doings.

Ideology and representation of people of color in advertising

Some attention has been given in recent years to the ways in which people of color are represented in advertising. Researchers have asked questions about the quantitative representation in ads of different groups in relation to their presence in the population, the situations and products most likely to include certain ethnic or minority group representation, and the role in which people of color are placed in ads. Mastro and Stern (2003) refer to these research areas as interests in frequencies, selective presentation, and presentation quality, and they provide a useful summary of prior research into these three areas. Much of this work is content analytic in nature, and it provides a valuable body of information about changes over time in the representation of people of color in ads.

In relation to the ideological implications of representation in advertising, each of the three areas is relevant, but in different ways. Quantity of representation is important to overcome the erasure of certain groups from the domain of product promotions—essentially to move these groups from a marginal status of non-recognition into some area of the frame that is available to advertising's consumers. Selective presentation in advertising associates particular groups with particular situations and products, which in turn reflect on the value of the group being represented. If Blacks, for example, are heavily represented in ads for Target and Sears but not in ads for stores like Bloomingdale's, their positioning as consumers may be devalued and stereotypes related to socioeconomic status activated. Mastro and Stern assert that presentation quality is "arguably the most illuminating measure of the value of the characterization" (p. 640). The ideological codes circulated based on the particular roles that are seen and heard in advertising moments incorporating diversity are important reminders of (1) how the society is structured, (2) what categories of people are in what positions, and (3) who in the society is most central.

Several studies offer useful perspectives on the status of advertising with regard to the representation of cultural diversity. Taylor and Stern (1997) analyzed 1,300 commercials aired in June 1994 on prime-time network television programs. Their findings about the representation of Asians raise particular concerns: although the proportion of Asian characters in the ads exceeded their proportion in the population, they were more likely than other racial and ethnically marked groups to appear in the background of commercials, and they were overrepresented in work situations. These researchers also considered what proportion of commercials in particular product categories were populated by the various race/ethnic groups. They found that Asians were most often seen in commercials "skewed toward products/services consistent with affluence and work orientation" (p. 55): retailers (11 percent of the entire sample of commercials in that category), cosmetics (10 percent), and telecommunications (close to 10 percent). Blacks were most often seen in commercials for food/beverages (30 percent of the entire sample of commercials in that category), and less but still quite often for retailers (29 percent). Latinos/as appeared most often in commercials in the automotive category (52 percent of the entire sample of commercials in that category), retailers (38 percent), and cosmetics (16 percent).

The study by Mastro and Stern (2003) mentioned earlier inquired about a range of attributes for those people of color who appeared in 2,880 network television commercials in February, 2001. They concluded that the overall representation of people of color in commercials had improved some over the years, but that there were still problematic issues. Although the frequencies of Black characters (12 percent) closely mirrored their presence in the population, this was not true for Asians (2 percent), Latinos/as (1 percent), and Native Americans (0.5 percent)—all of whom were underrepresented in the sample of television commercials. They found that Black characters were most likely to appear in commercials for financial services (20 percent of their representations) and food (18 percent of their representations); Asian characters were most likely to appear in commercials for technology (30 percent of their representations); Latino/a characters were most likely to appear in commercials for soap and deodorant (43 percent of their representations); and the few Native Americans who were depicted were most likely to appear in commercials for retailers such as Wal-Mart and automotives. Whites were depicted most often in commercials for technology (15 percent) and food products (15 percent). Furthermore, comparing the several ethnic and racial groups, Asian characters were seen significantly more often in work settings, Blacks and Latinos/as in outdoor settings, and Whites in the home. Neither Blacks nor Asians were typically represented as either giving or receiving orders.

Paek and Shah (2003) examined racial group representation in advertising placed in US news magazines that were published in the year 2000. Like Mastro and Stern, they found Asians models clustered in workplace settings as professionals, technicians and business people, as were Blacks and Latinos/as; but Blacks were also represented as athletes and Latino/as as blue-collar workers. The most frequent product categories for all of the ethnic and racially marked groups was, not surprisingly, business/finance/insurance because the ads were drawn from news magazines. Asian representation was also prominent for the product categories of electronics/computer and Internet companies. In comparison to Asians, for both Blacks and Latinos/as there was more dispersal in their representation across a broad range of product categories. These authors also noted that the language representations used in ads associated with Asian Americans stressed the work ethic.

Children's television commercials have also been the focus of several research studies. Studies of children's television focus on programs geared to children younger than is the focus in this chapter, but the profiles are nonetheless significant because they provide a baseline for understanding how race and ethnicity are represented in advertising to children, which is a "source of messages about social groups [that is significant] for children" (Bristor et al., 1995; Li-Vollmer, 2002). A range of studies that examined commercials aired during children's programming in the late 1980s and early 1990s found few "minority" representations; those that existed were almost always of Black characters (see Seiter, 1990; Greenberg and Brand, 1993; Li-Vollmer, 2002). A look at two more recent studies does not give one great cause to applaud the pace of progress.

Bang and Reece (2003) focused on commercials aired in the spring of 1997 in children's programs aired on the major networks (ABC, CBS, Fox, Nickelodeon, WB, UPN). Their sample included 813 commercials showing human characters. White characters appeared in 99 percent of the ads, Blacks and Asians were overrepresented based on their presence in the population, and Hispanics were somewhat underrepresented. Several findings provide a more telling view of what the child viewers were seeing. First, rarely were Black, Asian, or Hispanic groupings of characters seen without the presence of White characters, prompting the authors to comment that "Caucasian children may learn to believe that other ethnic groups are just like them, and thus fail to respect differences that exist among other ethnic groups" (p. 62). Second, Black characters were most likely to appear in commercials for food products (61 percent of the ads with Black characters compared to 46 percent with White characters, 17 percent for Hispanics, and 48 percent for Asians) and least likely to appear in toy commercials (only 18 percent of the Black characters compared to 33 percent of the White characters, 34 percent of the Hispanic characters, and 24 percent of the Asian characters). Third, Black and Asian characters were less likely than White characters to be represented in situations focused on home and family, which may convey a powerful message about the cultural integrity of these groups in relation to mainstream society— an especially powerful representation in an era steeped in rhetoric related to "family values."

A sample from a week of children's programming broadcast in 1998 on network and cable television was examined by Li-Vollmer (2002) to see what types of representation of people of color were present. The sample contained 2,429 people: 75 percent White; 20 percent African Americans, 2 percent Asian Americans, and 2.4 percent Latinos/as. Black characters were often seen in cereal ads (120 ads), and less often but with some frequency in restaurant (25 ads), snack/beverages/other food (23 ads), and toy (22 ads) ads. Asian Americans were present only in technology (12 ads) and cereal (16 ads) ads, and Latinos/as only in restaurant ads (29 ads). White characters appeared in ads for every category, but most often in ads for cereals (405 ads) and the snack and beverage category (260 ads). Role placement is a powerful form of representation, and these two aligned with racial identities: African American characters compared to Whites were relatively more frequently represented as athletes and musicians. When the race/ethnicity of the primary character in the commercial was considered, 29 percent of the African American primary characters were represented as laborers compared to 5 percent of the White primary characters and none of the other minorities. The few primary character roles given to other minorities were most often in the service worker category. The relation of speaking lines to race/ethnicity of the characters was also examined. Of all the speaking lines in the sample, 86 percent were uttered by White characters, and when the commercials represented integrated groups, over two-thirds of the speaking lines came from the mouths of Whites. Li-Vollmer concludes that although the presence of African American characters in children's television commercials "may give the casual viewer the impression that children's commercials are now multicultural, equitable, and progressive, a deeper examination suggests that this surface change masks continuing racial biases in the screen presence, casting, and direction of people of color" (p. 220).

The uneasy representation of cultural diversity in teen advertising

As a means for opening the lens on cultural diversity in televised commercials found in teen programming, this section presents a series of capsule profiles of specific program episodes. Knowing something about the program—its characters and plot lines—and then examining what types of representations of cultural diversity are present in the advertising moments found in these programs provides a qualitative view of how television advertising packages diversity for the teenage cohort. For purposes of this examination, the qualitative profiles are drawn from six different types of programs selected both because (1) they have been popular among teenagers and (2) they portray cultural diversity in various ways, ranging from programs populated exclusively or dominated by White people to those populated exclusively or dominated by people of color—in this case Black people, who with rare exception stand for "minority" in television programming.

Capsule profiles

One episode is highlighted from seven different programs in order to provide capsule profiles of how representations of diversity are embedded in commercials shown during teenage television programs. I selected three popular programs that feature largely or exclusively White casts and story lines (*Smallville, One Tree Hill*, and *The OC*). One program was selected because it has both a diverse cast and story lines that at times engage diversity to some degree as a subject matter (*Degrassi: The Next Generation*). Two programs were selected because the cast and story lines feature Black characters (*That's So Raven* and *One on One*), and one program was selected in the music/variety category because it is dominated by people of color and features rap artists (*106 & Park*).

Smallville

Smallville is the popular current-day spin on the life of Clark Kent as a teenager before he became Superman. The program is pure science-fiction drama filled with friendship, deception, romance, adventure, and secretive feats of power by Clark and those who have power from the green rocks that smashed into earth during a meteor storm. *Smallville*, which is rated TV 14, premiered in 2001 and is broadcast on The CW (a CBS affiliate previously known as the WB). The cast is White and as of this writing, the characters are young adults. The capsule summary here is from the episode aired on October 26, 2006. There were 46 ads from the pre-episode segment through to the ending scene and preview of the next installment. Of these, 10 were promotions for CW programs or ads for movies and DVDs. Among the remaining 36, six contained representations of cultural diversity in some form, accounting for 13 percent of all of the commercials and 17 percent of the product commercials.

#1: Chili's restaurant ran an ad for "Baby Back Ribs" that was quite diverse. In this ad there is (a) an Asian-looking female waiter who would be classified as a young adult, (b) an older Black man who is placed in what looks like a road side western style ribs joint and is seen holding a bottle (of beer?); and a couple that looks Hispanic. The speaking is done by the male voice-over, with the characters left as visual signifiers only.

#2: An ad for Citi Bank is presented as a comic parody of a White man with a pronounced accent who uses his Citi card in various places while a young man is trying to distract him through a range of antics. In the last scene, the man is buying a plane ticket to Istanbul, leading us to believe that he is being represented as Turkish. The ad presents a ridiculous series of events, showing the man as eccentric and dictatorial. Yet, this is one of the rare ads that uses English with an accent discernable as from a part of the world neither American nor European.

#3:   A young Black teenage male is featured in an ad for Verizon V-Cast. The male is placed in an urban street scene where we see him with his Verizon V-Cast, dancing to music that he announces to someone he meets (but who we do not see) is Fergie. He passes his Verizon wireless to the person(s) positioned to appear to be in front of him and in back of the camera. He is then distracted by two teenage girls who walk by (they appear to be Black). He grabs his Verizon and approaches the girls, saying, "Hey ladies, you like Fergie?" The teenage boy is represented in this ad as awkward and self-absorbed, but also apparently sure that his V-Cast of Fergie will win the babes.

#4:   A commercial for *NBA07 The Life*, Vol. 2 for PlayStation2 shows the rivalry between the real players, Kobe Bryant (Los Angeles Lakers) and the fictional player, Billy Joe Cuthbert, who was created and given a biography including his fame as a Guard on the Utah Jazz team. The name of Cuthbert is shown on the screen, as the two play against each other. Cuthbert—a White man—speaks in the commercial, and Bryant—a Black man—is silent.

#5:   Taco Bell advertises on *Smallville* with a portrayal of three young adults eating together (perhaps lunch): a Black woman, a White woman, and a White man. The voice-over is female, and the only one of the three who speaks is the White male.

#6:   We see three sports scenes in a commercial for the Massachusetts State Lottery. The commercial uses the explicit analogy that the lottery is like playing sports. The first scene depicts a baseball game that represents a White pitcher and a White first baseman. The second scene portrays a football scene, and we see two players from the New England Patriots: Quarterback Tom Brady, who is White, and Running Back Kevin Faulk, who is Black. The third scene is of a basketball game, and all of the characters represented are Black.

The commercials shown in *Smallville* that use characters who are identified as people of color rely for the most part on stock characteristics: a Black man in a rib joint, Black athletes, an Asian character placed in a restaurant in the server role. In one ad (Taco Bell) we see interactional diversity through the representation of a Black man with two Whites, but it is only the White man who speaks.

One Tree Hill

One Tree Hill (rated TV 14) is an hour-length drama in soap opera style that premiered in 2003 and airs on The CW and focuses on five White teenagers and their families. The characters experience a range of highs and lows, trials and tribulations—hooks-ups, break-ups, make-ups, accidents and death. The cast is White, with character names that sound White: Lucas, James, Peyton, Brooke, Nathan. "These five teenagers move through the everyday aspects of their personal and social lives as they face the cruelties of the high school world" (www.tv.com/one-tree-hill).

In an episode that aired on March 3, 2006, which was the third season finale, 50 commercials ran from the end of the program preceding *One Tree Hill* to the final scene; seven commercials preceded the first segment of the program and 42 were embedded in the program; and 13 commercials were for movies or other programs broadcast on the channel. Of these 50 commercials, eight (16 percent of the total) included characters who were racially represented as non-White; five of these show characters represented as Black or more clearly as African Americans. The ads in order are for:

#1: A commercial for Kashi Foods pictures various dark-skinned people in scenes that are represented as from countries with warm climates. Playing a dominant role in the ad is a White food buyer set in the various scenes and saying, "I go all over the world [to get Kashi ingredients]." The only speaker is the White male.

#2: Sunkist Orange Juice advertises by showing a pop music group that includes one Asian-looking teenage girl who appears to be playing a keyboard. She is shown quickly four different times during the ad, but the only speaking is provided by a male voice-over.

#3: A Secret Deodorant commercial depicts a White teenage girl playing a car racing video game with several boys. One boy says to another, "Dude, you lost to a girl." We see a young African American boy in the background as one of the losers, but he is not the person addressed in the ad. The speakers are the White teenage girl and one of the young White boys.

#4: Garnier Fructis Sleek and Shine Shampoo shows several different females in an ad that includes one Black girl with long, Afro-style hair parted in the middle; she is shown far in the background and at the end of the ad. The speaking is done by a female voice-over.

#5: Massachusetts State Lottery is promoted in an ad that tells viewers they can find out the winning numbers on the "10 O'clock News." The background for the ad is a scene of baseball players, all of whom are Black. The voice-over is male.

#6: INC Runway Collection (clothing for males and females) sold at Macy's represents one Black female model among approximately 10 runway models. The speaking is done by a male voice-over.

#7: Verizon presents a narrative-style commercial in which two White guys are making a documentary and asking different people if they are satisfied with Verizon. We are shown three satisfied customers in their natural settings. One is a White man in front of his pickup truck, which is filled with wood. The next is a White woman standing outside of her house on the driveway with her dogs. The third is a Black man who is standing in a stream fishing. When he speaks, his voice is phonologically stylized to represent an African American and/or southern intonation: "Ah got awl three [mobile phone, home phone, Internet] on one beel [bill]. It's great."

#8: An ad for Boost Mobile phone features Richard "Rip" Hamilton, NBA player for the Detroit Pistons. Hamilton is a heavily tattooed basketball player who wore a much commented-about clear plastic facemask for a couple years to protect his nose, which had been repeatedly broken. The ad is one in a series of ads that uses famous popular cultural personalities in a "then and now" narrative format, where Boost Mobile plays a major role in transforming the person from some ordinary status into their present fame. (One of these ads will be examined more closely in the next section.) The story is that "back in the day," a friend "chirped" Rip to a pick-up basketball game when he was young, and "the rest is history." The ad then presents an alternative scenario of what might have happened to Richard had he not been chirped. This section of the ad presents a parody of a Black funeral home—complete with a DJ next to the casket and a jiving, rocking parade of mourners. Richard is the funeral director presiding over a chaotic viewing, with the narrator telling the consumer that "Without Boost, he wouldn't be putting to bed the toughest defense. He'd be putting to bed the deceased as the hardest workin' man in the funeral business." The climax in this little narrative occurs when Richard accidentally sets fire to the place. We see him outside wearing Rip Hamilton's signature facemask. The ad ends as do all in the series with the voice-over narrator asking, "Where *you* at?"

What is striking about the Black figures that appear in ads in *One Tree Hill* is that they are either in the background and, thus, racially represented only by skin color appearance, or they are featured in ways that accentuate certain behavior or lifestyle features that quickly signify African American distinctiveness with social class overtones—the Black man fishing, the Black basketball star, and Black basketball background. These ads occur within the accompanying discourse of a program whose White cast navigates scenarios involving a range of teenage life experiences within a sanitized sub/exurban middle to upper-middle class environment. *New York Times* writer Charles McGrath describes the location of *One Tree Hill* and other television, movie, and literary environments like it as a place where "people tend to dwell in a classless, homogenized American Never-Never Land . . . [that is] an upgrade . . . from the old neighborhood where Beaver, Ozzie and Harriet, and Donna Reed used to live . . . airbrushed suburbs where all the cool young people hang out and where the pecking order of sex and looks has replaced the old hierarchy of jobs and money" (McGrath, 2005). McGrath doesn't mention that this "Never-Never Land" is a bastion of White people.

The OC

Set in Orange County, California, *The OC* is a TV-PG rated Fox television drama/soap opera that premiered in 2003. Set in the affluent Newport Beach community, the characters in this one-hour program are White and for the most part affluent. The kink in the class structure is a young man, Ryan, who "was taken in from the streets of Chino by then-public defender Sandy Cohen"—also an outsider to Newport Beach who married into a moneyed family. When the show debuted, the kids were teenagers in high school, but they have now graduated and are on to other things. The show is filled with romance, indiscretions, deceptions, and death. All of these entanglements involve White people, with only the rare appearance of a person of color. Black characters occasionally play a role, usually either in a background scene or as a character such a nurse in a hospital or a police or jail worker.

The episode considered for the advertising profile was the season premier for 2005, broadcast on September 8, 2005. This episode contains 44 commercials including those leading into the opening scene. Of the 44, 12 are promotions for other Fox programs and five are promotions for soon-to-be released movies or DVDs. Of the remaining 27, 10 include some type of representation of people of color. These 10 are described here:

#1: An ad for Filene's 2-Day Sale included a number of different visual representations of people to promote this department store's products in a trendy style accompanied by a male voice-over. The commercial shows six women, all of whom are White; two children, one of whom is an Asian girl; and three men, one of whom is Black. The Asian girl appears on the screen for such a short period of time that I missed seeing her the first time I watched the commercial.

#2: Sprint with Nextel is presented by showing a White male using his mobile phone in various urban scenes in which everything looks quite ordinary until he does something other-world-like, such as launching himself as a means of transportation. Black-skinned characters are present in some of the background scenes but have no conspicuous role—meaning that they could easily be missed.

#3:   A VW Passat commercial presents two 30-something men—one Black and the other White—throwing a football around in a neighborhood street. Both men are large, but the Black man is overweight, which is emphasized by showing his flabby belly hanging over his pants' waist when he jumps up to throw the football. This Black man has a speaking role, saying to the White man, "Who says you're outta shape"—after which he throws a long pseudo-pass, which the White man catches after crashing on top of a Passat that is parked on the street. The Black man comments, "Touchdown." A female voice-over provides comments about the car. In this ad, a Black person actually speaks, but he is represented in a stereotypical role of the out-of-shape former athlete. It is the White man who runs and is active, while the Black man pretty much stays in the same place.

#4:   Weight Watchers runs an ad showing 12 different short scenes with a varied sequence of women engaged in different activities to demonstrate that a broad range of women want to change their bodies for the better. Half of the sequences show White women only, and two of the sequences show women in silhouette, which makes it impossible to discern any racial or ethnic markers. The remaining four sequences include Black characters. In one, a White woman at a party is the central character, and among the partygoers in the background can be seen a Black male–female couple. Another sequence shows three women together, with a White woman prominently positioned in the foreground and a second White woman positioned slightly behind her and to the right. A Black woman is positioned farther behind and slightly to the left of the central White woman; of the three, she is least visible and the farthest in the background. The third sequence with Black characters presents a foursome of women at a table—perhaps in a kitchen—toasting one another; two of these women are Black, but the most prominent of the four is a White woman. The last of the scenes is of a Black woman with a "natural" hairstyle who is placed in a bedroom with two children. The children are energetically jumping up and down on the bed. This last scene is the only one to position the Black woman prominently and to provide a scene that is exclusively populated with Black people.

#5:   A commercial for Southwest Air to Ft Myers/Naples features a happy-looking White man in a business suit arriving in Florida. We see him in the airport and then waiting for and getting on a shuttle bus, smelling the presumably alluring air, which the male voice-over calls "destination smell." A Black man, who is casually dressed and looks pleasantly happy, appears three times in the ad, positioned behind the White man. We also see an Asian man (he looks Japanese) ready to board the bus, but he appears for less time than the other two men. In the scene where the White and Black man are getting on the bus, the Black man is positioned behind both the White man and a White woman who suddenly appears in the seat in front of the Black man and in back of the White man. The scene at the airport ends, and a screen is shown with information about Southwest Air, which is accompanied by the male voice-over. The "minority" representations in this ad stand out because the Black man is always behind the White characters, and the Asian/Japanese-appearing man appears to be a tourist.

#6: A DSW shoe store ad pictures a diverse range of women shopping in a typical, large DSW store, interspersed with close-up shots of various shoes. The only shopper who is positioned centrally in the ad is White. One woman who is by herself in a camera shot, but off to the side of the screen, appears by her manner to suggest that she is Middle Eastern. There is one shot where a Black woman and an Asian woman are clearly discernable, but they are in the background. Interestingly, we hear in this ad and several to follow it voice-overs using proper British-accented English.

#7: iPod Nano advertises their product in a clever sequence of hands touching the product. In some shots we see just one hand holding and manipulating the iPod, and in other shots, we see not only the iPod in a hand but also another hand unsuccessfully reaching for it because the hand holding it will not relinquish this product. Among what seem to be 12 different hands in the ad, two are Black—one holding the iPod and one in another scene grasping for the iPod.

#8: The T-Mobile Family Plan commercial is only marginally inclusive of diversity, but I've included it here because a Black person, and possibly an Asian person, is visible at the end of the ad. We first see several crazy, comic scenes between a White father and his White children. In each scene, the father is clutching his phone bill and chewing out the son or daughter for the number of minutes they have used, while at the same time the father is oblivious to something noteworthy or dramatic that is happening: the daughter calls to say she got an A+ in honors physics; the father barges into the son's room to protest the phone bill, and the boy is caught dressing up like a woman; the son has just accidentally crashed through the garage with the car, which was in Drive rather than Reverse. After these scenes, we see a mobile phone store with a number of people milling about; one of these people is a Black man, and another might possibly be represented as some indeterminate Asian-like female. The voice-over for the ad is male, and speaking with a proper British accent.

#9:   Various people are listening to Shakira sing "La Tortura" in a Verizon V-Cast commercial. Prior to a picture of the mobile phone and some product details, we see six scenes, each with different people. One of these scenes has a Black man positioned behind and to the side of a White woman. After the picture of the phone and product details, the ad cuts to the last scene, which depicts a middle-aged, balding Asian man wearing a white apron who seems to have just exited from some interior urban location. My interpretation is that he is represented as a restaurant worker who has come out of the restaurant for a break, and he's enjoying the V-Cast. In this ad, we again see representations of marginality and stereotyping, with a Black character positioned behind a White character and an Asian man represented in a manner whose connotation is of a stereotypic job category.

#10:   A musically rich commercial for Gap Jeans, which could be subtitled "Favorite Songs, Favorite Jeans," features six different people, two of whom are Black. The ad is composed of a series of cuts to different people, each of whom has their favorite song and favorite jeans (which we are to conclude are Gap jeans, although that is left unstated). One of the people is a Black woman, whose hair is long, wavy, flowing and definitely not in a curly, natural style. The Black man we see is at the piano playing and singing his favorite song "Hello it's me . . ." in mellow tones. He is handsome, with his hair in short braids, and he wears a dark suit jacket over a dark shirt. This Black man appears again at the conclusion of the ad, looking out to the camera and saying, "What's your favorite?" Three things can be said about the images of Blacks in this ad. First, one-third of the scenes focus on Black persons, which is quite distinctive among other ads. Second, the Black woman does not have natural or nappy hair, which is a certain type of representation in and of itself. Third, the Black man is presented in a professional manner and he not only speaks, but he also has the only speaking role of the on-screen people and his speaking is placed at the very end of the ad to provide the concluding thought.

What we have among these 10 commercials in *The OC* is a predominance of minority representations that are marginal and silent, and/or stereotypical and non-threatening. The woman in the Weight Watchers ad is confined to the interior domestic role of mother. The Black man playing football in the street is overweight. One of the Asians appears to be a Japanese tourist, and another

Asian man is represented as a restaurant worker. When positioned along with
Whites, most of the Blacks stand behind or are in the background. The Gap
commercial is a departure from this pattern, breaking the stereotypic portrayal
of the Black male and, in fact, giving him the last word in the ad. In some of the
ads, there also seems to be exploitation of the snob appeal of the British accent
for the voice-overs. For the US audience, this is a particular ideological claim
about language and the hierarchy of certain accents over others.

The OC draws an older group of viewers along with younger teens, and has
probably had much more draw for Whites than for people of color. The show is
White dominated, making the array of commercials completely compatible
with the type of drama/soap opera in which they are embedded. Minorities are
around the edges. They are sometimes obvious, but in the background. When
they do emerge against the grain of stereotyping, as in the Gap commercial,
they fit into the world of beautiful appearance. There's nothing wrong with
challenging the grain in this way, but the accompanying discourse for the ads
may provide a particular spin to what it means to step out of the minority
ghetto as a background figure.

Degrassi: The Next Generation

Premiering in the US in 2002, *Degrassi* is a gritty look at teenage life in the
context of a middle school and high school and, recently, a college environment. This program is broadcast on "The N" which is the night side of Noggin,
a daytime children's channel. The website for the channel (The-N.com) promotes the site and the N programs as "real":

> The-N.com is a site for you. It's a place you can come to let your opinion
> loose, play games, make stuff, and hang out. It's also the spot to find
> out more about the shows on The N, and about the stuff that happens
> in those shows. The-N.com is your community and it feeds The N on TV.
> So speak up, freely and often . . . The N is REAL . . . Real doesn't
> mean just "reality" programs, documentaries, or the news. It means the
> shows on The N are about your real life and the things you're dealing with
> every day.

The attempt here is to promote the representations as documentary-like rather
than fictionalized.

Degrassi is rated PG (parental guidance). One summary found on the Internet
reads as follows:

> This show is about a group of 7th to 12th graders at Degrassi Community

School. Kids at DCS deal with all kinds of issues (i.e. sex, drugs, dating, rape, abortion, sexuality, oral sex, religion and eating disorders). [Having spun off from earlier programs set in junior high school and high school, DCS has merged with another high school.]. . . . Some characters from these two [earlier] shows are in Degrassi: The Next Generation . . . and now have to deal with the real world now some of them are off to university and living on their own. (Degrassi, 2007)

The cast for this program is multiracial and diverse in many ways. Nineteen characters are featured on the website for The N. Among these are a Black brother and sister, a gay male named Marco Del Rossi, a girl named Manny Santos, and a male character (Black and possibly represented as Hispanic) who is now in a wheelchair because of a sports injury. When watching the show, the overall impression is that the White characters are much more central both because of their numbers and their prominence in the episodes. Yet, the show, unlike much of TV fare, has an urban, multicultural feel to it.

The one-hour program episodes average around 12 ads each, some of which are promotions for other programs airing on The N. In an episode aired on January 11, 2007, there were 15 commercials, four of which were program promotions. Of the remaining 11 commercials, only two represented non-White characters. The first one was for Sylvan Learning Centers, and featured three young people (the students) being assisted by three different tutors. One student was represented as Asian and given the name "Tiffany Moy." One of the tutors was represented as an Asian-looking woman. The choice of an Asian student, rather than a Black student or a student represented as Latino/a, plays into the stereotypic association of Asian Americans with academic perseverance and improvement. The second commercial was for the anti-drug website, abovetheinfluence.com. This public-service type commercial will be analyzed in detail later, but the main layout is of an older African American boy and a younger African American boy enacting a scene in an advertising setting in which the older boy is trying to get the younger boy to take drugs from him. Toward the end of the ad, each breaks character, which signals to the viewer that these boys were being portrayed as actors trying to make a commercial that is realistic. The ads are sponsored by the National Youth Anti-Drug Media Campaign (a program of the Office of National Drug Control Policy), whose web site states that, "Our goal is to help you stay above the influence. The more aware you are of the influences around you, the better prepared you will be to stand up to the pressures that keep you down" (abovetheinfluence.com).

That's So Raven

This show debuted in January, 2003, and has enjoyed a successful run on the Disney channel. Appealing to a tween and young teen audience, this half-hour situation comedy centers around Raven Baxter, an African American teenager who often has visions about the future. Pursuing these visions leads to problems for Raven and her friends, and her family also poses its own comedic challenges. Many of the Disney channel programs carry numerous promotions for the channel itself as well as for other Disney products, experiences, and destinations. This internal advertising approach is a means for promoting the Disney brand (see Preston and White, 2004). Many of the Disney ads include people of color interacting harmoniously with one another, which is an attribute of the company's brand. [There is, however, a dark side to Disney's promotion of cultural diversity, both in its purchase of cultural products by acquiring copyrights and in the particular ways in which cultural diversity is exploited and portrayed in many Disney films (Bollier, 2005; Lippi-Green, 1997).] A few non-Disney products are advertised on programs aired on the Disney channel. In each of two episodes that aired on August 29, 2006, just two non-Disney ads were shown: one for General Mills in the first episode (which originally aired in 2004) and the other for Gatorade in the second episode (which originally aired in 2005). The voice-over for the General Mills ad proclaims, "General Mills is a proud sponsor of Disney, where good nutrition is a part of every day." A White boy and a White man appear in the ad, with each speaking briefly after they race on foot through a tunnel. The boy can keep up with the man in this advertising moment because he ate his General Mills cereal. The Gatorade ad features the US women's soccer icon Mia Hamm as spokesperson. In the ad, we see visual images of both Black and White male and female athletes. The most conspicuous aspect of these ads is the absence of Black representations in central roles.

One on One

This show premiered on The N in 2001. A comedy/drama program rated TV PG, One on One features a middle-class Black family situation with a teenage girl and her widowed father. The father has a college degree in communication and is an on-air sportscaster. His best friend, who sells used cars, is a central character. The grandparents are also featured, and the grandmother teaches in public school. The program is in a 30-minute time slot.

An episode that aired on January 11, 2007 included 15 commercials, six of which were either ads for movies or promotions for other programs on The N. Of the remaining nine, two included representations of Black characters, and they were both for web sites. One of these was for Zwinky.com, which is a toolbar for kids. In the ad, both Black and White animated figures are dancing to a male rap tune that promotes the web site; the narrative tells the story of the boys waiting for the girls to be ready to go out, while the girls were dancing around and trying on different clothes. When I checked the web page for the toolbar, the figures represented were all of White teenagers (again, in animation and trying on different clothes). Perhaps the assumption is that only White kids have access to the Internet. The second ad was for The N's web site, which offers program features, fan links, games, music, and a range of other options. The ad included a number of clips from different The N programs, some in a large frame on the left of the screen and some in a small frame on the right of the screen. A male voice-over beckoned the viewer to come to the web site and "put yourself in the show with video commentary." All of the clips in the large frames featured White program characters, with only one Black character seen in one of the clips. There was one clip in the smaller frame of a Black male and female pair, but this was less prominent because of its placement on the web page. For a program with a Black cast and likely more Black audience members than many comedy programs for teens, the Black representation is neither substantial nor central. Yet, it is intriguing that both ads in which we see Blacks are for web sites—an appeal to the technology interests of the middle class.

106 & Park

BET (Black Entertainment Television) airs *106 & Park*—a program featuring the Top 10 countdown of pop/rap music. This 90 minute program, which airs each weekday at 6 pm and on Saturdays (with repeats at other times), is co-hosted by a Black man and Black woman, with guest music artists appearing as special hosts. There is a live studio audience. The profile presented here is for the first 60 minutes of the program that aired on June 14, 2006—"W.O.W. W.O.W. Wednesday with guest host Bow-Wow." During this hour, 55 commercials aired; 22 (or 40 percent) of these represented people of color in ads for products other than BET programs (four ads, all of which featured Black people) or movies and DVDs (six ads). Four of the 22 were repeated during the program, resulting in 18 different product commercials. Nine of the 18 product ads picture Black people only, and one ad pictures Black people but with the brief insertion of White hands at one point (see description that follows for the Bounty ad); in some of these ads, Black people speak and in others they are visually represented with the speaking restricted to the voice-over role. Clearly, the BET program site provides a racial niche for commercials in which Black characters (and a few other people of color) appear. The 18 different commercials with people of color are listed here, with those showing Black people exclusively marked with an asterisk(*):

#1:   Hershey's Chocolate presents a rare multi-cultural representation of society in its ad. In it, we see six different profiles: first an Asian female, then a White male, then two Black men, then a White man, then another Black man and finally a Black man with another non-Black man. In one way or another, each proclaims the virtues of Hershey's chocolate. The female who is represented as Asian actually speaks as the commercial begins, saying, "Hershey's milk chocolate is what I grew up on." In the third profile, we hear a Black man speak: "I'll never fumble one of these," and a Black man (this one with braids) again speaks in the fifth profile, saying "I can't share my chocolate with anybody else." This ad is repeated during the program.

#2:   *A commercial for FYE (For Your Entertainment) stores and Internet site pictures Black performing artists in the background with a male voice-over hyping the vendor.

#3:   Dr Pepper advertises using a narrative of a boxing match with White boxers and an elderly Black man as referee. The referee speaks when one of the White boxers is knocked down hard, saying, "Hey kid, how many fingers do you see." Dr Pepper is the answer to clearing his head.

#4:   *BET offers a special Mobile download product that is advertised as Rap City Hot Picks (with the first two words a skillful play on "rhapsody"). The male voice-over for the ad speaks in phonologically distinctive African American English. This ad is repeated twice in the program.

#5:   *Another FYE commercial promotes a "Field Mob" CD in the same format as the prior FYE ad.

#6:   *A commercial for the Marine Corps is exclusively composed of Black men. Created in a superhero style with pictures and real-appearing men imposed on scenes with graphics much like those found in stylized adventure games, the scenes are accompanied by a male voice-over who speaks with an authoritative-sounding tone: "In all the world there are a select few who at their very core are capable of incredible transformation under the most grueling conditions. They are shaped, hardened, sharpened, and ready to stand among the elite of all warriors. The proud Marines." The blatant appeal to African American men not only engages a separatist theme related to race and gender, but also appeals to Black men to achieve hegemonic White masculinity (Collins, 2004) by proving themselves in the Marines.

#7:   Fridays restaurant presents a scene with four guys being delivered a pig-out meal. One of the guys is Black, and the other three are White.

Each growls out the name of a food item (beef, pork, beans, sausage), and a male voice-over proclaims the quality and quantity of the food.

#8:   *A commercial for Crest Scope Extreme Toothpaste tells an urban story of two Black guys driving in traffic along a crowded city street. They are fighting over directions of some kind, when the guy on the passenger side lowers his window to ask the woman in the car next to him at the stop light. Two Black women are in that car, and once the guy's sweet breath wafts over to the female driver, she simply calls out her phone number in carefully enunciated, Standard US English. The frustrated driver seeking directions is then heard saying to his companion, "Ahh we evah gun git directions?" The language patterns of the female and male who speak display a polarity between the woman's careful language and the casual, dialect-inflected language of the man. The voice-over is female.

#9:   Andi, which is a game for X-Box and Playstation, is advertised by showing a simulated men's basketball game. We see two players closely—one Black and one White. The White player speaks briefly, but the Black player is silent. The voice-over is female. This ad is repeated later in the program.

#10:   A commercial for Wendy's restaurant features a White customer and a White server, both of whom have speaking roles. Several Black customers are seated at tables in the restaurant.

#11:   *A commercial for Sears Covington Polo Shirts engages diversity by featuring a male model for the shirts, who is clearly marked as Latino. His facial features seem Mexican, he is stocky, and he has a large (stereotyped) mustache. The Latino man doesn't speak but, rather, shows his pleasure through wide smiles. He is, in short, a visual stereotype who is accompanied by a male voice-over.

#12:   *An ad for Verizon V[ideo] CAST portrays visual images of cultural diversity by showing Blacks, Whites and Asians enjoying their music videos on the mobile devices. These characters are all silent, with the speaking left to the female voice-over.

#13:   *The Prudential Yahoo Real Estate commercial is unique in that it features a Black man in a position of professional authority and power. We see in this commercial a distinguished looking, gray-haired Black man in a business suit who has a valuable product to give to the consumer —in this case a younger White woman. He speaks in standard English and is presented as the quintessential businessman, but with a hint of parody added by a James Bond 007-style music playing in the background.

#14:   *Downy fabric softener advertises by showing three generations of Black women: a young girl, whose dressy dress is soft because of Downy, and what we are led to assume are her mother and grandmother. None of these Black women speak, however, and we hear only the standard articulation of a female voice-over.

#15: *Olay Daily Facials are cleansing pads whose presumed effects are shown in a commercial featuring a Black female model. She does not speak, and again, we hear only the standard articulation of a female voice-over.

#16: *Olay Quench Lotion is presented in the same format as the Facials. We see a Black female model, with the speaking role restricted to a female voice-over using standard articulation.

#17: *Panteen Totally You Tour presents an ad for its multi-city women's empowerment conference featuring various Black women celebrities and Black women known for their professional accomplishments. This ad is a set of images of women at these conferences with a female voice-over serving like a narrator. At the end, a Black woman who would clearly be an attendee rather than a featured speaker says, "This completely exemplifies sisterhood."

#18: *An ad for Bounty paper towels depicts a Black family composed of a mother and father, their son (likely a sixth or seventh grader) who is building a dinosaur for his school science fair, and a younger pre-school age daughter who is eating a popsicle. The scene is in the kitchen where the project is underway with lots of glue and paint. The father is assisting the son while the mother stands by. When a jar of paint spills, the mother is there to the rescue with a Bounty towel. Next we see a short demonstration of Bounty's absorbency; the hands holding the towels in this demonstration are White (perhaps this segment was produced for another ad featuring White actors). At the very end, the mother says, "nice"—either to refer to the science project or the absorbency of Bounty. What we have here is a typical nuclear family scene with the kind of stereotyped roles often seen in television ads. The family is Black but any American family could be substituted into the scene and scenario.

The verbal and visual images of Blacks are clearly more prominent in the ads presented in this BET program. The one commercial showing a Latino is also unique, but unfortunately its stereotyped quality makes it little more than a parody of the worst of ethnic essentialism. Like many ads, the spoken word in the commercials seen on *106 & Park* is mainly heard in voice-overs, but when characters marked for diversity do speak, it is men's rather than women's voices that we hear.

Two cases of racialized ads and their accompanying discourse

The seven capsule profiles provide glimpses of how diversity is brought into advertising images and how such images are placed within the accompanying discourse of their program contexts. From a marketing perspective, it appears that images of diversity in advertising are more numerous and more nuanced when the viewers are a combination of people of color and those of mixed racial and ethnic composition. Images of diversity appear to be less important when the advertising is placed in programs that invite a largely White audience through their portrayal of White social situations. Yet, it is precisely these latter programs where the larger cultural significance of advertising images related to diversity reflects ideological codes circulating more broadly in society. In this section, I examine two television commercials and their program placements as a vehicle for raising awareness of the potential racial and racist images that may be circulating in teen advertising for White consumption. The first ad is for Boost Mobile—a product of T-Mobile, and the second is for abovetheinfluence.com.

Boost Mobile as racial commodification

Boost Mobile (which is owned by Sprint/Nextel) presents their walkie-talkie mobile phone products through an advertising campaign that features edgy hip-hop narratives, most of which feature "cool" entertainers and sports stars such as Fat Joe, Eve, Kanye West, Ludacris, Richard "Rip" Hamilton and Nick Cannon. Marketed mainly to teens and young adults, the style of the advertising engages rap rhythm, vernacular language, and light parody. The brochures available where the phones are sold refers to the Boost service as "Chirp Days Chat Nights Plan." The lead text in the brochure assures the teen and young adult of the trendiness of this product: "Boost™ Walkie-Talkie lets you stay in the loop while our NEW RELAXED cell rates let you kick back and speak out—on your own terms, at your own pace." Appropriating the word, "relaxed" adds a metaphor of Black coolness, drawing as it does on the base meaning of "relaxed" for the loosening or straightening of tight curls (Smitherman, 1994).

Each television commercial in this Boost Mobile series is organized into a five part story: (1) a scene with an actor playing the featured star as a youth, in which she or he is called to some event or place by being "chirped"; (2) the youth arriving at the scene and either witnessing or doing something transformative, ending with a male voice-over saying, "And the rest is history"; (3) a somewhat silly scene (presented as parody) portraying what the person might have turned out to be had she or he not been chirped at the right moment; (4) a scene in which the featured star is shown in a way that magnifies his or her celebrity; and (5) the final voice over and visual verbal tag, "Where *you* at?" (emphasis added to show the stress pattern).

My interest in the Boost Mobile ads centers on their placement in programs featuring White casts and catering to White audiences. The ad I am focusing on here features the singer/songwriter/rap artist Eve Jeffers (formerly a stripper), and the accompanying discourse in which this advertising moment occurs is an episode of *Malcolm in the Middle* that was aired on September 5, 2005. The ad is part of the series that features Richard "Rip" Hamilton, NBA player for the Detroit Pistons, that is described (ad #8) in the capsule summary above for *One Tree Hill*. When pitched to White teen audiences, these ads are prime examples of how race is commodified as a style to be bought by White teenagers who deal with none of the liabilities of being a person of color in US society.

The program context for the Boost Mobile commercial is one of situation comedy broadcast on the FOX network. *Malcolm in the Middle* premiered in 2000 and ran new episodes through 2006. The story line revolves around Malcolm, who is a White adolescent in a close family including his parents and four brothers. Because Malcolm is a genius, he tends to hang out with an odd assortment of characters. The program overall and the episode in particular from which the commercial is drawn are not populated exclusively by White characters. There are students of color in Malcolm's school, and one character is handicapped. Yet, this situation com centers on Malcolm's life—complete with his White, somewhat quirky nuclear family.

The September 5, 2005, episode included 17 commercials including those immediately before the program began through the running of the credits. Of these 17, the only one to feature people of color is the Boost Mobile commercial. Three other commercials represent diversity: two show Blacks briefly in background roles and the third shows an Asian female and a Black male separately:

#1: A commercial for Fructis Shampoo for Color Treated Hair features a series of White women, in classic moving pictures of flowing hair. Interspersed are social scenes that include men, one of whom is a light-skinned Black male with long, curly hair.

#2: A training school called ITT-Tech is advertised by featuring a male who appears to be 30-something giving a testimonial for the training program. A number of still, close-up shots of younger students are shown briefly, followed by various out-of-focus background shots of students in a classroom situation—one of these students appears to be a Black female, but she appears very briefly.

#3: A commercial for Gatorade presents a series of black-and-white visuals of what appear to be six different athletes who are performing hard and sweating profusely, but with only a black background rather than in specific scenes. After the performance series, a series of quick frames represents the athletes, with moisture dripping from their faces and bodies, gulping down Gatorade. In the performance series, we see an Asian woman jump-roping and a Black male playing basketball; these two appear again in the "gulping Gatorade" sequence, plus there is another Black male with dreadlocks in this series.

The commercial for Boost Mobile is placed in the middle of the program. The transcript presented here (see Transcript 3.1) contains both the verbal elements of the commercial and descriptions of what is seen on the screen. Text without quotation marks is voice-over, and text with quotation marks is spoken by on-screen characters.

The short narrative presented in this commercial is steeped with images of urban, ghetto hip-hop culture. In the first scene, young Eve is represented in front of a brick building—suggestive of her urban apartment. The location to which she is chirped is an urban street scene. The verbal images throughout exude Black urban culture: the intonation is hip-hop, and both the phonology and syntactic features of the language that is spoken are typical of African American Vernacular English (AAVE; see Rickford and Rickford, 2000 for an excellent overview). For a short narrative, the verbal marking is especially noteworthy because it so forcefully carries the meaning of Black youth culture. "Where you at?" (lines 14 and 19) and "Where you goin'?" (line 16) represent a classic syntactic feature of AAVE called "zero copula" (also referred to as "copula deletion"), which is the absence, in comparison to mainstream US English, of the "to be" form—in this case the absence of "are" as would be the case in "Where are you going?" or "Where are you [at]?" This repetition of zero copula is the only syntactic feature of AAVE that we hear, which is consistent with a general trend, noted by Bailey (2001), for hip-hop and Black vocabulary to cross over into the mainstream but for AAVE syntax to cross over much less.

From a cultural perspective, placing the Boost Mobile ad in *Malcolm in the Middle* contributes to the circulation of Black discourse as a commodity for White middle-class kids. Embedding the ad in *Malcolm* makes it especially conspicuous since *Malcolm* is not in any focused way about urban culture or hip-hop kids. White middle-class kids can treat the Boost Mobile phone and its associated lifestyle as something that is for sale and that, if purchased, will signify their participation in a piece of "ghetto life style" (see Jones, 2007; Daniels, 2007). The discourse of the commercial commodifies the language through a synecdoche where the zero copula and phonological "sounding

Transcript 3.1 Commercial for Boost Mobile Featuring Eve Jeffers (September 5, 2005)

Line	On-Screen Description	Voice-over and Speaking Lines
1	Male VO	back in the day [Eve, back in the day when she was about 6 years old, is shown on screen]
2		Eve's friend Alexis chirped her
3	shows Eve as a young Black girl dancing in an urban street scene	to a block party
4	shows a Black	where she witnessed some dude get broken off by a
5	female MC with	female MC
6	the guys (all Black) and Eve looking on	and the rest is history
7	shows Eve as young	without Boost, she would have pursued
8	teen in dance show	a career in dance
9	shows Eve as adult	ultimately ending up as a ballet instructor in Eastern Ukraine
10	barking out "Russian" commands	[which is translated on screen to "Garbage"]
11	we see Eve	But luckily for us and for Eve
12	as rap star in a recording session	she has Boost Mobile
	phone rings	
13	Eve	"Hold on 1 sec" [addressed to a male production director]
14	Eve answers phone	"Where you at" [speaking into phone]
15	Director	"Cut"
16	Eve	"Chris [to the production director], where you goin
17		I'm almost done" [addressed to director]
18	VO	Where you at

Black" stand for vernacular Black culture. The language can be had for the price of the phone, with its "relaxed" rates appropriate for those who cannot afford a regular plan and whose parents likely will not be purchasing a family plan that extends to the kids.

The comic element in this commercial is the parody of what Eve might have become had she not been chirped. The joke is at the expense of a stereotypic representation of the Russian mode of drilling young dance students. Since we rarely if ever hear languages other than English in mainstream television commercials, using Russian-sounding language and calling it "garbage" perpetuates the cultural elitism attached to US English. In some ways, the comic element in the Boost Mobile ad featuring Rip Hamilton that was described above is even worse, because here the parody is of the Black funeral—which is not a cultural form that has passed over into more mainstream US society. Added to this is the placement of the Rip Hamilton version in *One Tree Hill*, which provides an almost whiter-than-white accompanying discourse. For the White viewer, the parody provides license to *laugh* at a ritual of historic significance in African American culture. For the Black viewer, there is the paradox of laughing with the White viewer, and thus being in an object position in relation to the comedy, versus laughing at yourself and your own culture, and thus being in a subject position in relation to the comedy.

abovetheinfluence.com *and the necessity of Black-on-Black*

The National Youth Anti-Drug Media Campaign (a program of the Office of National Drug Control Policy) ran an ad featuring two African American boys on a number of programs in early 2007. I saw the ad not only on *Degrassi* (described in the capsule statement earlier) but also on *Beyond the Break* (broadcast on The N), reruns of *Sabrina the Teenage Witch* (broadcast on the The N), and *Veronica Mars* (broadcast on the CW). Although *Degrassi* includes multiracial and multiethnic representations, the other programs are populated mainly by White characters.

The commercial in question is an interesting twist on the "mini-drama" style (Geis, 1982) of advertising narrative. The mini-narrative in this case presents a narrative within the narrative of the commercial (see Transcript 3.2). As the scene opens, we see two Black teenage boys standing against a chain-link fence that is in front of a basketball court and what looks like an urban school. Then a boy who is represented as elementary school age walks by. One of the older boys stops him, and the scene unfolds. The narrative is simple: these boys are making a commercial; the commercial begins with the older boy trying to introduce the younger boy to "weed" (lines 1–7); the two break character because of something that the younger boy says; they agree that they need better dialogue, but the older boy tells the younger boy that he "done good" (lines 8–10); a voice over delivers a message that, "Big brothers who live above the influence have little brothers who live above the influence" (line 11).

The scene is represented to be reminiscent of an urban ghetto. Both boys wear white t-shirts; the teenage boy wears baggy pants, and the younger boy wears shorts. Although not in black-and-white, the whole commercial is presented in black-white-gray tones, which underscores the concrete of the

Transcript 3.2 Commercial for abovetheinfluence.com (January 2007)

Line	On-Screen Description	Voice-over and Speaking Lines
	scene is of two Black teenage boys standing against a wire fence, behind which is a basketball court and what looks like an urban school a younger boy walks by and is stopped by one of the older boys	
1	teenage boy	hey lil man you wan some smoke
2	younger boy	no man I'm good
3	teenage boy	hey hey I'm not trying to hurt you I'm tryin to help you
4		I'm tryin to get you high
5		whada you say
6	younger boy	no man I don smoke weed
7		I smoke clowns like you on a b-ball court
	both boys break into laughter as they get out of character	
8	teenage boy	we gotta work up somtin else for you to say dude
9	younger boy	I know but it was the first thing I could think of
10	teenage boy	but you did good though lil brother
	the two walk away with the teenage boy's arm around the shoulders of the younger boy	
11	male VO web address appears on lower right side of screen	big brothers who live above the influence have little brothers who live above the influence

walkway and starkness of the urban landscape. The Black ghetto culture aspect of the commercial is also magnified through the speaking style of the characters involved. The language used by both boys—but especially the older one—is phonologically marked as African American Vernacular. Listening to the commercial, the contrast between the phonology of the boys' speech and the carefully articulated phonology of the male voice-over at the end is striking. Yet, the language too is highly stylized, with a small set of features taken synecdotally, to represent the whole of Black discourse.

Although anti-drug promotional ads are not inherently coded for race or ethnicity, the particular representation of two African American boys stands out for its racial overtones. In many ways, it's a low-risk racial representation because it feeds into an urban impression of Black male youth and drugs. Imagine the same commercial with a mixed-race representation: an older White boy and younger African American boy might seem too improbable and "unrealistic"; an older African American boy and younger White boy might appear to be explicitly racist. Another option using the same narrative would be for the commercial to feature two White boys, but this might be thought too alienating for the White audience. There are, in fact, a number of different television commercials for the web site; 16 of them are included on the web site for viewing. One of these was aired on the episode of *One on One* (the situation comedy featuring a Black single father and his daughter) described earlier in the chapter. This commercial includes only White characters who are engaged in bizarre activities involving putting leeches on their bodies (which is dubbed "slomming"); the moral of the narrative is that drugs can lead people to do some pretty weird things. The choice not to place the version with the African American boys in the program featuring a Black cast is itself some indication of the racial and racist overtones of the commercial.

The campaign for abovetheinfluence.com aims to reach youth through a range of engaging and witty commercials that, taken together, bear a unified message about the distorting impact of drugs on a person's life. Yet each particular ad as an advertising moment in its context of accompanying discourse carries ideological codes broadly available for interpretation. Two African American boys in an urban setting involving drugs inserted into programs featuring White characters and likely to be viewed by many White teenagers equals an opportunity for cementing the association of race with the urban drug scene.

Conclusions and implications

I posed several general questions at the beginning of the chapter. How are characters in ads marked for race and ethnicity? What relationships among people of color and Euro/Whites are represented? How is multicultural society depicted in commercials aimed at teenagers in relation to the programming context in which the commercials are placed? How might the representations of diversity in television commercials circulate broader ideological codes about multicultural society? These are far-reaching questions, and this chapter only begins to suggest answers that open up the domain of multicultural representation in television advertising aimed at tweens and teens.

The capsule profiles alone provide qualitative indicators that multicultural society is far less than a reality in advertising directed at teens than might be commonly thought. As much as multicultural/multiracial society is a fact of growing significance in the US, the advertising images remain limited, especially in television programming that centers on White casts and situations. Each advertising moment, understood in its larger context of accompanying discourse, bears some relationship to mediated ideological coding. In the capsule profiles, there is little indication that people of color are imaged (either verbally or visually) as a regular part of society, complete with complexity of appearance and role. Blacks tend to be in the background or sidelines, voiceless bodies, or represented in athletic or other stereotypic roles; they are Black bodies more than anything else, sometimes in moments of tokenism and sometimes in moments of integration. When Blacks are central in advertising moments, they tend to be represented in advertising moments of segregation featuring ghetto narratives or a hip-hop style of Black identity. The only array of Black characters with central roles in commercials that did not conform to this social placement were seen on *106 & Park,* where the emphasis on people of color in the program clearly matches the demographic profile of the show. Several commercials appear in this program episode that feature exclusively Black casts in separatist narratives (Marine Corps, Crest, Downy, Panteen and Bounty). At least one of these (Marine Corps) hails the Black male specifically, while others place Black characters in narratives that could be read both as hailing Blacks and as more generally applicable to a broad range of people. There is also some representation of more complex integration in a couple of the commercials in this program (Hersheys and Verizon). Yet, this program serves as the venue for the only commercial that I saw which clearly represented a Latino and did so by calling on the stereotype of the stocky Hispanic man with a big black mustache.

What especially interested me in considering how race and ethnicity are imaged in teen advertising is what happens in the context of programming that features Whites. Among the capsule profiles, these programs are *Smallville, One Tree Hill* and *The OC.* Many of the representations of people of color in ads in these programs occur through visual imaging primarily, with the images often showing Blacks in quick shots, as background figures, or in stereotypic roles. When the characters are given central roles, those roles tend to be stereotypic. Very few Asian-appearing characters are represented, as is true for Latinos and Latinas and for those who speak English with an accent that is not marked as "American Born." The overall impression is of advertising moments of tokenism in which people of color appear in marginalized positions or advertising moments that place people of color in central roles that magnify stereotypes.

The two case analyses—Boost Mobile and the abovetheinfluence.com commercials—spotlight how race is commodified for White consumers.

White youth's embrace of Black cultural style and products has been a topic of interest among academics and social commentators for some time. Bill Yousman (2003) has provided an insightful analysis of what he terms "Blacko-philia," or the love and consumption of Black popular culture, and it connec-tion to "Blackophobia," or the "fear and dread of African Americans" (p. 366). Yousman's argument is that consumption of Black culture by Whites is a way of trying to exert power by owning that which is desired while not having to deal with the challenges of its originality: "Blacks have neither the desire nor the option of adopting 'Blackness' only when it is convenient—they must experi-ence both the pleasure and the pain of being Black in America whereas White youth can opt for only the pleasures associated with Black music and other cultural creations" (p. 387). White consumption of Black cultural products and style constitute a new form of racism, says Yousman, because by consuming Blackness, White "retrench" (which in the military sense means to dig a new trench in order to protect) White control and domination.

A related line of analysis posits that Whites can embrace Black cultural forms by construing them as universal rather than specific to Black culture. This is one way of exerting power: that is, to take as applicable to oneself (and by extension to everyone) a commodified cultural product that is admired at its root source, in this case within its origins in Black culture. Eric Watts and Mark Orbe (2002) made this argument in reference to Budweiser beer's "Whassup" advertising campaign. Each ad in the series portrayed a scene in which guys (almost always groups of young Black men) were communicating with one another using language and conversational style marked as distinctly Black and vernacular; every ad includes the greeting "Whassup", and every ad, thus, uses Black male camaraderie as a source of humor. The researchers found that while Black college students interpreted these ads as specific narratives of Black experience, intentionally produced for them, White college students inter-preted these ads as universalized narratives of male identity. The humorous aspect of the commercials, these authors contend, "signifies the comic relief of white angst" about Black solidarity (p. 10). Watts and Orbe's conclusions about White viewers are consistent with Jason Rodriquez's (2006) ethnographic research in venues where White youth attend hip-hop events. Based on his interviews, he concluded that White concert-goers adhere to a color-blind ideology, which allows them to "justify their presence in the scene" and to use their "racial power, however unwittingly, to appropriate the culture of hip-hop, taking the racially coded meanings out of the music and replacing them with color-blind ones" (p. 663).

Like the Budweiser commercials, the commercials for Boost Mobile and abovetheinfluence.com bring humor into the discourse, which for White viewers provides a way to laugh at Blacks while at the same time embracing something seen as "authentic." Boost Mobile narratives position Black culture "for sale" through association with stars, but the comedic, caricature aspect pokes fun as a way of reminding the viewer that even though the star exists in reality, the product for sale exists in a cardboard text from which it can be removed as commodity. The narrative at the opening of the public service drug ad is positioned seriously, but when exposed as a skit within an ad, the comedic element surfaces. The urban scene and the vernacular language present a style that signifies authenticity—especially when the two actors walk away from the scene "as real people." In this case, no commodity is explicitly for sale, but the association of Black youth with drugs and Black urban style circulates an ideological message about race. The White viewer could easily see these Black youth as "other" but at the same time extract the "urban coolness" represented in the ad to do with it as she or he wants in the safety of decontextualized protection. Both cases fit the profile of "spectacular consumption" (Watts, 1997; Watts and Orbe, 2002), where the cultural forms identified as "authentic" Black are extracted and shaped for White consumption as part of commodity culture: cultural authenticity has been given a market value.

The advertising moments discussed in this chapter point to complicated ideological dimensions in the ways in which cultural diversity is represented in teen advertising. As the changing demographics reviewed early in the chapter demonstrate, cultural diversity is on the rise. Changes in the representation of race in advertising discourse have occurred in recent years, and taken as a whole, television programming for teens offers at least some greater frequency of multicultural representations. The important issues raised in this chapter concern the embeddedness of advertising within program contexts and the particular ways in which ideological codes of meaning are circulated about race and broader dimensions of diversity. There are still too many stereotypes and too often an equation of "Black = diversity." The near absence of people of color who are *not* Black skews the portrait of diversity just as much as does commodification of Black cultural forms, stereotyped imaging, silent roles, and marginalized representations. These matters are important, as Cortese (2004) emphasizes, because ". . . advertising and other media images help to shape attitudes about race and ethnicity . . . [and] ads can provide a barometer of the extent to which ethnic minorities have penetrated social institutions dominated by White males" (p. 15).

Chapter 4

Different tropes for different folks

Advertising and face-fixing

The cosmetics industry has grown to a multibillion-dollar branding competition conducted in the arenas of magazines, television, the Internet, outdoor and other public displays, shopping malls, and convenience and drug stores from coast to coast. In the culture of appearance, cosmetics promise enhancement, repair, and transformation. Advertising presents the terms of these promises through verbal and visual discourse. Most women know that you can't find a fashion or lifestyle magazine that is not filled with ads for cosmetic products—lipstick, face make-up, eye shadow and liners and lotions galore. In 2003, the global beauty industry topped $160 billion, with skin care accounting for $24 billion, make-up $18 billion, and hair care $38 billion (Pots of promise, 2003). Although men have been less of a target, the cosmetics industry is slowly paving an inroad to this consumer market through new products advertised in distinctly masculine ways.

The themes repeatedly circulated throughout the beauty industry are simple: everyone wants beauty and youthfulness, and beauty and youthfulness can be attained with the right combination of products. The repetitious barrage of these themes complement the larger discourse of beauty ideals and fantasies permeating daily life in a media-saturated society. Perpetually circulating visual and verbal images of ideal beauty tantalize the consumer with cosmetic products for attaining these images, and lace these images with messages about both youthfulness and sex. Women have been the overwhelming targets of ads to enhance beauty and hide age by fixing the face in one way or another. Yet, in recent years, men's faces have become consumer territory open for exploration with the introduction of facial creams promising a more youthful appearance.

In this chapter, I explore the particular domain of the face, and how discourse in advertising codes products for resurfacing what the cosmetics industry defines as in need of repair—what I will be referring to as "face-fixing." My focus is on those products promising change that is lasting or that make alterations in the face that cannot be wiped away in an instant, rather than on more ordinary products such as lipsticks and skin tone-matched make-up, which are offered for the more day-to-day purposes of beautification. Like many other products, those for the face are designed for and marketed to different segments of the population. These segments need to be hailed, that is "called into," the discourse of the ad and into the larger cultural ideology that is circulating through these advertisements. The analysis presented here aims to unpack the discourse images that thematically characterize appeals to different audience segments—teens, young adults, mature adults; and both females and males. Emphasis is given to the tropes—mainly metaphor and simile but also *metonymy* and *synecdoche* in some cases—running through the verbal images created by advertisers to call the potential consumer into the advertisements for resurfacing products. Advertisers frequently phrase their appeals using figures of speech (Leigh, 1994; McQuarrie and Mick, 1996), and this chapter examines the content of those figures of speech associated with doing something to the face. Current popular magazines with the highest circulation figures in several different audience segment categories were examined for instances of facial resurfacing advertisements.

The chapter is organized into four sections. I first discuss some general trends in the role of advertising in defining beauty standards and practices, including key critical analyses from the scholarly literature. The second section focuses on the cosmetics industry and on the rise of facial reconstruction as a background for cosmetic resurfacing. The third and major section presents analysis of the different tropes and other linguistic strategies found in ads for face-fixing products in magazines directed at five different groups: teenage girls, young women, women 40 and over, African American women, and adult men. The chapter concludes with a commentary on the significance of the discourse imaging involved in selling facial resurfacing products.

Advertising and beauty as a never-ending quest

It is old news that prevailing gender ideology in the US and many other parts of the world places especially pronounced demands on women's bodies and overall external appearance. I grew up in an era when 36–24–36 measurements were considered ideal, and voluptuous actresses like Elizabeth Taylor, Sophia Lauren, and Marilyn Monroe were seen as sex and beauty icons. Ideal beauty meant large, pointed breasts that stood up on their own, small waists, and firm, curvaceous hips. To help women who longed for this ideal, the Playtex Wonder Bra was invented to "lift and separate," tight belts cinched the waist, and a girdle could be worn to control too much bulge in the hips or jiggle in the derrière. Women who didn't measure up struggled with exercises to produce something more than they had. Teenage girls in my older sister's cohort used to do an exercise to the chant of "We must, we must, develop our bust!" Clearasil promised clearer skin to teenagers with acne, and Noxzema was pretty much it for deep-down cleansing. The models in magazines were thinner than the curvaceous movie stars, but larger than the models of today.

Anyone conscious of the world around them today knows that thinness is the ideal, and the range of options in the search for facial beauty has mushroomed. Although beauty images have changed somewhat over the last few decades, there is nothing different about the stranglehold that the ideology of the ideal body holds over women. The emphasis on thinness has led to alarming statistics on eating disorders, and the racks in clothing stores are filled with small sizes. The fashion industry has responded with some shows banishing underweight models (Hay, 2006). At the other extreme, daily news emphasizes the overeating and fattening of the US population. As a teenager, I don't recall ever seeing size 0 dresses in stores, and size 2 was unusual and not considered ideal. Reports are that Marilyn Monroe, for example—whose weight fluctuated between 118 and 140 pounds—stood 5 feet 5½ inches tall, hit the tape measure at 36–23–36, and wore a size 12 dress for much of her career (Urban Legends, 2000). By any measurements, she was bigger than Nicole Kidman, Angelina Jolie, Lindsay Lohan and most other female stars today. At the same time when the ideal woman was bigger than today, neither separate sizing for large women nor XXXL shirts for men existed.

Today's beauty ideals and the culture of beauty that surrounds our daily lives carry continuities from the past but also differ somewhat from the past. Thin is so "in" that eating is "out" for many women. A teenage boy recently told our family about a visit from his female cousin who is in college. He described the summer visit as a little awkward because the only meal she ate was lunch, and she didn't eat what the rest of the family ate even for that meal. The "fat is beautiful"/fat liberation movement notwithstanding, we live in a culture preoccupied with thinness, youthfulness, and notions of perfection.

The face

And what about the face? The face holds the central role in contextualizing beauty (which is not the same as sexuality) for women. Think about commonly heard comments in the US about women's faces in relation to the rest of their bodies. Sometimes an overweight woman is said to have "a pretty face," meaning that it's too bad she's overweight because she is fundamentally pretty. There are jokes about a man putting a bag over an ugly woman's face before he has sex with her, and cartoon jokes depicting a woman's curvaceous body, with a punch line showing an unattractive face—often with buck teeth. Certainly a man's handsome face holds power as well, but for him, the face is less critical, so long as his appearance doesn't diverge too far from the cultural idea of male-ness. If a man's face is too "pretty," he might be considered feminine. If he's too handsome in a polished way, he might be thought to be gay, which for many men is not desirable. And a light or spotty beard might not be the ideal of masculinity.

The face holds power, especially the face of a woman. Naomi Wolf (1991) comments that the face's "only power is that it has been designated as 'the face'—and that hence millions and millions of women are looking at it together, and know it" (p. 76). This idea of women being focused on women's faces differs from what is commonly thought about men and their faces. While the face of a man might be judged lacking in certain contexts because it is oily or unshaven or blemished or pock-marked, men by the millions are not cultur-ally taught to focus on their faces with laser precision. They are not taught to cultivate a "handsome myth" in the same way that women are taught from early age to cultivate a "beauty myth."

In the broadest view, the face is a site of cleanliness, which was not always the case. Clean skin became common practice in the nineteenth century, but even in the early twentieth century, cleansing the skin was not a daily ritual (Twitchell, 2003). Ideas about what exactly can be done to the face have also changed. The face is no longer just a canvas for make-up. The face is now a structure ready for renovation and remodeling. The face has parts, and advertis-ing magnifies those parts by emphasizing their association with particular products that can be applied to deal with particular problems and threats headlined in articles and advertisements.

For women, the search for youthful beauty is age-old, with ads for various face creams and treatments beckoning women with their promise of clear, smooth, youthful, glowing skin. Kathy Peiss's *Hope in a Jar* (1998) paints a portrait of women's early role in developing cosmetic products as a vehicle for freedom and expression of their sexuality, followed by a shift in the 1920s to mass production and male-defined standards for the beauty industry. For women in the US, facial creams have been the mainstay of the search for more beautiful skin. Early in the twentieth century, for example, Ponds launched a new product line with two creams that were pitched to women. Ads pro-claimed, "Every normal skin needs these two creams": Cold Cream for cleans-ing and Vanishing Cream for protection of the skin (Sutton, 2004). Cosmetics companies produced and advertised many products for the face during the twentieth century, but it was not until the anti-aging ingredients came on the scene that there was a major new product addition and opportunity for the beauty industry and its advertisers to spin new images of the face and to particularize the parts of the face. Paging through a 1978 issue of *Vogue* (for March), I found several ads for face creams that touted their moisturizing impact; among these ads, one bore news for women over 30: the ad promoted a cream named "Ultima II" by Charles Revson (the department store line of Revlon) containing soluble collagen, said to be "an ingredient of young skin." A number of other products were brought to market with reputed anti-aging ingredients—collagen, retinol, and alpha hydroxyl. Advertisements for these products offered new visual and verbal images of hope for the appearance.

In 1980, Dr Albert Kligman, a University of Pennsylvania dermatologist, named these new anti-aging products "cosmeceuticals" (Schillinger, 2005)—a label that stuck with an easy connection between the connotations of cosmetics and pharmaceuticals. Cosmeceuticals are not reviewed by the Food and Drug Administration, and "although cosmetics and cosmeceuticals are tested for safety, testing to determine whether beneficial ingredients actually live up to a manufacturer's claims is not mandatory" (Schwartz, 2006). Thus, the name "cosmeceuticals" potentially creates a verbal image of exact formulation in the methodology of pharmaceuticals but exists mainly to give status appeal for marketers to use in advertising.

Men's faces

Until recently, men's faces in the United States have, with rare exception, been targeted only for shaving creams and after-shave lotions. Now well into the twenty-first century, we are beginning to see more attention to full facial care, anti-wrinkle treatments, and the panoply of products that go along with this product orientation. Clinique was early to introduce a full line of men's facial products. Clinique could take advantage of its substantial department store business to interest women in buying these products for the men in their lives. Others have followed: Clarins, Biotherm, L'Oréal, plus separate men's lines such as 4VOO and Zirh. Estimated as a $7.7 billion business in 2004, men's cosmetic and grooming products are projected to reach $10 billion by 2010 (Ignelzi, 2004).

From acne treatment to plastic surgery

A life cycle chronology underlies the discourse in advertising for facial products, beginning with ads for acne treatment in early adolescence and moving through ads for the nebulous cleansing and moisturizing years to ads targeted specifically to the early mid-life onset of lines in the face that remain once the smile or frown is gone. Following the prescription of youthfulness that drives the beauty myth, the mid-life phase is arguably the "logical" entry for plastic surgery in the form of face-lifts and other procedures, because this is the phase of life when changes in the skin are most visible—the phase when dramatic measures to retain and restore beauty must be taken if the beauty myth is to be upheld. Face-lifts and other cosmetic surgeries used to be for the rich and famous but are now more commonplace. Just as from-the-ground-up home remodeling and renovation serves as an impetus for smaller remodeling projects—a new bathroom, kitchen or finished basement—so too is the facelift and surgical reconstruction the impetus for the cosmetics industry's forays into non-surgical solutions to culturally defined and culturally manufactured beauty. These procedures, thus, provide an important context for the advertising discourse used to promote facial cosmetics and especially cosmeceuticals. Most people cannot afford plastic surgery or would not spend their discretionary funds on such procedures, others are not willing to endure its risks and pain, while still others may simply dismiss plastic surgery as an intervention that goes beyond what they consider appropriate practices for taking care of oneself or for beauty enhancement. The backdrop of the face-lift and general growth of cosmetic surgery along with the intense quest for youth central to the beauty myth help position cosmeceuticals and their close relatives in the advertising discourse aimed at the face for early mid-life and beyond. Recently, both the cosmeceutical and plastic surgery options have moved into younger advertising cohort segments, a development that I will return to in the conclusion of this chapter.

Advertising, appearance, and the face

In an age of appearance, there is no product for sale more steeped in manipulating *signifiers of the image of appearance* than facial cosmetics. The image rather than the "reality" of appearance is an advertising staple. Shortcuts to that image, whatever it may be, give certain signifiers the power to stand in for the image, which stands in for the "reality." The face as synecdoche for total appearance has come to represent beauty itself. In advertising, the image of the *perfect* face stands in for the face itself, creating a double synecdoche where the part has come to represent the whole, and then an image of the part stands in for the whole. This process includes several components. First there is the larger cultural process of arbitrarily defining beauty, which occurs through repetitive interpersonal, institutional, and mass communication—with mass communication's role having moved into an increasingly prominent position. We do not—each of us—discover through every successive interpersonal engagement that clear skin is preferred or that wrinkles are disdained. Rather, those successive interpersonal engagements draw from multiple repetition of the same cultural message and also then contribute by repeating these established codes. This is the process through which gender is culturally produced and, as theorized by Judith Butler (1999/1990), sex is culturally defined as "natural." More specifically, according to Butler, "gender is the repeated stylization of the body, a set of repeated acts within a highly rigid regulatory frame that congeal over time to produce the appearance of substance, of a natural sort of being" (p. 33). Wrinkles, for example, are repeatedly defined outside the context of specific interpersonal interactions as a *negative signifier* of age (unlike wisdom, which is a *positive signifier* of age). Cultural gatekeepers are important in this part of the process, because not everyone is in the position to set the beauty standards.

Second, the consumer must objectify herself to imagine that the cultural constructions of beauty in their particularities provide a template that can be imposed on the body in general and the face in particular: "Do my hips fit the template?" "Is my tummy flat enough?" "Is my butt too big?" "Are my eyes large enough?" "Do my eyebrows have the right shape?" "Is my skin smooth enough, moist enough, wrinkle-free?" Or the even more abstract, "Does my skin glow?" All of these questions and the assessments that their answers provide require the individual person to see herself as both object and subject.

Third—and here is where facial products come in—the individual person must, after going through the second stage of subject–object assessment, go through yet another process of subject–object assessment, this time to make the judgment about product x. There are many products for sale for which we have no proof or material demonstration of their effectiveness. We don't, for instance, know if an item of clothing will look "as good as new" after it is washed, or if a particular ball point pen will be free of those globby ink deposits that make a mess on the hands and the page alike, or if we will like a movie as much as the friend who recommended it did. Some products for sale can be consumer tested for what their advertisements proclaim. "Satisfaction guaranteed or your money back within 30 days" might be the test in some cases. Demonstrations are available in other cases—for vacuum cleaners, lap-top computers, televisions, sound systems. Clothing falls into this category if bought in a store where we can see it, feel the fabric, and try it on for size and appearance. Even some make-up lines are advertised with a small free sample gooed onto the magazine advertisement, which is a technique adapted from the scented flap on perfume and cologne ads. Products advertised to enhance the face, like other body products and over-the-counter medications, differ because either (1) what they offer are promises with no specific due date or (2) the "due date" is in the future, as in the phrase "visible results in six weeks." For facial products, the effect must be imagined, and even if after time the product falls short of what we imagined, expectations can be recalibrated into some other imagined expectation. This is precisely the process captured in Kathy Peiss's book title, *Hope in a Jar* (1998).

Even though consumers consider many ads with skepticism and believe they are "personally exempt from advertising's influence" (Kilbourne, 1999, p. 27), when it comes to appearance, there is also what I term "despair-ism," or the willing granting of legitimacy to the images presented about a product because of the deep and unsatisfied longing for what the product promises. The terms of the longing are set culturally, and advertisers choose terms carefully because they want to engage the particular hopes that are relevant and attach them to the product as a valid path to its imagined effect.

Jean Kilbourne's now famous *Killing Us Softly* film exposé of the image of women in advertising has been seen in its various versions by thousands of people . . . and not just women. Now in its third version (Kilbourne, 2000), *Killing Us Softly* takes a look at the past 20 years of advertising images that continuously shape and resize the symbols of ideal womanhood and femininity.

Naomi Wolf's scathing 1991 critique of what she calls "the beauty myth" has been read by millions of people. Her incisive, landmark commentary on the role of women's magazines as a cultural source for promoting a myth of perfect beauty holds true over 15 years later. The magazines—through their advertising—perpetuate beauty standards that women cannot achieve, simply because they are mythic. "[The] beauty myth dosage the magazines provide," says Wolf, "elicits in their readers a raving, itching, parching product lust, and an abiding fantasy: the longing for some fairy godmother who will arrive at the reader's door and put her to sleep. When she awakens, her bathroom will be full of exactly the right skin-care products, with step-by-step instructions, and palettes of exactly the required makeup" (p. 70).

This myth and the preoccupation it generates in women compromises the gains won through the second wave of feminism, and Wolf adamantly asserts that "the magazines' message *about the myth* is determined by its advertisers" (pp. 73–4)—an assertion that seems valid given the support needed from advertising for magazines to survive. Wolf draws a useful comparison to men's cultural environment by noting two points. First, magazines read by men do not focus singly on anything similar to beauty; rather, they range by interests such as cars, skiing, fishing, skateboarding, etc. Second, the most important authority figures for men reside in education and in their jobs, but it is the genre of women's magazines that "gives women an invisible female authority figure to admire and obey" (p. 74). The analysis presented in this chapter will show that Wolf's cultural criticism, although read by millions, did not stop the beauty industry or the magazine culture fed by it. The book remains relevant. But it does not stop there. Wolf's thesis is underscored as the baby boomer generation ages and advertising creates a myth for this cohort about eternal youthful beauty.

Wolf and others identify the rebuilding of *Cosmopolitan* in the post-feminist era as pivotal to today's beauty myth. In an analysis of branding and discourse in *Cosmopolitan*, Machin and Thornborrow (2003) consider the similarities in the different national versions of the magazine that together constitute the *Cosmo* brand. As the best-selling magazine targeted at young women in the US,

Cosmo's branding functions as part of the ideological matrix for defining the ideal woman. The brand in this case features sex and appearance as the keys to power: ". . . women are fundamentally alone and must hold their own or advance through pleasing and/or manipulating others, and above all through the power which their body and sexuality affords them. . . . [T]his . . . defines women's agency" (p. 468).

Thematic tropes for fixing the face

Teen advertising

The insecurities of adolescence offer a plentiful field of possibilities for products and their promotion. Armed with psychological research, advertisers speak to teens by "exploiting their developmental vulnerabilities—the ways that their cognitive, social, emotional, and physical development influence decision making, likes, dislikes, interests, and activities" (Linn, p. 24). Most ads in teen magazines that address how to care for the teen face are for products to treat blemishes and acne. A few ads deal with removal of "unwanted hair" and with "plumping" the lips.

At the awkward developmental stage of puberty, already self-conscious kids have to deal with pimples, blackheads, and the transformation of a face once smooth and taken-for-granted to a face that teens experience as oily and unpredictable. Not surprisingly, advertisements directed at teens for "face-fixing" promote products to deal with these face problems. With upward to 85 percent of the population developing acne between the ages of 12 and 25 (Acne, 2006), the market for acne products is considerable. The production of androgens are a major causal element of acne, and the higher levels of these hormones in boys than girls accounts for higher acne rates in boys (American Academy of Dermatology, 2005). Acne often appears in girls starting at around age 11 and in boys starting at around age 13 (Acne, zits and pimples, 2006). Acne cannot be cured with medications, but treatment can control and lessen the symptoms (American Academy of Dermatology, n.d.). Although boys and girls alike suffer physically and socially from acne, girls are presented with various remedy alternatives in teen magazines—a genre that doesn't exist for boys. Boys receive their advice most often from their parents (usually mothers) and doctors, and increasingly through information available on the Internet. The paradox here means that the girls, who are less acne prone than boys, have more advertising directed at them than boys. This gender difference is important to distinctions in how females and males are courted as continuing consumers of facial products. Promotion through advertising of treatments for facial blemishes—from moderate to severe—ushers in the idea of facial maintenance as a regimen that needs to be dealt with through an array of products.

I scanned current issues of the most popular girls' magazines to see how the physical face is saved in product advertising (circulation data are from the Audit Bureau of Circulations and represent average monthly circulation for the second half of 2006): *Seventeen* (2,034,856), *CosmoGirl!* (1,443,482), and *Teen Vogue* (1,005,437). These magazines appeal to young teens, high school girls, and some college-aged women, and they reach far beyond their subscribers through sharing, browsing at magazine counters, and availability in places like dentists' and doctors' offices. Each issue of these girls' magazines includes about six to twelve ads for face products other than ordinary make-up and lipstick. Typical products are Clearasil Ultra, Neutrogena Rapid Clear Treatment Pads, Noxzema Blackhead Cleanser, and Proactiv Solution for acne.

Medical advice about acne has changed considerably over the years. Teens before the 1980s were cautioned not to eat foods high in fat, but more recent treatment centers on topical medications (both over-the-counter and prescription), and practices that keep heavy hair oils and oily lotions away from the face. Contrary to long-standing belief, there is no evidence that acne is related to dirty skin. In fact, scrubbing and alcohol-based cleansers irritate acne symptoms (American Academy of Dermatology, 2005). In a lively myth-buster internet entry, Binns (2006) proclaims that, "filthy-looking blackheads feed the misconception that acne grows on grime. In reality, sebum turns the color of mud when exposed to air."

The ads for anti-acne treatments and facial care for teens (girls because of the placement of ads in girls' magazines) stress several main metaphors for the skin and its treatment: skin that is clear, skin that is clean, skin that can be speedily restored, and—through synecdoche, the face and even the teen's entire identity as represented by a pimple.

Clear

To have clear skin is the underlying goal of the skin treatments advertised in girls' teen magazines. Related to the skin and complexion, *clear* is an adjective that engages a commonly understood meaning, i.e. "good in texture and color and without blemish or discoloration" (clear, n.d.). Drawing on the notion of clarity as signifying that which you can see through, this adjectival meaning is itself metaphorical in the first instance because it takes the idea of clear as "transparent" and extrapolates it to "clear from blemishes." The goal of *clear skin*, then, provides a metaphorical foundation for the verbal images in ads for anti-acne/anti-blemish products. Certain product names use the clear metaphor to ground their claims: Clearasil is the benchmark product that has been known for generations of teenagers, with its product name leading to the image of a future of "clear skin." Johnson & Johnson advertises a product named Clean&Clear, and Neutrogena advertises both SkinClearing® Oil-free Makeup and Rapid Clear Treatment Pads. When models are used in the ads, they have artificially blemish-free skin to demonstrate the visual metaphor that matches the "clear" headline.

"Clear" also appears in ad text to create the verbal pathway to the visualization of blemish-free skin. An ad for Clearasil Ultra tells the reader that "clearer skin" is "guaranteed" (*Teen Vogue*, August 2006). Neutrogena SkinClearing® Oil-free Makeup "Clears blemishes as it creates great skin" (*Seventeen*, August 2006), while L'Oréal Acne Response tells the potential user that this product "Rapidly clears . . . Cell by cell. Pore by pore. Day by day" (*CosmoGirl!*, June/July 2006).

Clean

Along with the metaphor of clear skin, the image of clean skin is used discursively to promote anti-acne products. The Clean&Clear product noted above suggests by its name that clean skin and clear skin go together. Neutrogena offers several products in different ads in the same magazine (*CosmoGirl!*, June/July 2006). One is specifically advertised for the cleansing part of the teen's facial program: Deep Clean Foaming Scrub will feel "So clean. So cool. So invigorating." The verbal text in an ad for Liquid Neutrogena Facial Cleansing Formula tells the teen to "get clean, clear, healthy-looking skin." The text for Johnson & Johnson's product, Clean&Clear Oxygenating Fizzing Cleanser, contains a visual metaphor of movement to tell the teen that this product "Fizzes up to Clean Deep Down" (*CosmoGirl!*, June/July 2006). Noxzema's product line includes Microbead Cleanser and Blackhead Cleanser. The ads (*CosmoGirl!*, June/July 2006) for Microbead Cleanser playfully feature a stick figure of a young woman with text plays on the word "Microbead"—such as, "Microbeads are good for your face. Macrobeads make cute bracelets" On the tube for this product is the statement, "Continuous clean," which engages a metaphor of movement through time into the future: this product will not only clean your face, but it will continue cleaning after it has been applied. The Blackhead Cleaner explicitly names the culprit on your face as "dirt": "If anyone's talking dirt, it won't be about your face." The consumer is told that this product is a "Purifying Blackhead Cleanser."

While it might seem to the average person that clean skin for acne sufferers is a "no-brainer," this particular verbal image is, based on current medical information about acne, simply misleading. At best, it is a fiction supported by a metaphor drawn from the cleaning of hard, grimy surfaces. At worst, it is a lie offered to draw vulnerable teenage girls into the consumer market for facial cleansers.

Speed

Ads for cleansing and acne products often rely on an underlying metaphor of time, where the metaphor points to the product's ability to get to the problem quickly and deliver a solution swiftly. One prescription medication, BenzaClin, carries the verbal image "fast" in its ad, with no further specification (*CosmoGirl!*, June/July 2006). Other ads are more lavish with their promises of speed. Neutrogena Rapid Clear Treatment Pads are said to not only be "Fast!" but to give "clearer skin in hours, not days" (*Seventeen*, August 2006). Ads for Clearsil Ultra make strong claims, "Clearer skin in just 3 days. Guaranteed" (*Teen Vogue*, August 2006). These ads also offer a visual metaphor of a timeline anchored at day one by a Dalmatian dog with spots and at day three by a Dalmatian with only a few spots (see Figure 4.1).

In this case, the visual metaphor of the Dalmatian dog carries the image of pimples and blackheads—neither of which is mentioned in the ad's text. I found one ad that uses the on–off switch as a metaphor of speed: Zeno is advertised with the message that "Pimples now have an off button" (*Seventeen*, August 2006); all you need to do is touch the applicator to the pimple, and a "precisely controlled dose of heat [is applied] directly to the pimple."

Ads like these offer a discourse of promises to the girl who might pursue the product. Yet these promises stand against medical information that acne is not just impossible to cure but is slow to subside. Material on Web MD cautions that "it often takes six to eight weeks for acne to improve after you start treatment [and that] some treatments may cause acne to get worse before it gets better" (Acne Vulgaris, 2005). In this case, the speed metaphor does not equal the cautionary medical information.

The pimple as synecdoche

The message to teenagers is clear: *the pimple is the person*. Ads for teen facial products contain an underlying synecdoche that uses the pimple as a sign to represent the face, which represents identity. Most adolescents with even mild acne magnify the image of pimples on their faces and think this is all that others see. The discourse in the facial product ads builds on that insecurity and creates it as a condition leading to insecurity. Much of this message is carried through the interplay of verbal and visual images in the ads. BenzaClin (a prescription medication) is a product associated verbally with "confidence," and the visual representation in the ad is of two heterosexual teenage couples having fun

Figure 4.1 **Clearsil Ultra** (*Teen Vogue*, August 2006).

on the beach (*Teen Vogue*, August 2006). An ad for Clean&Clear Acne Spot Treatment includes in its ad the statement that "in a clinical study everyone saw a reduction in size, redness or number of pimples *in just one day*." (*Teen Vogue*, August 2006). Right below the statement, two smiling girls are pictured with porcelain clear skin—not a blemish on them (see Figure 4.2), so we can assume

Figure 4.2 **Clean&Clear** Acne Spot Treatment (*Teen Vogue*, August 2006).

that they were totally cured. Here, as elsewhere, once the pimple is no longer the synecdoche for the face, beauty, happiness, and fun with friends are possible. One product goes so far as to label their formulation "vanishing cream" (sounds like the early twentieth century Ponds product). Nature's Cure Two-Part Acne Treatment is one part pill and one part "Acne Medication Vanishing Cream": not just cream, but *vanishing* cream (*Seventeen*, August 2006). If the pimple can vanish, then it will no longer stand for the whole face, and the face (and the entire person) can be restored to its totality.

Cultivating the facial care regimen

Advertising not only brings the teenage girl into a discourse of the face that relies on underlying metaphors for clear, clean skin in just a short time, but it also introduces her to a facial regimen for women that will play out over the course of her life. A girl, and subsequently a woman, does not just treat the face; she treats it with a variety of products making up the facial regimen.

A number of ads present two- and three-step solutions for the care of unwanted blemishes. The Nature's Cure Two-Part Acne Treatment noted above is one example. St Ives Swiss Formula presents three products: Apricot Scrub, Apricot Cleaner, and Apricot Face Wash. These products are verbally presented with second person imperative statements for each, followed by what you will achieve, "You scrub. You cleanse. You fight blemishes. You Glow." (*CosmoGirl!*, June/July 2006). In a two-page ad, Johnson & Johnson's Clean-&Clear offers a three-product solution of cleanser, spot treatment, and "invisible" acne patch (*Teen Vogue*, August 2006). The left-facing page describes the "regimen" that will be needed to achieve "Great Skin for School" (*Teen Vogue*, August 2006). The magazine ads for Clearasil Ultra feature four products: wash, astringent, cleansing pads, and stick. If you follow the web site address (www.clearasil.com), which first shows a girl happily dancing in the arms of a boy, the Ultra link takes you to not just four, but eight products, one of which is an Acne Scar Care System, which contains three products—for a total of ten different bottles and tubes. The web page active in September 2006 also shows a men's line, with just three products in containers that are dark blue and silver in contrast to the other products which are in containers that are aqua, white, and light purple: Energizing Acne Scrub, Skin Clearing Shave Gel, and Skin Clearing After Shave Balm. There are other products too, with a total of 24 different products plus three identified as "for men." By linguistically marking three products as "for men," the implication is that the other 24 are for girls and women. Typical of web sites for teen and young adult products, there's also a game—this one called "Clearahill Sweepstakes" with prizes including music downloads and iPods.

Natural looking skin

Underlying many of the advertisements for these teen products is the verbal image of either a product that will look "natural" when applied to the face or that will yield "natural" looking skin as a result. The word "natural" is sometimes also combined with "healthy" looking skin. The pictures of teen girls (and boys where they appear) in these ads are overwhelmingly of White models. When models of color are used, their skin is very light, as is shown in Figure 4.3, which is an ad for BenzaClin (*Teen Vogue*, August 2006). The only other ads that I saw with Black models were those from Noxzema for the Microbead Cleanser, where stick-figure drawings were shown; and Nature's Cure, which shows before and after pictures of girls—sometimes with one light-skinned Black girl. The web sites for many of the products advertised also offer images that almost always picture White youth. One wonders about the motivation behind this erasure of black skin from the skin care product lines for teens. One possibility is that the niche for the girls' magazines is largely White, but White girls do function in a larger society. More importantly, given their prominence, we cannot assume that Black girls do not see these magazines. The discourse of these ads portrays clear, clean, natural looking skin as normatively belonging to White faces, which reinforces the metaphorical association of clear as transparent.

Advertising to the cosmo generation

Cosmopolitan magazine claims to be "the lifestylist—and cheerleader—for millions of fun, fearless females who want to be the best they can be in every area of their lives"—fashion, beauty, romance and sex, entertainment (*Cosmopolitan*). The "Cosmo generation" can be described as trendy or wannabe-trendy young women in their twenties and early thirties who cultivate the urban lifestyle made famous by the *Sex and the City* women. *Cosmopolitan* tops the magazine circulation figures for this generation, but the general vibe of the generation is also reflected in other magazines—magazines decidedly beyond teenage and with distinctive discourse for face-fixing.

I was surprised to find one "adult" ad for an anti-acne product in a teen magazine: *Teen Vogue* (August 2006) ran a two-page ad for L'Oréal Acne Response, billing the product as the company's "First Adult Acne Program." The ad contained testimonials from five women, two of whom explicitly mention that they are past their teen years. Seemingly misplaced in *Teen Vogue*, this ad effectively shows the continuum from teenage girls to young adult women, and does so by linking these age groups through a common problem—acne—and a common solution—a regimen for skin care. Since a continuum can be read in both

Figure 4.3 **BenzaClin** (*Teen Vogue*, August 2006).

directions, the appearance in magazines for the 20-something group of several facial care ads that appear in the teen magazines is not surprising—especially those ads composed in the discourse of clean, clear, healthy skin. As a transitional generation in the life of the face, the young adult "Cosmo generation" women still experience acne and the occasional unwanted skin breakout, but this is an age cohort that also needs to be cultivated by producers of the massive facial care industry to build on the practice of the facial regimen as the key to perfect skin. The woman who reads beauty and fashion magazines such as *Cosmopolitan* and *In Style* is given the face message clearly: she is at war with her face and nothing short of tactical weapons are needed. In fact, this is the time of life to start building an arsenal.

The "Cosmo generation" corresponds to what has been termed "Generation X"—those aged roughly mid-twenties to about 40, but also to the upper end of "Generation Y"—those in late teens and early twenties (Johnson and Learned, 2004). The major magazines in the market for this group and their 2006-paid monthly circulation (data from Audit Bureau of Circulations, 2006) are *Cosmopolitan* (2,947,220), *In Style* (1,760,542), *Marie Claire* (962,025), and *Vogue* (1,282,589). I scanned current issues of these magazines to locate ads for facial care products. These magazines typically include five to 10 ads for face products other than ordinary make-up and lipstick. Typical products are Olay Total Effects, Neutrogena Healthy Defense Daily Moisturizer, Aveno Clear Complexion Correcting Treatment, and Revlon Age Defying Makeup with Botafirm.

Two tropes carry over from the teen audience and three new tropes appear in the ads directed at the Cosmo generation. The tropes of *facial care as regimen* and *healthy skin* continue in the ads for this age cohort, and a number of ads appear for moisturizers and cleansing products. The new tropes stress (1) *metaphors of control and restoration*, in which the face is metaphorically separated from the person who can then exercise control over its features, (2) *metaphors related to war* (with the face), and (3) *metaphors of restoration*.

Control your face!

The discourse of control permeates many of the ads for facial care products promoted in magazines like *Vogue* and *Cosmopolitan*. The young woman is now past the more direct procedure of dealing with a problem by applying various products: she's at a stage where she needs to take control. An ad for L'Oréal Acne Response (*InStyle*, July 2006; see Figure 4.4) instructs the women who look at the page to "Take charge of your skin's clarity." The image created here is one of a determined executive officer of the face—a woman who will not let her face control her. Rodan & Field's Proactiv Solution offers the same message, but in the form of a question: "Are you ready to take control of your skin—and your life?" (*Cosmopolitan*, July 2006). The Cosmo generation woman needs to deal with her face through determination and action. This control metaphor dovetails nicely with the even more serious business of metaphorically creating the face as the field for war.

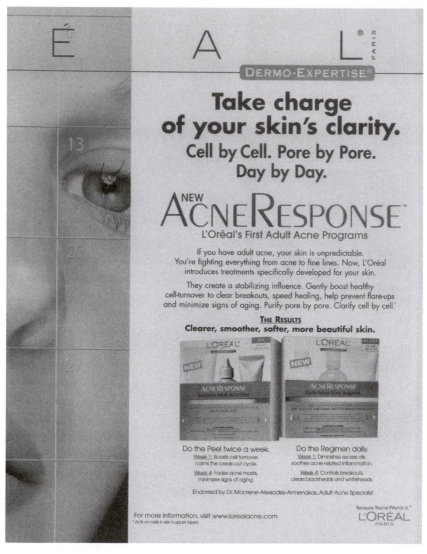

Figure 4.4 **L'Oréal Acne Response** (*InStyle*, July 2006).

The battleground of the face

Although not prominent, a few ads in magazines directed at the Cosmo generation open up a discourse in which the face is metaphorically presented as a battleground in need of weapons. Send in the troops and arm them with the most sophisticated weapons possible! This metaphor is conveyed through both the use of war words and the use of more elaborate images of the face as battleground. An example of war words appears in an ad for Aveeno Clear Complexion Correcting Treatment. This ad tells the reader to "Fight your blemish. *And* the mark it leaves behind" (*InStyle*, July 2006). The product being promoted is billed as a "blemish fighter"—thus a weapon in the war being waged on the face. The L'Oréal Acne Response ad shown in Figure 4.4 is for a product that also appeared in one of the teen magazines, but it appears in *InStyle* with different tag lines aimed at the younger end of the Cosmo generation. The young woman who reads this magazine is told that, "You're fighting everything from acne to fine lines" (*InStyle*, July 2006). This second-person pseudo-descriptive statement bridges the acne phase of life and the onset of lines (notice that they are not called "wrinkles") with a war metaphor telling the woman that she *is* fighting—not that she might be or will soon be, but that she is waging this fight in the present and better recognize this fact. Making the statement in the present tense ("You're fighting . . .") rather than in the future tense ("You're fighting acne and will soon see wrinkles/lines") or conditional construction ("You may be fighting acne and fine lines") speaks directly to the young woman about the condition of her face and places her immediately in the object position of being looked at for her flaws. Especially interesting in this ad is the visual image of a monthly calendar superimposed over the face of a young woman, which seems to indicate the menstrual cycle as the culprit of what's "beneath the surface" of her face. This woman has no lines, but the verbal text is telling the reader that lines are part of what she is fighting and not just pimples brought about by the phases of her menstrual cycle.

These few war-related ads are significant for their role in opening the discourse to a metaphor that will be significant in ads for facial care directed at older women. They also dovetail with the metaphors of control found in a number of ads directed at this audience of younger women. As the discourse images build up with the chronology of age, we see the carry-over of the facial regimen moving toward the battlefield that is the face. As with the occasional reaching up to an older age cohort found in teen magazines, the occasional appearance of a facial product designed for older women shows up in the formula for younger looking skin, as illustrated in an ad for Dermacia Breathable Foundation where a specific formula is provided for the potential user that boasts "younger, smoother skin in just 17 days" (*Cosmopolitan*, September 2006). The model for the ad is actress Rachel Hunter, born in 1969, which places her at the outer limit of the Cosmo generation. The formula is displayed as follows:

more OXYGEN =
more COLLAGEN =
YOUNGER LOOKING SKIN

Bringing the "collagen" ingredient into the discourse of this ad moves the product into a next phase of facial care in which tools and weapons become more precisely defined.

Time for restoration

In ads directed at the Cosmo generation we begin to see discourse tropes dealing with the face that revolve around restoration and remodeling—a trope that creates the idea that the face must be brought back to its original condition. Restoration suggests authenticity, and ads using this trope entreat women to become restoration specialists and then apply their tools to the face they presently have—a face that has fallen into ruin and is *not* in its natural or original state. The assumption, of course, is that the "original" face, the face that was "new" at some point in time, is a face that now looks worse.

Some ads introduce what I will call *restoration "light"* by using less edgy terms for the work to be done. Physicians Formula Cover ToxTen^{50TM} Wrinkle Therapy Concealer is advertised with a shocked-looking female model spewing forth a narrative about the horrible discovery of "a wrinkle" (*Vogue*, September 2006). "Is that a wrinkle?" she asks. "That *is* a wrinkle," followed by "Terrific, I have wrinkles," and finally, "And a date." She then announces, "I'm 35, single, and wrinkled." The answer is to apply a product that will *conceal* the wrinkle (this product is said to also reduce the appearance of "dark circles").

An ad for Noxzema Blackhead Cleanser uses the idea of "Detoxifying" (see Figure 4.5, *Cosmopolitan*, July 2006) the face. Here, "detox" as a metaphor calls upon two established meanings of the term: (1) the more fundamental "detox" as a program to cleanse addicted individuals of drugs or alcohol and (2) the newer "detox" as a more beauty-oriented process of body cleansing through a regimen of purifying ingredients and experiences.

Other ads are less "light" and more direct with the restoration trope. St Ives Apricot Skin Cleansing Products are said to "Refine. Renew. Reveal younger looking skin" (*Marie Claire*, July 2006)—suggesting a pentimento in which the valuable original face that lies beneath the overlay of dirty skin can be revealed, just as a valuable painting that underlies a less worthy painting overlaid on it can be revealed through careful restoration work. An ad for Olay Regenerist (*Vogue*, October 2006; see Figure 4.6) actually pictures the offensive layer of a woman's face being peeled back to show beautiful skin beneath—as one would peel away old wallpaper to expose the original surface. The discourse of this ad assumes, of course, that the woman's skin and facial appearance were flawless and conventionally beautiful at some point in her life.

Another Regenerist ad (*Vogue*, May 2006) positions the cream as an alternative to more invasive procedures, by announcing to the potential buyer, "If you

Figure 4.5 **Noxema Blackhead Cleanser** (*Cosmopolitan*, July 2006).

Figure 4.6 **Olay Regenerist Daily Regenerating Serum** (*Vogue*, October 2006).

think cosmetic procedures are too drastic, do we have an alternative for you."
An ad for Olay Dual Action Cleanser and Toner instructs the woman to
"Restore your skin's harmonious balance . . ." (*Marie Claire*, July 2006), and
promotion of Olay Regenerist amplifies the metaphor through the product
name by telling the woman that this tool will yield "skin that looks beautifully

regenerated. What better way to reactivate your skin" (*Vogue*, July 2006). The temporal implication here is that the woman's skin *was* in a state of "generated" something (but it's not clear what) that now needs to be activated and re-started. This last ad appears in *Vogue*, the Cosmo generation magazine that reaches up the most in the age of its readership. *Vogue* also runs some ads with more explicit messages about aging—ads that use the euphemism of "mature skin." In an ad indicative of how far up the age ladder *Vogue* reaches, Lancôme's Absolue Premium βx with Pro-Xylane™ boasts that this product "visibly rejuvenates and replenishes from within" (*Vogue*, September 2006). The ad tells its reader, "Face 50 with our new standard in skincare to fight visible effects of age and hormonal changes and see younger-looking skin emerge" (here the artistic metaphor of pentimento creates the image of the original appearing underneath the surface appearance). Even for the younger reader of *Vogue*, this ad offers promise of rescue for the face when the time comes.

Advertising reaches out to the 40-something generation . . . and beyond

After the Cosmo generation comes the move through the mid and late thirties to the fortieth birthday, which in US culture is often considered a major threshold for women's entry into the socially constructed world of youth's decline into "middle age." It is for this age cohort that cosmetic surgery and less invasive Botox injections provide the backdrop against which products are advertised to get rid of the signs of aging.

The first ads that I saw for Botox Cosmetic (which is a prescription treatment) appeared in *Newsweek* in 2004. These ads clearly were aimed at the middle-aged generation of women. An ad that ran on April 28 pictured an invitation to a twenty-fifth High School Reunion, with the caption reading, "Still waiting for the right time to ask your doctor about Botox™Cosmetic? It just arrived [with the invitation]." Another ad (May 3, 2004) pictured an ornate off-white photo album with gold filigree and the words, "Our Daughter's Wedding." The tagline read, "Can you think of a better reason?" The first woman I knew who had Botox injections was exactly in that target group: late forties and working to keep pace with her 23-year-old daughter. Recent ads that I've seen for Botox Cosmetic in *Vogue* verbally present the product as something for the self. One ad (*Vogue*, August 2006) shows an attractive woman with long brown hair whose skin is clear and has that airbrush glow. The woman represented in this ad wears a pinstriped suit and tailored blouse, and her business portfolio holds a lavender colored folder on which it says, "I did it for ME." The past tense verb implies that this woman has already had Botox injections—thus, the beautiful skin—and there was no other reason for doing

the "after" image rather than the "before" image because she has no visible wrinkles or lines.

The first line of an ad for Estēe Lauder's product "Perfectionist Correcting Concentrate for Deeper Facial Lines/Wrinkles-with Poly-Collagen Peptides," invites "every woman who says no to Botox®" (*More*, July/August 2006). An alternative to surgical face-lifts also appears in an ad for Avon's Anew Clinical ThermaFirm Face Lifting Cream, which is "the new wave in face lifting." The ad for this product implores the female consumer to "get a tighter, firmer, more lifted look in just three days" (*Vogue*, September 2006). An attractive and perfectly clear woman's face in this ad shows only slight wrinkles and creases around the eyes and mouth—perhaps intended to suggest that she has already used the product. L'Oréal's Revitalift, named to elicit the connotation of the face-lift, uses the actress Andie MacDowell (48 years old at the time the ad was published) in its advertising, with the ads portraying a regimen of many products for treatment day and night. One of these ads (*Vogue*, 2006) is for a product that is redundantly named Revitalift® Double Lifting. To make sure that the potential consumer gets the picture, the ad, as seen in Figure 4.8, shows circular motion arrows on the model's face and two straight upward-pointing arrows on the product display. Clarins Advanced Extra-Firming Neck Cream gets into the face-lift trope through the image created in the phrase "to help lift, firm, revitalize and soften for a younger-looking, truly beautiful neck" (*Vanity Fair*, October 2006). An ad for Neutrogena Advanced Solutions Facial Peel (*Vanity Fair*, June 2006) is headlined "The extreme skin makeover without the extreme measures [of acid peels]," which gives "visible age-minimizing benefits with results up to a professional 35% glycolic peel." Olay Regenerist Microabrasion and Peel System is termed a "refinisher" with the ad addressing the potential consumer with a statement in the second person that invites a comparison to professional facial resurfacing through the restoration trope: "You get the strength of a microdermabrasion plus the smoothness of a mini-peel" (*Harper's Bazaar*, May 2006). The emphasis on doing something over again, in this case redoing the face, boldly appears by naming the product *Regenerist* (emphasis added) and by taking up the metaphor of furniture restoration through the metaphor of re-finishing. And you get "strength" just as you would in a good house restoration project that shores up the beams. Another ad for the same product shows a woman actually applying the product to her face, with the imperative statement, "Do try this at home" to suggest the comparison to procedures done in a professional's office space (*Harper's Bazaar*, May 2006). Both ads include small print disclaims that, "Results not equal to medical procedures." Disclaimers aside, these ads depend on the meanings associated with surgery and injections and borrow the metaphors of lifting and refinishing. Not only do these ads define beauty as wrinkle-free but they also set a standard for early intervention.

Figure 4.8 **L'Oréal RevitaLift Double Lifting** (*Vogue*, February 2006).

A note of explicit sexuality is added with a product by Elizabeth Arden. Prevage™ Anti-aging Moisturizing Treatment was created by Arden and Allergan Dermatology "who brought us Botox" (*Vogue*, December 2006). The first-person headline for the product, combined with the seductive look on the

Figure 4.9 **Prevage Eye Anti-aging Moisturizing Treatment** (*Vogue*, December 2006).

model's face that is shown in Figure 4.9, connote sex between an older woman and younger man: "Actually, he's my boyfriend. My son is slightly older." Not only can the hailed "older" woman look younger, but she can have an affair with a man younger than her son! On the website for this product (http://prevageskin.com/flash.asp), a dermatologist speaking with a British accent actually advises that the "ideal" is a combination of Prevage and Botox injections. Here the "medical" and "cosmeceutical" are combined.

Other evidence of the structural/restoration trope appears in many ads for the mature woman's face. One ad that I encountered for Channel's Précision Rectifiance Intense Eye actually pictures an angular, contemporary building in the background presented in black and white—more suggestive of architecture than of restoration (*Harper's Bazaar*, May 2006). Figure 4.10 shows the left page of a two-page spread; the right page displays a close-up black-and-white facial shot of a classically beautiful woman.

The signification here seems to be that just as the design of this sleek building needs to be precise, with nothing suggesting less than perfection, so too must the woman's face; the model on the opposing page is strikingly beautiful in her simplicity, with the product name (Rectifiance Intense Eye) overlaid on the building. The product name itself is a slick combination of "rectifying" and "defiance," proclaiming, "Now telltale signs of age are a thing of the past." The structural dimensions of restoration surface in L'Oréal's ad for Age Perfect For Mature Skin Anti-Sagging and Ultra-Hydrating Cream, which will "*reinforce* mature skin's network" and "*tighten* sagging skin" (*More*, July/August 2006; emphasis added).

One of the newer products on the market for the "aging" woman draws not only on tropes of war directed at facial lines and wrinkles but borrows its name from the currency of high definition technology to chart a new battlefield. Definity by Olay will do battle with the degradation of the facial color by bringing high definition to the surface: the potential consumer is hailed with the imperative to "Fight discoloration, dullness and wrinkles for highly defined luminosity" (*Vogue*, November 2006). Elsewhere the product is described as "highly defined anti-aging." And—to usher in 2007—the invitation comes as a New Year's resolution: "resolve to fight what ages you most—discoloration, dullness and wrinkles. Because fighting just wrinkles is sooo 2006." The web site for this product regimen—which includes Deep Penetrating Foaming Moisturizer, Intense Hydrating Cream, and Correcting Protective Lotion—expands on the "highly defined anti-aging" approach by verbally spotlighting the association of "luminosity" with "high definition" (www.olaydefinity.com). Definity gives "luminosity from within" by "unlocking luminosity." "Highly defined luminosity" is tied to the battle against aging with the pseudo-scientific results of research: "a recent study suggests that there may be a 'new wrinkle' in the fight against aging: brown spots, dullness and uneven tone." The scientific study claims results, reported in bullet form, for 78 percent of the participants using a dependent measure called "Skin Tone Analysis"; we are not told who did the study or anything about the dependent measure.

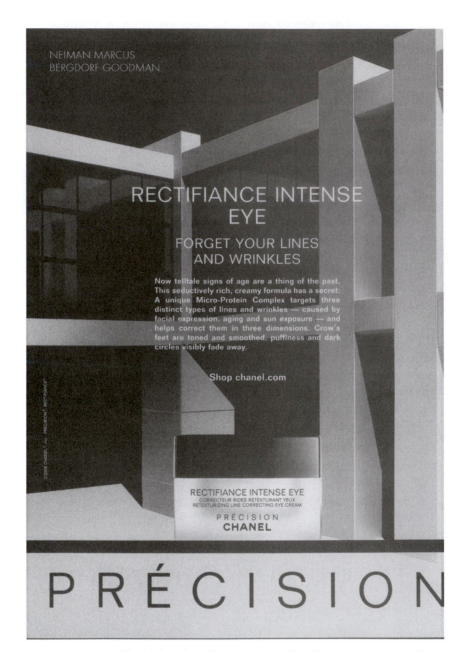

Figure 4.10 **Chanel Précision Rectifiance Intense Eye** (*Harper's Bazaar*, May 2006).

At about the same time that Olay's Definity was introduced to consumers, *Vogue* ran an article (Reed, 2006) that begins with the concerns of models, actors, and newscasters about their facial appearance on HDTV. The article moves to "real women" who are "seen in close-up all the time" and for whom "there is help, in the form of an increasing number of products taking advantage of new technology—and HD terminology" (p. 588). Several products are described, including Definity. Although Definity ads employ verbal imaging in an especially novel, up-to-date manner, other products also get at this newer battleground on the face. Clarins UV Plus Ecran Protective Day Screen uses a much more descriptive approach in talking about the need to shield the face from the sun, yet still calls upon the trope of remodeling by proclaiming both its "high-tech formulation" and its "White Tea extract" as the key to "*reinforced protection against pollution*" (*Vanity Fair*, June 2006; emphasis added).

Some advertisements for the 40-plus woman explicitly hail her by naming her age. L'Oréal's Revitalift Anti-Wrinkle and Firming Moisturizers mentioned above are "For 40ish Skin," and this company advertises its Age Perfect For Mature Skin Anti-Sagging and Ultra-Hydrating Cream as "50+ Years, Mature Skin" (*More*, July/August 2006). In this ad, 57-year-old Dayle Haddon —an actress and regular as the Health and Wellness Expert on CBS's *The Early Show*—speaks to the potential consumer with what is presented as a quotation: "Look as young as you feel." Another ad for this product, also featuring Dayle Haddon, leads with the statement, "Because 50ish skin demands full support"—directly invoking the restoration trope in suggesting that the skin needs bolstering for stability (*More*, May 2006). An ad for Roc® Retinol Correxion Deep Wrinkle Serum features a woman with tilted head and mouth open in speech saying, "I'm 40" next to which is the promise, "Get 10 Years Back" (*Vanity Fair*, June 2006).

Television programs during the day that focus on women (morning variety shows and soap operas running throughout daytime programming) are increasingly saturated with commercials for the same products advertised in magazines. The tag lines are the same as are the models, although the television mode allows for live models and voice-overs to tone the message. For example, Covergirl's product named Advanced Radiance Foundation is advertised on afternoon soap operas as "the most advanced age defier yet" (*As the World Turns*, February 2, 2007). Christie Brinkley is shown on screen with a label that says "age 52." The voice-over proclaims that this product is "reducing the look of wrinkles by 84%," while relatively small print on the screen reads, "84% on average." Of course we have absolutely no idea about the origin of this number.

What about women of color?

Women of color read most of the fashion and beauty magazines that Euro/White women read, but there are also specially targeted magazines carrying features and advertisements catering especially for them. Wondering about possible differences in discourse strategies, I examined the ways in which advertising for face-fixing hailed the Black woman. I chose *Essence* magazine as the main focus, whose average paid monthly circulation for the last six months in 2006 was 1,075,622. As a major magazine for Black women, this magazine draws readers mainly from the late teen to late thirties age cohort. *Essence* is described as focused on "general interest . . . male/female relationships, health and fitness, beauty, diet, parenting, financial management, careers, recipes, decorating, fashion, and travel . . . from an African American perspective" (LaGuardia, 2005, p. 449). The web site description reads, "The preeminent magazine for contemporary African American women, focusing on such topics as fashion, relationships, career and family. Every issue addresses cultural, political and social issues as well, catering to the well-educated African American."

The cosmetics and personal care items advertised in *Essence* are dominated by hair care products, such as Softsheen Carson Dark and Lovely Moisturizing Relaxer, Doo Gro Smooth & Straight Relaxer, and Panteen Relaxed & Natural Shampoo and Conditioner. Other common products are various make-up formulations, including those that are skin-tone matched, such as Covergirl Queen [Latifah] Collection and L'Oréal HIP-high intensity pigments, and body lotions, such as Jergens African Shea Butter. This concentration of products is marketed to the particular hair and skin needs among African Americans—many of whom experience dry skin and hair. Given that the age range for the *Essence* audience cuts across the late teen, single young adult female, and married female groups, the advertising is somewhat different from that in women's magazines such as *Vogue* and *InStyle* and more comparable to *Cosmopolitan*. With few exceptions, ads in magazines for women of color that are completely identical to those in magazines for White women present text and product displays but lack models. For example, an ad for Clinique Turnaround Concentrate Visible Skin Renewer (*Essence*, August 2006) shows the product under a filmy blue surface that is ripped to expose the product name underneath—suggesting that the film is like the surface of the face and, thus, needs to be removed to be renewed. The visual metaphor bears a clear association to wallpaper removal.

Some ads for products from major cosmetics manufacturers replace White models with Black models or add Black models to the ads that are placed in magazines such as *Essence*. An ad for Olay's Regenerist Thermal Contour and Lift uses a dark-skinned Black woman and stresses the moisturizing aspect of "lifting": the "Lifting Complex infuses moisture deep within skin's surface" (*Essence*, December 2006). In an advertising section for Mary Kay cosmetics, a two-page spread features a picture of a Black woman holding lip gloss on the right page with general information about Mary Kay products on the left page. An eight-page tear-out insert has four pictures of women, only one of whom is Black, and this one is the same picture as on the two-page spread for the same product. Interestingly, the face-fixing products in this regimen (Cleanser, Age-Fighting Moisturizer, and a day cream and night cream) are presented with a White model, which may be a way of avoiding specific verbal references to the Black woman's face. Avon also advertises their anti-aging product, Ageless Results, using a White and a Black model in the same ad (*Essence*, August 2006).

Face-fixing ads in *Essence* that are produced especially for the Black audience deal with evening out skin tone and fading spots on the face. Dr Susan Taylor (2004), who is Director of the Skin of Color Center at St Luke's Roosevelt Hospital in Philadelphia and author of *Brown Skin* (Taylor, 2003), describes the challenge of dark spots for people of color: "For women in particular acne bumps cause dark marks. When the acne bump goes away a woman of color is often left with a dark blemish. In addition, any type of rash on the skin, for example eczema, can resolve with a dark mark. Cuts, scrapes, burns, and abrasions may all heal with a dark area on the skin . . . Unfortunately, despite the exact cause, it can require several months, if not years, for the dark mark to fade."

Formulations known as fade creams are sold to treat various types of dark spots. A main ingredient in these creams is Alpha Hydroxy. Tropes related to health, consistency through "even tone," and richness—in its meaning of deep, complex, and strong—are key to the verbal images in the advertising and the visual images showing the Black woman's face. An ad for Ambi Fade Cream promotes "smooth, even-toned skin" by addressing "women with richer skin tones [who] face unique challenges in achieving smooth, even-toned skin" (*Essence*, December 2006; see Figure 4.11).

Similarly, Palmer's Skin Success regimen, which includes Eventone "Fade Milk," "Fade Cream," and "Facial Milk," offers the promise of "A healthier, eventone complexion" (*Essence*, December 2006). Both of these ads include text that promises results in two weeks or "in as little as two weeks (Palmer's, n.d.), which may be unrealistic (as are many claims made in cosmetics advertising). Contrasted to the magazine ad, the Palmer's website projects a longer wait: results can be expected in six to eight weeks (Palmer's, n.d.).

One skin tone product advertised in *Essence* is for a "concealment" cosmetic, which is a make-up, rather than a fade cream. Unlike the fade cream ads, where the audience is Black women, this ad does include visual reference to White people. The product is Dermablend Total Coverage Corrective System, which

Figure 4.11 **Ambi Fade Cream** (*Essence*, December 2006).

claims "Total coverage of moderate to severe skin flaws for up to 16 hours" (*Essence*, August 2006). The Black woman's face is shown in a "before" shot of one side of her face with some blotching and moles; the side-by-side "after shot," which shows the full face, has no blotching, although the moles remain. Four sets of small before–after pictures are shown in the bottom right corner of the ad, with each set labeled for the condition being concealed: one is a young, White woman for "birthmarks"; one is a dark-skinned Black person (gender is not clear) for "vitiligo" (a skin condition whose symptoms are irregular pale patches); one is a young, White man for "acne"; and one looks like a White version of the Black woman shown on the top of the ad, who is using the product for "post-op bruising." This last set presents interesting ambiguities: is it the same person as in the picture of the Black woman? why use the same picture? if not, why the similarity? I thought that checking the web site might clarify the picture, but although 33 before–after shots are included on the web site, the pictures from the magazine ad are not among them. In fact, only three of the 33 pictures on the web site are of Black people: two females for hyper pigmentation and one male for vitiligo.

The most striking differences in the ads for face-fixing in Black-oriented and White-oriented magazines have to do with the near-absence of "anti-aging" tropes and the presence of specifically race-targeted fade creams that draw on the trope of consistency and richness. As a White woman, I have often heard White women remark (and have remarked myself) on how young most Black women look in relation to their chronological age. The reason has largely to do with melanin. Dr Susan Taylor (2004) explains this: "Often women of color will look 10 years younger when compared to their counterparts with white skin. The melanin in the skin absorbs the ultraviolet light and prevents many of the changes that we associate with aging." The negative of more melanin is more spots; thus, the emphasis on fade creams. Yet, Olay is trying to reach the market of Black women with its anti-aging cosmeceuticals, although with terms drawing from the lifting metaphors rather than those explicitly about wrinkles and lines. It will be interesting to see how successful Olay and other companies who may follow suit are in bringing Black women into the discourse of wrinkles, lines and other facial signs of aging. Or perhaps they will gain entré into this market of Black women's faces through new products in the fade cream category that grow from the latest frontier in face-fixing: discolorations and spots that are now being defined as the new enemies on the battlefield of the face—enemies to be fought with products like Olay's Definity. Yet, just as Definity is not termed a "fade cream," complete crossover is unlikely in the terms used to hail women who are market-segmented through race and skin color. In fact, just recently, a Definity ad in *Essence* (March 2007) spoke directly in the second person to the Black woman using the metaphor of even surface but no reference to wrinkles: "You've always aged gracefully. Why not help your skin age more flawlessly too?"

Do "real men" care about wrinkles?

The vast cosmetics industry has for decades been all about women. Baby-boomer American males grew up with after-shave lotion, a few hair preparations depending on the style of the day, deodorant and an assortment of colognes for special occasions. Black men have always attended more to managing their hair than have White men, but other cosmetic products have been minimal for them too, except as "prescribed" by their mothers, sisters, and wives. In the last few years, we have seen a vast increase in personal care products for men. There are more shampoos, deodorants, after-shave lotions, body sprays and colognes "for him" than ever before. The cultivation of the male consumer for these products has also dropped a substantial age bracket with the successful introduction of Unilever's Axe, and on its heels, Tag. These products are aimed at teens and young men and have been marketed mainly as the key to attracting girls and women. Gillette even went so far as to keep its company name off Tag and its advertising as a way of disassociating this new teen product from possible old school associations (Abelson, 2005). But what about facial care? Is the anti-aging push in cosmetics restricted to women, or are men targeted for face-fixing discourse through new products and their advertising?

Magazine culture does not exist for teenage boys as it does for teenage girls, nor is there an array of men's magazines compared to those published for women. Magazines like *Sports Illustrated* and *Car and Driver* are popular among teenage boys and men of varying ages. These magazines rarely include ads for facial products with the exception of shaving creams and after-shave lotions. The 2006 Swimsuit Issue of *Sports Illustrated*, for instance, included only five ads for personal care products: two cologne ads, one shampoo ad, and one shave cream ad. There are several lifestyle magazines for men in different age groups that are logical venues for advertising cosmetic products, and I focused on these to learn more about the products being advertised and the discourse strategies used in the advertisements. Magazines in this group and their average monthly paid circulation for the second half of 2006 as reported by the Audit Bureau of Circulations (2006) include *Maxim* (2,501,175), *Stuff* (1,247,825), *Details* (455,374), *Esquire* (709,151), *GQ/Gentlemen's Quarterly* (1,005,303), and the new *Men's Vogue* (which Condé Nast launched with a run of 300,000 copies).

We might expect the publisher's overview statements for these men's magazines to provide some grounding for the type of advertising in the magazines. Certainly the fashions and personal care products such as cologne are codable based on the publisher's definition of the men's image they are working to create. If more advanced face-fixing products are to be advertised, they would presumably be consonant with the magazine's image of men. The statements below are from the publisher's web pages (active in February 2007) for each of the men's magazines. The first two magazines (*Maxim* and *Stuff*) cater to a younger male audience focused on sex and "guy stuff." The last three (*Esquire*, *GQ*, and *Men's Vogue*) appeal to a more sophisticated men's audience—to men with varied and more mature interests that are less dominated by sex. *Esquire* is somewhat of a bridge between the two magazine types, although it is more consonant with the latter than the former grouping.

- *Maxim* "delivers the best of what guys want, hot women, big laughs, and cool gear every month!" (Dennis Publications; website includes soft porn).
- *Stuff* has no description, but the words used at the top of the web site include "gear, girls, hype! laughs, mayhem, sex, style" (Dennis Publications; web site includes soft porn).
- *Esquire* "is special because it's a magazine for men. Not a fashion magazine for men, not a health magazine for men, not a money magazine for men. It is not any of these things; it is all of them. It is, and has been for nearly seventy years, a magazine about the interests, the curiosity, the passions, of men" (Hearst Communications).
- *GQ* "is the authority on men . . . providing definitive coverage of men's style and culture. GQ embraces every aspect of a man's life, from fashion and politics to travel, entertainment, sports, food, technology and relationships . . . [The readers] are hip, affluent, and above all influential and they look to GQ for what it takes to look sharp and live smart" (Condé Nast).
- *Men's Vogue* "presents a colorful portrait of a world in which a man's *intellect, accomplishments, and appearance converge in the creation of a well-lived, well-balanced life.* It combines far-reaching curiosity with a regard for the kind of *style* that emanates from *success and substance.* Through coverage of art and architecture, travel and food, politics and finance, culture and sports, bespoke tailoring and fine watches, the leading writers and photographers of the world will define *a new male sensibility—smart, worldly, mature*, and ready to discover more" (Condé Nast; emphasis in original).

Ads for the Maxim-style male

Face-fixing products are rarely seen in the macho, "sex and girls" oriented magazines. Those that do appear are for shaving products that moisturize the face. Conspicuous in these ads is discourse related to male–female relationships. Ads for Gillette Fusion Hydra Soothe, which is an "after shave moisturizer," appear in both *Maxim* (July 2006) and *Stuff* (August, 2006). The language of these ads calls on sexual intercourse metaphors with suggestive phrases such as "hydrating emollients and *lubricants* . . ." and "from the first *stroke* to the last" (emphasis added). The ad is spread over two pages in a web layout format (see Chapter 5), and the phrase on the bottom corner of the right-side page reads, "The Best a Man Can Get"—again with a suggestive connotation that invites the metaphor of sexual intercourse. An ad for Edge Active Care Shave Cream makes an explicit connection between the product and male–female relations. In this ad, a clean-shaven, wide-eyed young man is shown with a woman's hands on his face and told, "Keep her hands to yourself" (*Stuff*, August 2006). Avon's line of men's products is also advertised with the ladies in mind: "Impress her with your charm, not your lines" (*Sports Illustrated*, October 31, 2005). In stressing the orientation of men to sex and women, the discourse in these ads is consistent with ads for body sprays and deodorants, which stress their connection with attracting women. This discourse corroborates a more general conclusion that Christina Baker (2005) draws from her analysis of the images of women's sexuality in men's and women's magazines: "in women's magazines, the idea was to try to obtain beauty through a certain product, whereas in men's magazines the idea was to obtain an attractive woman through a product" (p. 25).

Ads for the more "mature" male

The second group of magazines, like the first, has only a few ads focused on the face, but here we see the first appearance of ads for "anti-aging" products. L'Oréal introduced a new product line called Men's Expert in May 2005, which many reviewers described as directed at the gay and metrosexual consumer (Wilke, 2005). Products in this line have been advertised in magazines but are also more fully explained on the L'Oréal website. The gay target audience for the products is clear on the website, which features Kyan Douglas, the grooming expert on "Queer Eye for the Straight Guy"—the show that brought gay male style to the uncultivated heterosexual man. Yet, just as Queer Eye holds out hope for even the slobbiest of straight men, so too does the advertising discourse. The first ad that I saw for a Men's Expert product was in the July 4, 2005 issue of *Sports Illustrated*—not exactly a gay publication. This ad shows two pictures of a handsome man, one of which is a facial close-up under which is written "You think you look wide awake" and the other an even closer cropped picture of one side of the man's face under which is written, "She thinks you need a wake-up call." The product is called Hydrapower Invigorating Moisturizer. An interesting element in this ad is the association of skin appearance with heterosexual attractiveness by using captions to speak directly to the male reader of the ad. Another ad in this series appeared in both the September 19, 2005 issue of *Sports Illustrated* and the premier issue of *Men's Vogue* (Fall 2005) (see Figure 4.12).

Figure 4.12 **L'Oréal Men's Expert Stop Lines Anti-Lines** (*Men's Vogue*, Fall 2005).

The product advertised was Stop Lines Anti-Lines Moisturizer with SPF 15 Sunscreen. Using masculine words such as "ADS, *Active Defense System*" and "*powerful*, soothing formula [to] *strengthen* your skin's natural *defense against daily aggressions*" (emphasis added), the product associates anti-aging with the metaphor of war and combat. Again, the discourse in this ad associates facial care, in this case lines, with heterosexual attractiveness through the captioning: "You think lines add character. She thinks lines add years." The consumer who is hailed is neither gay nor clearly metrosexual. An ad for another version of this product, Vita Lift SPF 15 Anti-Wrinkle & Firming Moisturizer with UVA/UVB Sunscreen (*Esquire*, July 2006), also uses a manly metaphor in its heading, "How Many Wrinkles Can You Press?" Because weight training might be the domain of either straight or gay men, the manly trope has elasticity across audiences.

L'Oréal's website presentation for Men's Expert (http://www.loreal parisusa.com) provides the full array of products plus a how-to guide that is led by Kyan Douglas. The manly trope is clear in every aspect of the product line, as metaphors of both aggression and cars permeate the advertising presentation. Of the ten products, the word *power* is used in three names: Hydra Power Moisturizer, Power Clean Anti-Dullness Face Wash, and Power Buff Anti-Roughness Exfoliator. In each of these, a change in the last word would make the name appropriate for a car detailing service: . . . *wash*, . . . *car wash* and . . . *polisher*, respectively. The web site also has a link to Sports Updates, and the tutorial/product demonstrations by Kyan Douglas for how to choose and then use the "customized" product regimen "that's right for you" is grunt and click in its no-nonsense simplicity. The web site also engages technology language by introducing the product line as L'Oréal bringing its "grooming technology and expertise to men."

A scarce few additional face-fixing products are advertised in men's magazines. *Men's Vogue* has carried ads for Pevonia Botanica, which is a lotion billed as "a dynamic in-spa treatment with Caviar (anti-aging) and Escutox™ (wrinkle-smoothing)" ingredients. The text in the ad carries sexual connotations in the phrase, "Prolong your results," and exploits a sports metaphor to tell the potential consumer that this product is "Raising the bar to youthful skin." Unlike the heterosexual appeal in the ad that ran in *Sports Illustrated*, this ad pictures a tall, sculpted and heavily muscled, bare-chested White male model who appears to be wearing white linen exercise pants—a presentation that is easily interpreted as both gay and metrosexual-oriented, or upper class, refined male. The premier issue of *Men's Vogue* also carried an advertising section called "Face~Time." The products advertised had simple, clear masculine imagery. The Zirh line of anti-aging products is called "kit," and the strength training metaphor is clear: "Stay Young. Stay Strong. Strong Skin." The verbal images carry connotations of Lance Armstrong. Shiseido Men is advertised as a "high-performance skincare system" that will "Power Your Skin." And Bionova is given the technology aura with the term, "Nano Skin Tech™."

While there are still not many products or advertisements for men's facial care, those that exist hail the potential consumer with tropes well suited to manliness (whether gay or straight) and distinct from the discourse directed at women. Heterosexual relations, sports, combat, and aggression prevail as the main elements enabling the advertising discourse to create images associated with these face-fixing products. Alongside of this approach to men, there is also evidence that women are the target for these products as the purchaser for their special man. On September 24, 2006, I saw the first Macy's full-page ad in *The Boston Globe* (and probably many other newspapers) for a variety of men's facial products that was unequivocally directed at women: "*There's a new sensation across the nation. For Fall, pamper him.* Help him clean up his act with exciting new skincare products" (p. A15). The discourse here invokes conventional gender ideology of the man who is unconcerned about his appearance and the woman who will be in charge of his daily upkeep and will tame his unruly appearance. The race for male face-fixing has begun, and if consumer culture prevails, the next generation of young men will be madly comparing products. Market researchers (Ignelzi, 2004) project that by 2010, sales of men's grooming products will reach $10 billion—no small change, even if the changes in men's use of these products appears small.

Conclusions and implications

Across the lifespan—and when it comes to face-fixing, it's still primarily the lifespan for females—we find a growing avalanche of advertising discourse proclaiming the possibilities for face-fixing as part of the "beauty myth" that mass media present. Teens learn to attend to the face and to cultivate facial care as a regimen of practice. As women get older, they are presented with many different products for the face, often hawked with the tropes of repair and renovation. The image is one of constant battle against the enemies of the face and the enemies, ultimately, of aging. Underlying this discourse is the age-old quest for youth. What has changed, however, is the broad and ever proliferating array of products that offer promises to fix "this or that" problem. With the backdrop of Botox injections and surgical intervention, which are much more readily accessible than in the past, the cosmeceutical industry has exploded with discourse, the purpose of which is not only to persuade the potential consumer to buy face-fixing products but also to buy these products because they are cheaper/less invasive/less frightening than injections or surgery. Yet, the promotion and use of injections marches on, with the American

Society for Aesthetic Plastic Surgery reporting that $1.3 billion was spent on Botox injections alone in 2005, and the number of injections rose over a 10-year period from about 65,000 to close to 3.3 million (Botox Product, 2006). The greater popularity of Botox and the targeting of younger women with taglines such as "I did it for me" and "I was curious" will keep pushing cosmeceutical producers to introduce innovations in both their products and their advertising, as will the growing popularity of cosmetic surgery.

What is clear today and will likely be clear tomorrow is that ads for cosmeceuticals use both visual and verbal imaging strategies that draw on conventional beauty ideals and the quest for youth. In the cultural flux of meanings, we are seeing advertising discourse about facial degradation directed at younger and younger women (a trend to which I'll return).

Although most of the advertising discourse about face-fixing focuses on White women, there are other targets as well. Women of color are interpolated somewhat differently than are White women, with Black women more often approached about spots and uneven skin tone. Yet, the remedies available to dark-skinned women fit squarely in the newest profile of face-fixing products for the mainstream woman—"correcting" products said to get rid of skin's unevenness—which is presented to mainstream women as the ultimate sign of aging and, thus, the newest battle to be fought with the most innovative weapons. The most recent advertising foray for the anti-aging remedies aims at men—sometimes directly, but more often through direct appeal to women who are placed in the position of attending to the facial needs that matter to women, who want them to look young.

The overview presented in this chapter on face-fixing products and the ways in which advertising discourse represents images to be pursued raises all of the issues about the pressure on women to conform to particular—and in almost all cases unattainable—beauty standards. There are, however, several other issues that arise from the analysis that I have presented. Five issues are noted here: face-fixing and people of color, especially women; the movement of advertising discourse about aging to younger target audiences; the exploitation of common, culturally meaningful tropes; the saturation of various media with face-fixing imaging through the discourse of advertising; and the more general accelerated pace in the culture of appearance and semblances through which advertising tropes are contextualized.

The first set of issues arises in relation to people of color. The ways in which advertising hails the non-White consumer draw attention to several issues about the future of cosmetic intervention. One issue raised in respect to people of color has to do with the reach of hegemonic gender ideals for the face, *which are inscribed on the White face*. Beauty standards for Black and Asian women are not identical to those of Whites (see, for example, Baker, 2005, for a comparison of how Black and White women are represented in advertising), yet the mass-marketed reach of face-fixing products guarantees that Blacks, Asians and non-White Latinos/as will continuously be exposed to White hegemonic ideals of beauty and attractiveness. Milkie's (1999) research indicates that although African-American high school girls were very familiar with White hegemonic beauty standards, they were less likely than White girls to judge themselves by these standards or to think these standards were relevant in how their beauty would be judged by African-American boys. More recently, there are indicators that women of color in the US are succumbing to the White beauty myth and what it implies for the face. Das (2007), for example, writes about the growth of cosmetic surgery among non-White groups. Eyelid alterations for Asian women and nose shaping to create a slimmer appearance for both Asian and African American women are on the rise. For Asian American women, the context is not only the western beauty myth that is propagated through advertising, fashion, and media representations, but also the growing trend in Asian countries for facial surgery to create features less marked for Asian-ness and more conforming to European and American beauty standards (Cullen, 2002).

Another issue raised by the analysis of face-fixing images in advertising pertains to age and market segmentation. In reflecting on the progression of treatments for the female face across the lifespan of the teen years to middle age, the question arises as to the relationship between the pounding discourse of advertising and the perceptions that girls and women have about the appearance of their faces. One journal narrative (Damsky, 1999) focuses on the loss of "natural" appearance during the teen years. Here, the author writes about the war with her face at age 12 related to acne: "In a short period of time, I become completely alienated from my own reflection. Each morning I stare at myself in the mirror with a cold and critical eye trying to assess the state of my complexion. Everything I do to my skin is an exercise in powerlessness since my acne doesn't respond" (p. 135). At age 16, she refers to her "adversarial relationship with my own face" (p. 136). Yes, the acne is there, but the particular metaphors in this personal account bear a striking similarity to the verbal hailing found in advertising. This young teen is likely not alone in her perception that she is at war with her face. The discourse imaging running through advertising for numerous face-fixing products across the lifespan carries the same metaphors—the battleground of the face with enemies to be conquered and, later, the massive rebuilding project that continuously faces the "mature" woman. Yet, what also appears in the advertisements considered in this chapter is a movement of the image of aging downward. Recall the ad for L'Oréal Acne Response in *InStyle* that was described earlier in the section on the "Cosmo generation." That ad appropriated the war metaphor to bridge the more common face "ailment" of this generation (acne) with the enemy more commonly imaged for the next generation of older women (wrinkles): the second-person, present tense statement reads, "You're fighting everything from acne to fine lines." This accelerated discourse of aging further propels the idea of the body in general as commodity, and the woman's face in particular as an object to be manipulated. At the other end of the age spectrum, ads are directed at women in their fifties, and it would not be a surprise to see face-fixing products and their discourse images moving upward to older "senior" women in the years ahead. As baby-boomers age, there is a ready market for more and more face-fixing appeals—especially for a cultural group that is obsessive about health, fitness, and looking good (meaning not looking like your mother or grandmother).

The degree to which face-fixing products will be successfully promoted to a male clientele is an open question. The saturation of every age group with advertising promotions for products aimed at women is less likely to be easily duplicated for men. Many of the leading theorists of masculinity view its definition as hinging on the repudiation of femininity, and by extension, of homosexuality (see Collins, 2004; Connell and Messerschmidt, 2005; Kimmel, 1994). Upper class and upper-middle class men have more latitude in using an array of cosmetics and in practices such as manicures, but the majority of mainstream American men continue to be circumscribed by a hegemonic masculinity that bars practices associated with the feminine. This places con-straints on the types of discourse that can be effectively used in direct appeals to men. To move too far risks what many heterosexual men fear, that is, being associated with homosexual images. These conclusions are not meant, however, to preclude the possibility that cosmetics manufacturers might not make inroads into the male market. Connell and Messerschmidt (2005) call attention to *embodiment* as part of hegemonic masculinity, with embodiment entailing "circuits of social practice linking bodily processes and social structure" (p. 851). Embodiment changes over time, and it may be the case that we are seeing the early stages of what will become more elaborate face-fixing practices among men in the US. Any speculation, however, must consider the differential poten-tials for face-fixing products to appeal to men from different racial and cultural groups.

The third issue arising from this analysis is squarely in the domain of dis-course and culture. Advertisers often call on familiar forms of discourse that can be truncated through ellipsis. We might not usually think of tropes as forms of ellipsis, but figures of speech work similarly to ellipsis. When advertisers represent their products using familiar tropes, such as the metaphor of war and the metaphor of restoration and rebuilding, they are relying on the consumer not only to fill in the missing elements left blank but also to expand the meaning of the advertising discourse with images carried through the tropes that are used. In a society steeped in war metaphors that are refreshed daily by discourse about real wars, advertisers can rely on verbal metaphors of war to convey the seriousness of the problems they want the consumer to accept. Especially interesting in the face-fixing business is the targeting (pun intended) of women with war metaphors. It is not unusual to hear reports of war casualties in which statements like "innocent women and children" are used to characterize the victims of war—thus giving women and children a special status because of their presumed helplessness in the face of war. In the cosmetics business, there is also this underlying image of women as helpless against the enemy of facial degradation unless saved by the latest cosmetic product, in short, saved by the weapons and strategies used to combat the enemy in an all-out war. The tropes used to advertise face-fixing cosmetics for (mainly) White women are becoming so common, almost universal, that they are coming to be first-order "reality." The war metaphor also stands out in a number of advertisements focused on the teenage face. The teen audience targeted by the ads is, like the female audience, innocent; they did not do anything to create the facial enemy of acne, and the products advertised can both fight the enemy and protect them.

Restoration is also a timely metaphor for cosmetic products because of the fast-growing industry in home repair and renovation. Just as Home Depot and Lowes are just a few miles away and loaded with supplies for the home projects that need to be undertaken, so too are face-fixing products only as far away as the cosmetics counter at the local pharmacy or department store. For men, the metaphor of war is more likely to emerge in images related to attracting women. We might, therefore, expect future attempts by advertisers to bring more men into the face-fixing regimen to work with tropes either drawing on the war of the sexes or drawing on completely different tropes—perhaps gaming or auto detailing.

The fourth issue of interest has to do with the potential of various media to be the advertisers' field for blanketing consumer awareness about facial care products. New products and advertising for face-fixing treatments—especially for women approaching and deep into middle age—are appearing at a rapid pace. Television programs from daytime to prime time slots are interrupted with commercials that beckon the woman to take some significant interventions to repair and rebuild her face. These products also now show up as subject matter for talk-TV. The *Today Show*, for example, included a feature in its January 25, 2007, program in which wrinkle creams were the focus, and an expert compared various products, concluding that price was not a factor in effectiveness. And what did she say? Essentially that, by some measure not made clear in her report, all of the products were good moisturizers, and that a "10 percent improvement" was noticed with the use of some of the products—

modest results indeed for a product category that is flooding the market with advertising discourse offering visions of before–after remodeling. For any product advertised on television or in the pages of the many magazines available for purchase or perusal while waiting for appointments, the presentation on the Internet is surely more expansive. Sometimes, there is simply more information about a product or more specific products from the same manufacturer. Other times, the web sites offer the consumer an extended discourse that includes narratives of success. Whatever the medium of advertising, the market potential for facial products will lead advertisers to saturate the outlets available to them for reaching consumers.

Finally, the potential of expanded product development and advertising venues, combined with a growing cultural acceptance of the body as flexible and open to changes, suggest that discourse used in advertising will keep pace with cultural changes, with the face only one of several stages on which to mount a production. New tropes are appearing to supplement the established metaphors: Olay, for example, recently released a product for the eye named Regenerist Eye Derma-Pod Anti-Aging Triple Response System, which is recommended as a thrice-weekly product; one wonders if the "derma-pod" verbal image was someone's brainchild to engage connotations related to the iPod. In mid-2007, the makers of Botox introduced an injectable gel product named Juvéderm. Ads in magazines and on television urge the consumer to talk to her doctor about this procedure, which is said "to instantly smooth those 'parentheses' lines on the sides of your nose and mouth." In this case, it appears that the metaphor of punctuation has been used to soften the invasive images of Botox. "Body firming" cosmeceutical products and eye creams are already widely available, and we are seeing ads for dealing with more parts of the face and body—lips, legs, hands. Culturally, the idea of "naturalness" and what is "natural" is undergoing a meaning shift. Advertisers have long used the appeal to a "natural look" to promote facial care products, making ideas of facial and whole body restoration just an easy metaphorical step away. Natural now seems to be nothing more than an appearance, and for the aging adult cohort, advertising discourse is positioning it as an appearance that can be restored and rebuilt. With metaphors of renovation and war so firmly fixed in facial care advertising, it is interesting to speculate about what tropes might emerge in the future to draw concepts of cultural currency into the discourse of advertising. Perhaps we will see and hear advertisers position the body as a surface to be "navigated" or appearance as an attribute amenable to the "shuffle." Or perhaps advertisers will hail the consumer with promises of endless transformations through "Bod-casting." Whatever the different tropes might be, facial and body remodeling, restoration, and regimens are expensive and time-consuming propositions for the consumer. From a critical discourse analysis perspective, it is time to talk back to the discourse that places higher priority on appearance and the quest for changes to the physical body than on the critical problems facing society. In the face of rising health care costs, global environmental threats, and ethnic and racial conflicts around the world, just how important can the restoration of one person's face be?

Chapter 5

Madison Avenue meets Silicon Valley

Technology imprints on advertising

The first images that come to mind when joining the words "technology" and "advertising" are likely to be of technology products that appear in magazines, television programs, billboards, buses and subways, and Internet pop-ups. Computers and printers, cameras, mobile phones, global positioning systems for your car, copiers, and web sites for a range of products and services appear in ads proclaiming speed, cutting-edge innovations, sleek style, and a host of other attributes. Less obvious, however, is an array of non-product specific images of technology that appears in ads for both technology products and products that we do not think of as technology-based, such as hair care, snacks, and cigarettes. This second image level marks a technological imprint on the discourse of advertising, and it reaches far beyond the technology products advertised and what consumers usually think about in association with "technology."

This chapter is devoted to laying out the different ways in which this technological imprint can be seen in current advertising and considering the implications that technologically marked discourse in advertising may have for our thinking, our sense of connection to or alienation from others, and our cultural milieu overall. I will demonstrate several different ways in which we see, read, and hear technology in advertising and how technology enters not just explicitly into advertising discourse but more pervasively through its intertextual presence by modeling or mocking technology. When we encounter the "texts" of technology where they might not be expected and in ways that they might not be expected, we are in the domain of discourse framing on the order of what Lakoff and Johnson (1980; 2003) brought into focus in their explication of how war metaphorically structures the ways in which we express many non-war experiences: not just the "war on poverty," but "*attacking* a problem," "*retreating* from a bad relationship," and "*battling* the bureaucracy." Lakoff and Johnson's fundamental idea was that metaphor is ever-present in language, and that metaphors both structure thinking and direct action. Technology, then, may be today's intrusion on our thinking and action not only because the products of technology are ubiquitous—DVD players, digital cameras, mobile phones, the computer and its transport to web surfing, e-mail, and instant messaging—but also because we speak and understand language laced with technology metaphors.

In a short time, electronic technology has become prominent in the practices of daily life. Technology envelopes us. As recently as 20 years ago, I had access to only a cumbersome e-mail system and felt fortunate to get on-line information about the library catalog at my university. I plugged my telephone into a receptacle on the wall, went to the photo store to have my films developed without the advantage of instantly seeing the shots I had taken, and did my home shopping by calling an 800 number or filling out the order form and dropping it in the mailbox. My computer had very limited memory, and "viruses" attacked the human body. The younger generation now in their late teens has grown up with the Internet as a daily source of information, entertainment, and shopping; communication via e-mail and instant messaging—especially for youth and young adults—happens throughout the day; and mobile phone contact and text messaging create the possibility for contacts with others never before possible. Indeed, the culture of "24/7" (a new technological metaphor) exists because of technological advances and the toys brought with these advances; one can stay "virtually connected" to friends and family even when away, and your presence to others can be "on" to the extent that a business person might even set an alarm clock for the middle of the night to check messages through a Blackberry and do business across time zones.

As with any innovation, technological changes spawn new language—vocabulary being the most recognizable. For technology specialists, an *argot* (which is a specialized language used by a specific group of people) developed just as in other specialized professional fields. New terms and abbreviations were born, and some old terms were given specialized meanings: CPU, RAM, ROM, mainframe, memory space, bits and bytes, hard drive, protocol, encryption, to name a few. As Internet technology became more accessible and moved beyond the specialists, terms like "file sharing" (meaning something different than lending your manila folders to another person), "downloading" (different from "unloading" your problems on another person) and "user" (not of drugs but of computers) were added. Technology terms ushered in new modes of expression. We do not simply share our work with others; we share the file it is in. We do not simply get something from someone else; we download it to our local computer from somewhere else (up?—but up where?). We do not simply work on a computer; we are "users" who often have user names and numbers. What we write in e-mails is labeled "messages" rather than "notes" or "communications"; the content of anything sent over the Internet is referred to as "information" rather than differentiated "ideas" and "facts." The cybernetic model that had been taken up by some communication scholars in the 1960s to frame communication as a process of transmission between senders and receivers dominates the Internet lingo of "sending" messages as opposed to "expressing" or "communicating." Today's lexicon includes new meanings for "screen" and "page" distinct from the "big" screen and the television screen and from pages in a book. We "channel surf" with the remote control or "surf the web" with a mouse, even if we aren't skilled, inclined, or fortunate to be in a location to hit the ocean waves. We can even "bump into" something on the Internet, just as we might bump into another person accidentally while rushing to cross the street before the light turned red. In short, the specialized argot of "information specialists" and computer geeks gradually spread outward in the culture. You don't have to be a computer or information specialist to have a pretty good idea what a fair amount of the lingo signifies, and new technology terms enter the lexicon all the time: "spam" (whoever created that one must have detested the canned meat wannabe), "web master" (or the nonsexist version, "webster"), "pop-up" (not as cute as a Jack-in-the-Box), and a host of e-words made comprehensible by our understanding that the "e" in "e-mail" means electronic mail over the Internet using a computer. Transfers of the "e" idea have given rise to terms such as "e-commerce," "e-trade," "e-tailer," and sell-anything-you-want "e-bay." No longer restricted in meaning to a skin irritation on the dog's tail that he chewed and licked or the best night club in town, we have learned that a "hot spot" is also a place to connect with the Internet, and "Wi-Fi" means that wireless fidelity is present in that café we love to frequent. What had been argot became vernacular and then moved into more general American lingo.

Ever so slowly, new editions of dictionaries have carried the terms of technology. Randomhouse.com includes a page titled "New Words: Sixty Years of New Words," which begins in the 1960s. They include some well-known new technology words for each decade: "megabyte" in the 1960s, "diskette" and "personal computer" in the 1970s (although only a privileged few owned a PC in that decade), "emoticon" and "virtual reality" in the 1980s, and "intranet" and "web site" in the 1990s. Askoxford.com lists a *Word of the Year*, posting "text message" in 1998 and "pod casting" in 2004. The publicity for the 2006 American Heritage College Dictionary headlines two of the newest entrants to the technology lingo: "blog" and "wiki." Once these words are in the standard dictionaries, we know they have made it past the fad stage and have likely passed into broader usage.

The growth of terminology and of practice related to technology products have their place referentially and culturally. We adapt language to meet the circumstances and experiences in which we live. For example, the personal diary format on the web page became known as the "weblog," then the "blog" whose participants were dubbed "bloggers." In this case, a practice and the means for talking about it have a short history, yet are part of today's mass cultural idiom. The term "blog" is dated to 1999 (*Webster's New Millennium Dictionary*, 2003–2005); shortly thereafter, *New Yorker* magazine was carrying its first story about blogging (Mead, 2000). Today, most people know about blogs even if they have never read one.

Innovations change practice—both materially and linguistically. But has technology stayed in its place? Or has it seeped into other areas of life? These are questions about both culture and mind. The presence of technology in advertising for non-technology products shows that technology reaches farther into the cultural landscape than the particular practices that define it. Why should we be interested in this? My critical judgment is that advertising provides one important source of language change—one source for the ways in which technology may be reformatting (to use a technological term) our thinking and expression. The language of technology is moving through culture, circulating in various media, making certain discourse moments more accessible to some than others, and changing lexicon, punctuation, and visual orientations to language. Advertising, because of its prominence in everyday life, is one circulator of this new contributor to the American idiom.

I have chosen the term *technographic discourse* for the fusion of verbal and visual signification of technology in advertising. Technographic discourse creates the semblance of technology through the manipulation of text and the format through which text is presented. Like the term "telegraphic," *technographic* implies both reduction and broadcasting. The telegraph as a means of communication extracted basic elements of syntax and vocabulary and then sent them across distances to be deciphered in a remote location. The resulting "telegram" format contained only the barest of items, leaving elements out that could be filled in by the recipient. The telegram was sent to a person distant from the sender, for example to someone who would pick up the sender at the train station upon her arrival, in the form of:

WILL ARRIVE 7 PM SUNDAY. MEET AT STATION. NED WITH ME. MONA.

The meaning of the telegram would easily be retrieved by a person fluent in English to mean, "[I] will arrive [at] 7[:00] p.m.[on] Sunday. [You or perhaps someone else should] meet [me] at [the] station. Ned [will be] with me. [From] Mona." The person sending the telegram relied on the ability of the person receiving the telegram to fill in the ellipsis points to complete the meaning, that is, to be involved in actively rendering the full linguistic signification.

Precisely this form of ellipsis and the retrieval of missing elements shape technographic discourse. Advertising in general relies on ellipsis to create an atmosphere of proximity and intimacy. As Cook (2001) explains it, ads "draw parasitically on the genre of 'conversation': the prototype of interactive reciprocal communication in which formalities and differences of rank are often diminished or partially suspended" (p. 173). In the case of ads that draw on the discourse associated with technology, the use of ellipsis occurs not only linguistically but also when a broad array of assumptions about technology-enhanced products and interactions are important to interpreting the ad, but remain unstated: some of these assumptions are that technology improves products; technology cuts out many steps for the consumer; and technology is about virtualities deemed to be as good as or better than the "real thing." And technology balances on the edge of the public–private split by juxtaposing personal use and privacy with the mass circulation potential of the Internet and the loss of personal identity through public access. When presenting techno-graphic discourse elements, the advertiser provides publicly understood dis-course templates for the consumer to personally navigate: technology is or can be global, but any particular product is for you personally to select just as you would select one of the (finite) choices available through technology.

In this chapter, four different domains of technographic discourse will be charted:

- technology terms, which are a direct representation of argot through vocabulary;
- technological symbols such as the @ sign, now commonplace because of e-mail, and the > sign used to guide a link or to signify forward on a video device;
- terminal punctuation and short programming commands used on com-puter applications such as might be found in World Wide Web addresses; and
- discourse presented in the format of technology templates such a text messages and web page layouts.

As introduction, a brief overview of technology use—especially use of the Internet—is provided as context.

The who and what of technology use

The idea that everyday social life occurs through learned *practices* is central to the Critical Discourse Analysis perspective that was introduced in the first chapter. Practices are defined by Chouliaraki and Fairclough (1999) as:

> . . . habitualised ways, tied to particular times and places, in which people apply resources (material and symbolic) to act together in the world . . .

> The advantage of focusing upon practices is that they constitute a point of connection between abstract structures and their mechanisms, and concrete events—between "society" and people living their lives. (p. 21)

Practices are, thus, not isolated quirky actions of an autonomous individual but, rather, socially formed ways of doing things and representing experiences and ideas. Chouliaraki and Fairclough further note that practices have three main characteristics (p. 22): (1) they are "forms of production" (in the case of technology, using a local area network to share resources and set up meeting times, file sharing, downloading virus protection software, installing and using the Instant Messaging system, using a mobile phone or Facebook to contact friends, family, and work colleagues); (2) they are located "within a network of relationships to other practices" (for example, using a personal computer or laptop, buying a digital camera, driving or riding in a car with a navigation system, using a hand-held scientific calculator); and (3) they have a "reflexive dimension" such that people "generate representations of what they do as part of what they do" (statements such as, "I'm going to check my messages"; "See what you can find on the Internet" [about a particular topic]; "I think myspace.com is dangerous for kids and I'm going to monitor my daughter's computer"; "You can design your own computer and order it on-line"; "I'm getting a picture phone"; "He has a blog about the political campaign"; "This is a WiFi location."

Because so much of what is referred to as technology is accessible through a computer application (or what are metaphorically called "information systems"), the hardware and software involved have become a major signifier for technology use. Hardware and software are the tools available for uses to localize practices. We tend to think of the technologically savvy person as one who understands how the technology "works" and how to gain access to it, and as one who uses various innovative gadgets. But most people are "end-users" only—meaning that they use but do not necessarily understand the technological devices available to them. They may be rich in practices but poor in underlying knowledge, leading them to ask those who are computer savvy for advice and help when problems occur. The end-user wants the product to be easily operated but also wants to be secure that the technology behind the product will make it effective for its particular use. The end-user may know some of the terminology, but often does not really comprehend the underlying meaning of the terms he or she encounters, such as "RAM," "encryption," and so forth. This type of surface level of technology knowledge is what makes it possible for advertisers (and other mass communicators) to communicate the newness of technology discourse broadly within society.

Technology in the consumer's hands

The explosive growth in technology uses of all kinds marked the lead-up to the new millennium and has continued to dramatically reshape social relations, business practices, and communication of all kinds. Video recording, cordless phones, word processing, sophisticated hand-held calculators are some of the products of technology that first put technology in our hands and established new cultural practices. Cell phones gave the individual freedom to be connected to others by voice in many parts of the country, and by 2004, about two-thirds of all adults in the US had cell phones (Rainie and Keeter, 2006). The meaning of "being out of contact" dramatically changed for many people as cell phones came of age to the point that we need to be reminded in movie theatres, concert halls, classrooms, lectures, and places of worship to "please shut off your cell phones." Then came the quintessential tool of technology: *the Internet*. Using the 1994 launch of Netscape's Mosaic browser as the initiation point for the World Wide Web, the Pew Internet and American Life Project concluded that "a decade later, the Internet has reached into—and, in some cases, reshaped—just about every important realm of modern life. It has changed the way we inform ourselves, amuse ourselves, care for ourselves, educate ourselves, work, shop, bank, pray and stay in touch" (Rainie and Horrigan, 2005, p. 56); in short, the Internet revolutionized many cultural practices and introduced entirely new ones. In 2005, 78.6 percent of Americans were going on-line an average of 13.3 hours per week (Center for the Digital Future, 2005). By 2004, 83 million people in the US had bought products on-line, and as many as 97 million had navigated web sites (Rainie and Horrigan, 2005).

The Internet is in many ways the icon of technology. If you don't use the Internet, you're "old school"—really old school, and you're not part of the "new normal" (Rainie and Horrigan, 2005, p. 61). The Internet provides quick access to communication, information, entertainment, and commerce. Not using the Internet can shut a person out from cultural practices that have become commonplace (such as YouTube, receiving photographs of grandchildren, or conducting financial transactions on-line), and can create serious problems. As the Internet has expanded, the youngest generations take it for granted while many of today's elderly remain totally left behind and confused when forced to do things like choose options for government-supported prescription drug coverage. The Pew Internet and American Life Project (Fox, 2004) reported age cohort data for Internet use in 2004 that clearly show a generational shift toward the Internet: 77 percent of those aged 18–29 have access to the Internet compared to 75 percent of those aged 30–49, 58 percent of those aged 50–64, and only 22 percent of those aged 65 or older. Another study in the same year (Lenhart et al., 2005) showed teens (defined as 12–17) in the US to be the most broadly engaged in Internet use at 87 percent. These differences are displayed in Table 5.1:

Table 5.1 Percentage of population who use Internet by age group: 2004

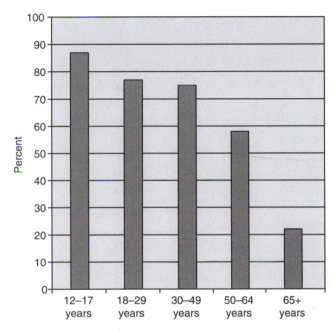

Source: Fox, 2004.

Diversity and Internet access

In all age groups, Whites are more likely to be Internet users than are African Americans and are more likely to be Internet users for all age groups of Hispanics, except for senior citizens. In a Pew study (Fox, 2004) conducted in 2003/2004, only 11 percent of the "senior" age group of African Americans reported using the Internet. This compares with 22 percent of the Whites who were sampled. At 21 percent, the number of older Hispanics surveyed who use the Internet is very close to the usage of Whites. The Hispanic user data, however, are limited to those who are English speaking; if the sample included non-English speakers as well, the percentages for Hispanics would likely be lower. The picture for those under 65 clearly places Whites as heavier users than either African Americans or Hispanics. For the 55–64 age group, Hispanics outnumber African Americans as Internet users (32 percent to 22 percent), but this difference is not evident in the 18–24 year old cohort. Research findings for the 8–18 year old group shows greater parity among Whites, African Americans and Hispanics in the practice of going on-line, with all groups exceeding 90 percent (Rideout et al., 2005). Even though the "diversity gap" is closing, it still remains, giving the White person a greater likelihood of being digitally connected at any given time because of in-home access (see Table 5.2). White youth lead in having Internet access at home: 80 percent compared to 67 percent of Hispanics and 61 percent of Blacks (Rideout et al., 2005).

Youth and technology access

Not surprisingly, the youth cohort is defined as the technology generation. Survey data gathered in fall 2004 for the Pew Project (Lenhart et al., 2005) documented the high teen use of technology options for communication and entertainment:

- 84 percent of teens say they own at least one media technology device—a computer, cell phone or Personal Digital Assistant;
- 87 percent of teens use the Internet, with 51 percent reporting that they go on-line daily;
- 81 percent of teens play games on-line;
- 76 percent of teens get news on-line;
- 45 percent of teens own a cell phone;
- 33 percent of teens use text messaging;
- 32 percent of teens use Instant Messaging every day, and 77 percent use e-mail (but consider it the medium of "older people").

These numbers have undoubtedly grown substantially since 2004. Yet, within the data lie important demographic differences. First, there are the differences based on race and ethnicity already mentioned. Second, there is an economic issue in that the teens who do not use the Internet tend to be from lower

Table 5.2 Percentage of population using Internet by age and race/ethnicity: 2003–2004

Race/Ethnicity	Age*			
	65+	55–64	18–24	8–18
Whites	22	58	83	96
African Americans	11	22	68	92
Hispanics**	21	32	70	95

* Statistics for 55–64 cohort and 18–24 cohort from Fox (2004); statistics for 8–18 cohort from Rideout et al. (2005). Asian Americans were not included in these reports.
** English speaking.

income families, while almost all teens from households with earnings above $75,000 per year use the Internet. Third, children reaching the seventh grade show a surge in Internet use, with the lag up until then mainly accounted for by boys (44 percent of sixth-grade boys compared to 79 percent of sixth-grade girls reported being on-line). Fourth, contrary to what might be common wisdom, older teenage girls (15–17) outpace teenage boys of the same age in the range of activities they engage in using the Internet. These activities include not only on-line communication but also information-seeking about health, colleges, topics of interest, and entertainment websites.

The Pew Project also reports on type of media used and time spent on various media (Rainie, 2006). Looking at the most prominent technology toys and modes of access for the 8–18 age group, home is a place with a VCR/DVD player (97 percent), video game console (87 percent), computer (86 percent), Internet access (82 percent), and, less so, high speed Internet access (46 percent). Average time spent using a computer is 62 minutes per day, compared to 1 hour 44 minutes of music and 3 hours 51 minutes of television/videos/DVDs (with simultaneous use common). A 2003/2004 study by the Kaiser Family Foundation (Rideout et al., 2005) on the ways in which teens use the computer for recreational purposes (not for school-related purposes) showed more detail in the racial and ethnic differences. Overall, this research found White youth more likely to use computers (57 percent) than both African American youth (44 percent) and Hispanic youth (47 percent). Considering those who do use computers, African Americans aged 8–18 were less likely to play Internet games or to use instant messaging on any given day than either Whites or Hispanics.

Technology streaming through advertising discourse

As we think through the relationship between technology uses (especially those common in the youth environment) and the appearance of technology discourse in advertising, the particular growth areas become important in shining light on what originates in technology and then moves *outside* of technology into a broader discourse space. For advertising to incorporate words, concepts, and formats common in technology applications (for example on the Internet), there must be some threshold of familiarity with what is imported into advertising. The cultural practices must be established at least at some level beyond the specialist. At the same time, advertising can serve to solidify and reinforce the significance of technology in several ways. Advertising can repetitively call upon discourse elements found in technology for use as metaphors ("reboot your relationship" with mouthwash *x*; "improve your connectivity" with chicks by getting a smooth shave of razor *x*), and can use the word "technology" to engage a set of ideas about what has gone into a product ("cushioning technology" for athletic shoes, "lysine technology" for a product to strengthen hair). Advertising can also appropriate larger formats found on web pages or in communication modes such as e-mail or IM. And because advertising exploits ellipsis, it can reinforce the consumer's identity as current and in-the-know through using technology elements that can be understood but, at the same time, marginalize other consumers' identities by placing them outside the circle of understanding. Advertisers are likely going to be very skillful in the types of technographic displays they choose for a particular product based on the targeted consumer and the placement of the ad. Based on demographic factors, we would, for instance, expect fewer technographic elements in adverting in *AARP The Magazine* (published by the American Association of Retired Persons) than in *Spin* (a magazine focused on current popular and rock music and its surrounding culture).

Technographic discourse types in advertising

In her chapter on "Cooking Nature," Judith Williamson (1978) dealt with the ways in which representation in advertising appropriates form without content—in this case *the image of science without science as performed*. The cooking process, says Williamson, defines and then supercedes the image of nature. Although the image of science is still discursively present in many ads, Williamson's ideas seem to me well suited to what is now presented as the image of technology as a new way of "cooking" the referent system to create *the image of technology without technology as performed*. Similar to advertising appeals that refer to science ("scientific breakthrough," "scientific studies have shown," "Science Diet" dog food), appeals to technology as a rational foundation for positive orientation to a product are constructed to engage only a superficial level of understanding: the form of technology rather than its performance, the surface rather than the workings, and the practices that have grown to access the products of technology without having to be a techno-genius. Rarely will a consumer be presented with deep technology, meaning the complete explanation of how technology was used to create a product or what technological advances or processes are contained in the product. This would be true even for what are explicitly recognized as technology products (digital cameras, specialized web sites, car design features, navigational devices); here, most consumers wouldn't understand the intricacies of technology, but the superficial reference to it suffices to provide the semiotic grounding for some general meanings of technology as associated with newness, precision, and so forth.

As cultural citizens become increasingly knowledgeable about the surfaces of technology and the consumer goods it produces, they also form what are called *communities of practice* (CofP) in relation to their uses of technology. Penelope Eckert and Sally McConnell-Ginet (1999) define the CofP as: "an aggregate of people who, united by a common enterprise, develop and share ways of doing things, ways of talking, beliefs, and values—in short, practices" (p. 186). As e-mail has grown from a restricted mode of communication used in some business environments to a major way to communicate with friends and family, so have the practices associated with e-mail (e.g. e-mailing someone your travel itinerary, sending an invitation via e-mail), and the community-based understanding of those practices. My in-laws, for example, are not part of the e-mail CofP, which means more phone calls and probably less day-to-day information about family events, moods, and so forth. Instant messaging works the same way. There are groups of "users" who form a CofP—in this case, a CofP whose practices include greater rapidity in communication, "away messages" as a normative everyday practice, and a host of spelling and abbreviation conventions. All of the communities of practice involving technology use have implications for deciphering the imprints of technology on advertising; they can entice or distance the potential consumer, depending on that consumer's practices related to the semblance of technology appearing in a particular advertisement.

Technographic discourse in advertising, then, provides a glimpse into the ways in which technology, especially the Internet, weaves through culture. Because advertising is so prominent and occurs across a range of media (including the Internet), its discourse patterns both tell us about broader cultural practices and at the same time accentuate those cultural practices. As recently as a decade ago, there were virtually no technological terms or discourse structures in advertising. Even the web site for a company or brand was not often part of advertising. Instead, consumers were directed to "800-xxx-xxxx" telephone numbers for post-advertisement communication. The situation has changed as will be seen in the following sections.

Technology terminology

The first and most obvious type of technographic discourse in advertising is the use of technology terms, the most basic of which is the word "technology." The word "technology" offers the consumer a sign that the product has credibility and currency. Clairol, for example, promoted its "Renewal 5x Shampoo" with the claim that "5 TECHNOLOGIES WASH IN STRENGTH" (*People*, August 20, 2001). Other words in the technology lexicon invite the consumer to be "in the know" about technology. Sometimes these are presented with the conventional "wink" suggesting that "we" (the advertisers) know that "you" (the potential consumer we are addressing) know that we are playing with technology language. At other times, the terms are offered more seriously to associate the product with the aura of competitive edge over other product offerings or a refreshed image of how a known product has been improved.

One rather straightforward use of technology terms found in advertising is for products and services that promote Internet use. Examples include the US Postal Service's ad for their on-line services, which is headlined "IF YOU CLICK IT, WE WILL COME" (*Newsweek*, October 4, 2004); an ad for *Allure* magazine's on-line shopping web site with the techie name, "allure *connect*" (*New Yorker*, emphasis added); and an ad for ebay (*People*, November 28, 2005) that features a large

i t

in the center of the page, playing on the abbreviation for the term "information technology" and placing the tag line, "you can get *it* on ebay" at the bottom right side of the page as a bit of word play. In this type of ad, there may be explicit manipulation of double meanings, but the technology reference can easily be seen as belonging to its referent. There are, however, many technology terms that are used in ads for products where the product itself has nothing to do with technology (even though the production of the product will likely have involved various technologies). Five types of such usage are covered here: (1) use of the term "technology" with an adjective before it to brand or characterize the technology, (2) use of the term "technology" along with other terms that signify newness or advances, (3) use of the term "technology" with another contrasting feature of the product, (4) use of technology terms other than "technology," and (5) product names that use technology terms.

Appropriating "[fill in the blank] technology" to entice the consumer

Appropriations of the meanings associated with the word "technology" are evident in many ads. One type of appropriation appears in the linguistic form of *adjective + technology* where the adjective provides an additional association for the product. Various cosmetics and beauty products are promoted in this manner. Consider the ad for Adidas anti-perspirants for women shown in Figure 5.1, which is said to have "Smart™ Technology" (*Shape*, June 2004). In this case the adjective associated with the word "technology" has been registered, and the term is presented in a no-nonsense font.

This ad, like many others that appropriate the word "technology," incorporates a number of other features to signify the advanced nature of the product. Here, the words "ACTIVE Anti-Perspirants For Women" appear in a forward-

Figure 5.1 **Adidas Active Anti-Perspirant for Women** (*Shape*, June 2004).

moving, right-leaning font, suggesting movement and activity. The schema for sweat and bacteria at the lower right of the ad suggests a computer graphic rendering of biological information, and it is the "Smart™ Technology" that works on the biological interaction of *bacteria + sweat = odor*, which appears in small font size at the very lower right.

The *adjective* + *technology* vocabulary format in ads is used for various product types. Advertisements for women's hair and beauty products in mainstream women's magazines (and also on the web sites for the products) use a number of creative, vivid adjectives to tell the consumer what kind of technology boosts the product. For hair products, some examples follow:

- Garnier Fructis Style Shake Effect Liqui-Gel with "*fruit micro-wax technology*" (*Jane*, October 2004).
- Mizani Beyond Conditioning Crème Haircolor is "Infused with *Oleo-Technology* to condition and care for the hair" (http://www.mizani-usa.com).
- Redken Addictive Hair Transformer with "*breakthrough nano-emulsion technology*" that "instantly transforms the feel of dry hair" (*Elle*, October 2003). The ads for Redken men's hair products contain no technology terms.
- Soft·Sheen Carson Optimum Care No-Lye Relaxer System, which "Features *lysine technology* formulated to give you 4 times less breakage" (*Essence*, June 2004).

Make-up ads are equally creative in their suggestion that technology has added a distinctive element to the particular product being sold:

- "*Opti-Match*™ *Technology* creates precisely calibrated skin-true shades" to produce L'Oréal's True Match make-up in multicultural shades (*Essence*[1], September 2004) or, for the more "White" audience, this technology "creates precisely calibrated skin-true shades" (*Shape*, September 2004).
- L'Oréal offers a hair straightening cream called "Studioline Hot Straight Cream" by hyping its "technological innovation" of "*Thermo-Protect technology*" (*Elle Girl*, December/January 2006).
- Lancôme offers "*Patented Juicy Seal*™ Technology" in their Juicy Wear lipstick and top-coat (*Harper's Bazaar*, January 2004), and "*Smooth-Hold Technology*" for its line of Sensational Effects Lipcolor (*Vanity Fair*, March 2006).
- Neutrogena's cleansing pads for acne, named Rapid Clear, are headlined to have "*Exclusive MicroClear*™ *Technology*" (*Seventeen*, July 2006).
- "*Cutting-edge technology* without the cutting edge" is the caption for Avon's Clinical Eye Lift (*More*[2], March 2006).

1   *Essence* is one of the magazines marketed to African American women. Advertisers will sometimes run the same ads in magazines for different racial/ethnic readerships, but will often change the race of the model and slightly alter the wording of the ad when it appears in a race-targeted magazine such as *Essence*.
2   *More* is a magazine targeted at "older" women, defined as those 40 and over.

Although there are fewer examples for men's products, technology does show up as part of the sign system:

- A Gillette ad for its Fusion manual and battery-powered razors touts "*5 Blade Shaving Surface*™ *Technology* for ultimate comfort" (*Maxim*, July 2006).
- Gillette's anti-perspirant is said to contain "*Power Stripe*™ *technology*" (*Gentlemen's Quarterly*, August 2005 and *Sports Illustrated*, January 2, 2006).
- An ad for Bionova high-end skin products for men boasts "*patented NANO SKIN TECH*™" (*Men's Vogue*, Fall 2005)—with the term "skin tech" resembling the term "high tech".
- L'Oréal's Vive Daily Thickening shampoo for men makes hair look thicker because of "*Regenium-XY technology*" (*Rolling Stone*, August 11, 2005).

Even some shoes are claimed to be improved because of a certain type of technology. It may be the case that technology is used in designing shoes, but the terms used by advertisers to create the connotations associated with technology are not drawn from the lexicon of computer-aided-design:

- Rockport men's shoes feature "*patented kinetic air circulator footbed technology*" (*Esquire*, April 2004).
- New Balance offers "*Cushioning Technology*" for "long lasting impact protection" (*Sports Illustrated*, June 26, 2006).
- "The first shoe with SmartWool's *temperature regulation technology* built right in" is proclaimed in an ad for Timberland (*Sports Illustrated*, December 5, 2005).

Cars are also hyped to the consumer for their built-in technology. Here the product is more clearly a result of technology-aided design and testing, but the names once again bear the advertisers' flare for language:

- The Infiniti FX has "*intelligent Key technology*" (*New Yorker*, August 9 and 16, 2004).
- The Audi Q7 has "*Race technology*" (*Boston Magazine*, May 2006), and "*direct injection technology*" (http://microsites.audiusa.com/AudiQ7/html/flash.html, May 2006) while the Audi A6 has the more general "greater power, *technology* and design" (*Money*, December 2004).
- Toyota's Avalon is billed as the product of "*serious technology*"—"filled with an available array of *mind-boggling technology* . . ." (*New Yorker*, June 19, 2006).

- If you want technologically enhanced tires for your vehicle, Bridgestone has them with "*touring technology* in motion" (*Black Enterprise*, May 2005).

"Technology" and newness

Other advertising examples of the *adjective* + *technology* formulation appear throughout magazines, commercials, and web advertisements. A number of these show a second type of technology vocabulary by strategically using phrases that signify newness or innovation. This language not only appropriates technology, but also explicitly uses it for seeking the consumer's interest in state of the art products. Words like "new," "advanced," "innovative," and "breakthrough" combine with "technology" to create this effect. We see the newness strategy especially in women's cosmetic products, but in ads for other products as well:

- Redken Soft Addictive Hair Transformer uses "*breakthrough* nano-emulsion technology to provide smoothness, conditioning" (*Elle*, October 2003).
- Hairspray by Aveda is offered with "*breakthrough* pine resin technology," allowing the spray to dry upon application (*Vanity Fair*, July 2004).
- Elizabeth Arden's skin cream Prevate is "a *revolutionary* new skincare technology" (*Vogue*, December 2005).
- L'Oréal offers something for men in Vive shampoo with "Regenium-XY technology," that is "*new* technology" (*Newsweek*, March 29, 2004).
- "*Breakthrough* technology" is the headline in the ad for Gillette's Fusion razor mentioned earlier.
- The Lands End catalog heralds Sea-to-Shore Sport Shoes for their "*new* aqua drainage technology" (Early spring catalog, 2006).
- Avon's Anew Wrinkle Corrector is advertised as containing "*revolutionary* derma 3x technology . . . that rebuilds collagen for firmer skin" (*Essence*, June 2004).
- Moving into the domain of the home, Hunter offers ceiling fans that have both "legendary quality and *innovative* technology" (*Architectural Digest*, June, 2004).

"Technology" as complement to tradition

The ad for the Hunter ceiling fan also conveys a juxtaposition of something old and something new, with "technology" being the contrast to "legendary quality." This is yet another discursive strategy for using technology to promote products but at the same time nodding to tradition or to aspects of quality that are not products of modern design. Several examples illustrate this strategy:

- David Yurman men's watches are described as having "Artistry and Swiss technology" (*Architecture Digest*, June, 2004). By using the "and" conjunction, the two features are separated, inviting an interpretation that the artistry is not borne of technology.
- Bridgestone Tires are advertised as "Elegant SUV technology" which could be read as combining aesthetics with engineering (*10 O'clock News*, NECN, Boston, June 29, 2006).
- An Electrolux vacuum cleaner is proclaimed in an ad to have "MicroSeal™ fresh air technology," although it is not clear what the microseal is doing to or with the fresh air (*New Yorker*, November 7, 2005).
- The caption on an ad for GE Profile appliances reads, "Superb marries supersonic." The verbal elements of the ad marry "sculptured handles" and "trivection technology"; and the contrast is shown in a photo of a space age looking woman and a male chef holding an artistic culinary creation (*Food and Wine*, May 2004).

Other words from the technology lexicon

There are words other than "technology" that are drawn from the technology lexicon—mainly the Internet—that appear in ads for non-technology products to create the image of technology without its substance. Most of these verbal elements work as metaphors, drawing on the foundation of technology to give meaning to something entirely different. As we would expect, these words are familiar ones to even the unsophisticated technology user, yet they serve to anchor the vocabulary of technology in a special way by extending it beyond even its creative adaptation for ads proclaiming certain technology attributes for a product.

One of the key words is "connect" and its related "connection." Kool cigarettes has brought the current usage of "connection" into its branding by linking it to the culture of cell phone usage. In the ad displayed in Figure 5.2 (*Essence*, December 2004), the green cigarette box is graphically represented as a geometric montage of various cell phones displayed against a blue background of digitized area codes. The words "SMOOTH" and "CONNECTION" are part of a rectangular frame around the pack of cigarettes. The juxtaposition of these two words offers yet another example of linking the old and new: in this case "smoothness" carries a long association with menthol cigarettes and Kool in particular, while "connection" links cool to the currency of the cell phone generation.

Acura recently drew on the signification of "connection" in its advertising with the tag line "YOUR LIFE. YOUR CAR. CONNECTED" (*Newsweek*, March 6, 2006). In this particular ad, we see a man with a look of satisfaction in

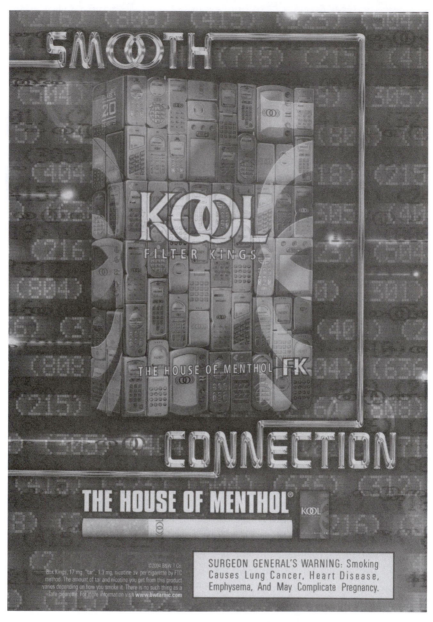

Figure 5.2 **Kool Smooth Connection** (*Essence*, December, 2004).

the foreground; he's wearing earphones with a cord trailing off to the background of the ad and into the Acura displayed there.

Several other creative and sometimes whimsical uses of technology terms can be found in ads:

- An ad for Sephora.com, the web site for Sephora beauty products, plays with both the practice of clicking on a link in a web page and labeling on-line communication as "virtual" with its phrases, "beauty that clicks" and "virtually beauty-full" (*O—The Oprah Magazine*, September 2005).
- MSNBC.com's Real Estate section is headlined "HomePages™" (*Newsweek*, April 24, 2006) as a playful and product-appropriate use of the now well-known idea of a home page for a web site.
- Readers are directed to "Power up your day." in an ad for Nature's Path Optimum organic cereal (*Shape*, June 2004). In the ad's text, we are told that "Optimum™ powers you up with [various ingredients]."
- SoftSheen·Carson names one of its hair products for dark-haired women "HiRez™ High Resolution Haircolor," which appropriates the concept of screen resolution to create the impression of exact color creation through its "breakthrough technology" (*Essence*, June, 2005).
- Fuzion™ HRi tires, which are for fancy maneuvers and fans of skidding, are advertised using the tag at the upper left which reads, "The serious art of instant messaging." Below are tire tracks made from "one slick-looking set of asymmetrical treads" (*Stuff*, September 2005). This ad, shown in Figure 5.3, contains many elements drawing from the semiotic domain of technology: font style and graphics, use of the term "advanced technologies," the tire tracks in the format of the smiley face text symbol expressed as :), and the vernacular, "How cool is that!" at the lower left corner.
- An ad for Ashford.com, which offers luxury items such as watches, handbags, and fountain pens on-line, predicts that gifts purchased from this web site can "reboot the relationship."
- Even Public Broadcasting System (PBS) advertising made use of a cell phone term in promoting its living history program, "Texas Ranch House" with a large triangular cowboy dinner bell labeled "Cowboy Ring Tone" (*New Yorker*, May 1, 2006).

Technology imprints on product naming

The fifth way in which technology terms are used in advertising for non-technology products is in product naming. The name of the product can be the branding strategy for giving currency through technology connotations to whatever that product may be. Consider these examples:

Figure 5.3 **Fuzion HRi Tires** (*Stuff*, September 2005).

- Footjoy offers a line of golf shoes named "eComfort™" which is presented in a magazine ad layout showing four different shoe lines for women (*Golf for Women*, July/August 2004).
- KFC has named its kids' meal "laptop meals" (commercial during

"Smallville," October 31, 2005; http://kids.kfc.com/), spreading what's on the lap beyond the small computer.

- One new-age looking Swiss watch is named "TechnoMarine," and one of its styles features "Technodiamond Chrono Steel" (*Vanity Fair*, June 2005).
- One line of lightweight outdoor footwear is named "Hi-Tec® Outdoor" (*Shape*, June 2004).

For any of these ads with technology terms, recognition of the terms hails the reader as part of the community of practice familiar with the specific domain involved—the Internet in general, web sites, cell phones. The linkages being made between the products advertised and the discourse signs associated with technology seem to convey trendiness and currency of a particular kind. These linkages also add to the broader cultural saturation with technology and its various products, practices, and discourses. For a person without special knowledge of technology practices or lexicon, the ads may still be comprehensible but at the same time somewhat flat or devoid of the catchy quality strived for in today's advertising. Although "technology" is a god term for our age like "science" was in the first half of the twentieth century, a person not savvy about technology might wonder what an ad means when it uses technology terms or discourse structuring, and might dismiss the ad as not intended for her or him. "Derma 3x technology"? Does that mean you put the cream on three times? How about "Instant messaging"? Is that when your tire dealer calls back right away? Go figure if you're not tech savvy.

Technographic symbols

The second type of technographic discourse found in advertising brings symbols that have technological meanings into the text of the ad. Many specialized symbols make up the discourse used for specific technological applications, but advertising understandably draws on those most familiar to the consumer, usually those encountered in navigating the Internet, sending e-mail, ordering consumer goods on-line, playing a DVD, using a digital camera, etc. Familiar symbols might be the @ sign used in e-mail or the > sign used to move from one command to another, from one part of a web page to another, or to forward or fast-forward (>>) a DVD or CD.

In this section, various usages of technographic symbols will be illustrated to show how they have made their way into advertising. Some of these symbols are occasional, while others have become almost mainstream in advertising.

Some of the symbols commonly used in technology applications are only occasionally used in advertising. Given how common the @ sign is as part of e-mail addresses, we might expect it to be frequently seen in the language of magazine advertising. Not so. Yet, the sign does appear occasionally. An early appearance of @ occurred in an ad for Virginia Slims cigarettes showing a woman's face with a full laugh expression and captioned, "I am allowed to laugh @ myself." A department store ad for a Bloomingdale's sale tells the potential customer that the items advertised are "only@Bloomingdale's" (*Boston* Globe, April 4, 2004, A9).

The typed smile symbol is another commonly used e-mail and IM symbol that occasionally is seen in advertising. The Fuzion tire ad shown in Figure 5.3 uses this symbol, as does a 2005 Toyota magazine ad (*Newsweek*, November 14, 2005) promoting their "Hybrid Synergy Drive®" by positioning "mpg:)" in a 1-inch high headline. The tech-savvy person knows that this symbol, consisting of a typed colon and closed parenthesis, is a simple 90 degrees counter-clockwise rotation of the smiley face found on young children's school papers. The symbol is likely meaningless to the tech-challenged person.

Highlighting that visually resembles what is generally available in word pro-cessing (which mimics the basic hand-held marker) also appears in some printed advertising. Highlighting, unlike the use of some technology symbols, would be well recognized by most people—tech savvy or not—but the par-ticular way in which the highlighting is presented signifies its importation from computer text conventions. The style is completely angular and regular—no curves or variation in height as would be the case if using a hand-held high-lighter from the local office supply store on a piece of paper. An ad for "beyondpetroleum.com" used yellow highlighting in the words shown in ital-ics: "To find solutions to *global warming*, we went to Princeton [text follows]. To inspire solutions to *global warming*, we went to kindergarten [text follows]" (*New Yorker*, November 2005); Beyond Petroleum also uses similar highlighting in their television commercials. An ad for the Blackberry PDA serviced through Nextel includes the following in highlighted text at the bottom right of the full page ad: "NEXTEL.Done." (*Newsweek*, April 12, 2004). It is more common to have a reverse highlighting, in which white or light-colored text is placed with a dark highlighting-type block. When this style is used, the word or words highlighted usually stand alone rather than being contained within a phrase or sentence. For example, Ideology (the women's line of clothing) uses this format to show its brand name as **IDEOLOGY** (*Jane*, January 2005). An ad for Danzka Vodka, a Danish vodka, picked up the reverse highlighting on the liquor's bottle, which is shown in a bowl of ice, for the tag, **MADE TO CHILL** (where the background is red; *Details*, April 2004). And one of T. D. Waterhouse's ads, in which we see a head shot of "Law and Order" star Sam Waterston (are we supposed to think that the actor trusts his finances to Waterhouse? or that lawyers put their trust in TDW?), uses green highlighting on white text for **FREE TRADES FOR A MONTH** (*Money*, February

2006). We more frequently see text boxes (those geometric figures where text is placed inside the shape) in ads than these types of highlighting, but text boxes too are familiar to the word processor and anyone working with layout for web pages. These are the kind of text effects that would be commonly available to anyone working with word processing.

There are other symbols drawn from the discourse of technology that are more commonly used in advertising to link back to technology discourse. The most frequently used technology symbols in advertising discourse are the forward arrow or caret (>) and the underscore typing symbol that is used in many e-mail addresses (e.g., carmella_fudge1499@hotmail.com). Both of these are symbols new to advertising, and their broad usage reflects standardization of the symbols in computer applications.

The forward arrow

The forward, left to right arrow (and variations on single > or multiple >>) are now seen frequently in advertising: variations include the open arrow (>), the double or multiple open arrow (>>), and the filled arrow (▶). The open forward arrow is a vintage symbol in computer programming language. For those old enough to be familiar with the DOS system, arrow symbols were used in the program to move, for example, from one drive to another. The forward arrows were quickly incorporated as universal symbols in audio and video equipment, and later in digital cameras and DVD machines.

Advertisers for both Audi and Toyota use the forward arrow extensively. In 2004, Audi launched the "It's greater to lead than follow" campaign with an inventive 7-inch × 7½-inch magazine insert for the Audi A6 (*New Yorker*, November 29, 2004). With center opening pages, "Lead" was placed on the left side and "Follow" on the right, with the open forward arrow set in the middle across the center opening page cut (see Figure 5.4). The arrow points the way into the ad brochure, but also has a double meaning that is clear once the first opposing pages are opened. The forward arrow now takes on the mathematical meaning of "more than" as we see an engine on the left with the text, "More than simply horsepower" and a picture of galloping horses on the right. Ads for the Audi Quattro showed a large forward arrow followed by the numeral "4: > 4" (*Black Enterprise*, May 2005). The text at the bottom of the ad began with "Greater than four-wheel drive"—again engaging the double meaning of the forward arrow for a symbol that leads you forward and also that signifies "more than" in mathematical language.

Toyota introduced their "moving forward" tag line is 2004, which is accompanied by the filled forward pointing arrow. In many of the ads, the tag in slanting forward white font and arrow are placed at the top right of the ad,

Figure 5.4 **Audi** *(New Yorker,* November 29, 2004).

under the Toyota insignia—all in a red rectangular box: *"moving forward* ▶*"* (Highlander ad, *Newsweek,* December 20, 2004). In other ads, the tag and arrow appear at the bottom right (Tundra truck ad, *Newsweek,* September 19, 2005; Rav4 ad, *Car and Driver,* May 2006). The arrow leads off the page—to the right—in all of these ads, creating an association with forward movement to complement the tag line.

A broad range of other products use the forward arrow. All of these ads promise some result if the reader does something related to the product. In this sense, the forward arrow is an icon for progress and results.

• Accenture (consulting, technology, and outsourcing services for business) features Tiger Woods in its "Go on. Be a Tiger" campaign. The company name in these ads is presented with the open forward arrow placed above the letter "t" as shown in Figure 5.5 (*Black Enterprise,* March 2005; *Forbes,*

Every great accomplishment
is at first impossible.

Go on. Be a Tiger.

Never. Can't. Impossible. These are words that inspire the high performer. By working to close the gap between what is and what could be, Accenture can help your business become a high-performance business. See how at accenture.com

• Consulting • Technology • Outsourcing

accenture

High performance. Delivered.

Figure 5.5 **Accenture** (*Forbes*, April 18, 2005).

April 18, 2005). The web site for the company (www.accenture.com) also offers a screen saver version of the lead ad in the campaign.

• The American Express Blue Cash card is advertised showing the filled forward arrow symbol on both the card itself (lower left side) and as part

of a text element standing alone on the page presented as "FORWARD ▶"
(*Money*, April 2004).

- The open forward arrow is used to point the way to the inside contents of
  a pull-out multi-page advertisement for Vanguard money funds (*Money*,
  February 2006). Here, the arrow is placed to the right of forward-slanting
  text that reads, "Introducing the world's best mutual funds and ETFs
  [exchange-traded funds]."

- An ad for Bell South that focuses on its Supplier Diversity Program uses
  the double open arrow (>>) as the end of a triangle that is pointing to the
  right of the page. Inside the triangle shape, we see a photograph of a young
  Black girl holding a paintbrush and the words "graphic artist." (*Forbes*,
  December 13, 2004). The tag above the triangle is "This might just be a
  future . . .": the triangle and >> constitute what McQuarrie and Mick
  (1999) describe as a visual rhyme—in this case mirroring the verbal tag
  line and also coordinating with the forward leaning text font of the company name, all creating forward movement signifying the future.

The forward arrow is used in some ads as a marker for bullets (similar to what
is found in word processing software). In these cases, the arrow will appear to
the left of text, just as any bullet format would, rather than at the right of the
page or to the right of text:

- Fidelity Investments ads use the filled forward arrow before a statement
  about account features and again before the statement "▶ Open a Fidelity
  no-fee IRA today" (*Newsweek*, February 6, 2006).

- A newspaper ad for Merrimack College uses the open forward arrow
  twice, once in front of the statement "Summer Registration Underway"
  and again in front of the listing of dates for Open Houses (*Boston Globe*,
  June 1, 2006).

- The Philip Morris tobacco company advertises its "Quit Assist" web site
  using open forward arrows as bullets (*Car and Driver*, June 2006). The
  arrows are all in gold, with the main text set in green:

  > If you decide to quit smoking,
      this is a good place to start.

Information in smaller text appears below, with each point bulleted with
the forward arrow symbol.

Cosmetics companies also bullet with the arrow:

- Lancôme's "New Color Design" lipstick is characterized with arrow bulleted statements, as seen in Figure 5.6 (*Vanity Fair*, March 2006). This ad also uses the term "smooth-hold technology" and places the word "new" in reverse highlight font effect.

- An ad for Sally Hansen hair removal product, "Express Wax," employs the open arrow to point to three characteristics:

    FAST >EASY >FUN (*Seventeen*, August 2006).

A variation of this bullet style occurs in ads when the forward arrow is used to mark different points in a continuous stream of text, much as terminal punctuation would:

- An ad for the Dodge Charger describes the vehicle as follows:

    DODGE CHARGER > 425 horses of SPT HEMI[fi] V8 power > 420 lb-ft of torque > All-speed traction control > Electronic Stability Program with three-position switching > 5-speed Auto Stick[fi] transmission > Visit us at . . . (*Sports Illustrated*, December 19, 2005).

- Sprint uses a variation of the forward arrow in its recent advertising campaign following acquisition of Nextel (these ads appeared in a broad range of magazines, television programs, and on the Internet). The new Sprint logo looks like a slightly feathered arrow with smooth edges, with the arrow appearing after the brand name.

The underscore

Most people are familiar with the underscore symbol (_) because it is a standard key on the keypad for computers, as it was years ago on the typewriter. The underscore became part of the ASCII code of binary digits used in microprocessors (Underscore, n.d.), and more recently has been used rather than a space in a number of computer operating systems, file names, and in various World Wide Web applications, specifically in addresses (for example, "ad_ junkie@post.org"). In this more recent application, the symbol underscores nothing because it is a place-holder. This use of the underscore may now be the most common for many computer users; even in typing, word processing software allows underlining by either clicking a button on the toolbar or performing a simple keyboard command (ctrl + u)—thus no need for using the underscore key as such. The newer usage of the underscore has spread widely because anyone who has sent e-mail messages needs to know how it is used in names. Omitting the underscore and joining the two elements it divides or substituting something else for it will lead to returned mail.

Figure 5.6 **Lancôme Color Design Sensational Effects Lipcolor** (*Vanity Fair*, March 2006).

As a newer sign for technology, the underscore has made its way into advertising. Its placement at times looks like a partial web address, such that the reader can fill in the missing elements of the ellipsis and get the point that this is a take-off on web discourse conventions. At other times, it is used as a divider of two content elements, not unlike the use of the forward arrow in the ad described earlier for the Dodge Charger (p. 181).

Nissan is famous for making use of the underscore in advertising. In the hands of the TBWA\Chait\Day advertising agency, Nissan launched its Shift_ campaign. The Shift_ tagline has been plastered throughout magazine, television, Internet, and mobile phone advertising. The tag line is, of course, a play on the word "shift" as both specifically the movement from one gear to another in a car and more generally as movement or change in direction, purpose, motivation, and so forth. Each ad in this campaign presents an attribute associated with the Nissan model being advertised and, presumably, appropriate to the ad's placement and target audience. Here are a range of tag lines (the Nissan model and one or two magazines in which the ad appears are listed):

- SHIFT_obsession (The Nissan Z sports model, *Maxim Blender, GQ*);
- SHIFT_superride (2005 V6 Altima, *Black Enterprise*);
- SHIFT_style (2005 V6 Altima, *Shape, Newsweek*);
- SHIFT_superstyle (2005 V6 Altima, *Essence*);
- SHIFT_adventure (Pathfinder, *Sports Illustrated, Car and Driver*);
- SHIFT_adventure (Murano urban SUV-style in San Francisco setting, with journal entry titled "ascending the Eastern Face of Nob Hill"—play on mountain climbing);
- SHIFT_landscape (Murano in mid-town Manhattan setting, with journal entry titled, "Traversing the 7th Avenue River," *Newsweek*);
- SHIFT_passion (Murano in New Orleans setting, with journal entry titled, "On the Trail of the Elusive Gumbo," *Food and Wine*);
- SHIFT_power (Frontier 4×4 truck, *ESPN Magazine*);
- SHIFT_exhilaration (2005 V6 Altima, *Money*);
- SHIFT_convention (2003 Quest van-style, *Money*);
- SHIFT_expectations (2004 265-hp Maxima, *New York Times Magazine; Food and Wine*);
- SHIFT_hotness (2005 265-hp Maxima, *Essence, Black Enterprise*);
- SHIFT_freedom (Xterra SUV, *Stuff*, August 2006);
- SHIFT_design (Quest, *The Oprah Magazine*, September 2005);
- SHIFT_respect (260-hp Altima SE-R driving through streets with a bull-fight run (*Sports Illustrated*).

Each of the attributes that the ads promise bears connotations related to lifestyle positions and aspirations. This is exactly what Nissan is working to accomplish in this campaign. Shortly after the Shift_ campaign began, Steven Wilhite, the Vice President of Marketing for Nissan North America, described it by saying this:

> Actually, Shift_ isn't merely a tag line. Shift_ is a communication platform . . . to capture Nissan's core values, characteristics, and attitudes and to create a more comprehensive . . . . brand . . . The Shift_ tag . . . can change a person, a life, the world, or it can simply change the way you move through it . . . . [It] is a way of communicating that we must always question our assumptions and strive to look at things in a different way.
>
> (Mamos and Saw, 2002)

The tag line, then, is central to a branding strategy, which then makes its way into the advertising presentation. If successful, Shift_ is an ellipsis for a message telling its target person that if you drive Nissan model x, then you will be shifted into the realm of fill-in-the-blank, depending on the attribute associated with the model being advertised. Nissan's web site scrolls a number of these attributes, including "joy, individuality, originality, inspiration . . . ."

The Shift_ campaign has taken several new directions since its 2002 beginnings. In 2003, the campaign was extended to mobile and wireless devices (Nissan Takes "Shift," 2003), naming this advertising strategy "Mobile Concierge." The Shift_ tag line leads in to expanded information on the model as well as entertainment information (restaurant, nightlife, hotel, etc.) through Nissan's connection with a destination content company. This innovation made Shift_ just a PDA away! Next came "Inside Stories"—aptly named and advertised as "SHIFT_stories"—very short stories about particular cars, engines, and innovations at Nissan. The layout for magazine ads featuring SHIFT_stories places the tag line at the bottom right of the page, but without a characteristic or attribute (Car and Driver, March 2006). The story is placed in a textbox positioned in the upper right quadrant of the page. In 2006, Nissan introduced another discourse element drawn from technology into its advertising by incorporating the designation of "2.0" (for instance, "2.0 Passion") in the style of software update numbers (Solman, 2006). Television commercials for Quest (ESPN, July 2, 2006) and Maxima (CBS, July 10, 2006) present "Shift_2.0" with the three elements moving up quickly in succession from the bottom of the screen, left to right, to form the technology imprint. These commercials also include the "intelligent key technology" phrase. The "_2.0" signifier also shows up in statements about product characteristics, as in the ad for the Maxima that includes "Mission Control_2.0" (Newsweek, July 17, 2006).

Nissan has the corner on the underscore symbol, but it is seen in a few other advertisements:

- W Hotels offers a strikingly modern visual image of angular lines in orange and yellow tones, with the tag line at the bottom reading:

    WARMTH OF COOL_THE BALANCE BETWEEN STYLE AND SOUL

    Here, the underscore seems to serve the same purpose as would a colon or a dash (*Vanity Fair*, July 2005).

- Microsoft recently directed advertising to the business customer with the lead, "Your people are your company's most important asset" (*Newsweek*, April 10, 2006). The bottom left of this two-page ad showing a scene in what appears to be an airplane plant poses the question, "Are your *people_ready?*" A silhouette of a person is standing above the _ mark. Another ad in the series (*Newsweek*, May 28, 2006) places "ready" and the underscore ("ready_") next to people pictured in the plant site. In this case, a technology company is using a technology symbol to sell technology, but the use of the underscore is an extrapolation from its use in practice.

Square brackets

Like the underscore, square brackets—represented as "[ ]" when both sides are typed—are familiar keys on the typewriter keyboard or computer keypad. Used in various mathematical expressions, most students also learn somewhere along the way that brackets can be used in writing to insert some comment, explanation, or words in the middle of a quotation. In this sense, the bracket means that something is added. Brackets are also used in the ASCII computer code to delimit an expression and are frequently used in various forms of technology communication. E-mail and IM users call upon the square brackets (left, right, or both) for various emoticons, such as ":-]" for "polite smile," ": [" for "bored" or "sad," and "[ ]" for "hug."

Several examples of the square brackets placed in advertising text demonstrate how this symbol is used with its more technological meanings:

- An early example is seen in a 1995 ad for the GMC Jimmy truck (*Ebony*, February 1995). Each page of a two-page layout uses the brackets for headlines above the text below:

    [COMING ON STRONG.] and [COMING ON SHARP.]

- Hankook tires for racing and other high performance driving are advertised with the tag line of: "[Fast Track . . .] *Technology*." Here, the placement of the ellipsis within the brackets might call on the reader's imagination to fill in his own fantasy, especially considering the text following the tag line, which promises that "Hankook brings pure *driving emotion* to the track" (*Sports Illustrated*, May 2006).

- A full-page advertisement billed as "A Message From America's Oil and Natural Gas Industry" appeared in the *Boston Globe* (November 8, 2005, and other papers) not long after the devastation of Hurricane Katrina. The text, in gray tones, addresses the uses of natural gas and implicitly asks the reader to have confidence that the industry will act responsibly to develop this valuable and highly demanded energy resource in areas currently off-limits because of government restriction. A bracketed comment appears in the middle of the page and in bold:

  [Thoughts about natural gas]

  The placement of the bracketed statement and the text contained in it seem to invite the reader to ponder the advertisement—to think about the possibilities that still remain for development of natural gas.

- A text-intensive ad for the Chevrolet Silverado (*Car and Driver*, January 2006) emphasizes the power of this truck (345 horsepower, "Chevy Vorrtec™ Max powertrain," "whopping 380 lb.-ft. of torque"). Right beneath a picture of a gold, four-door truck and placed in the middle of a two-column text, is this bracketed message:

  [LONG LIVE THE TRUCK]

- Casella Estate, an Australian winery, has named its line of wines "[yellow tail]". An ad in *Entertainment Weekly* (November 11, 2005) displays the name boldly at the top of the page (the square brackets are part of the name) in yellow font on a black background. A bottle of [yellow tail] Shiraz is shown at the bottom right of the page, with its name on the bottle. More than two-thirds of the page is taken up with a shiny black lobster with a bright yellow tail. The use of the square brackets as part of the wine's name, and thus of its identity, seems positioned to invite the potential drinker to ponder what it might be like: think about what this wine might be like . . . .

- In a few cases, only one side of the square bracket is used. One illustration is in a Subaru WRX ad where we see Lance Armstrong on the top and the car on the bottom with text in the middle reading, "Control your POWER and you'll own the road" (*Details*, April 2004). The description at the bottom of the page is square bracketed at the right side only.

- An inventive use of the square brackets appears in a two-page ad for NAS-DAQ's group of non-financial companies called QQQ (*Forbes*, April 18,

Figure 5.7 **NASDAQ QQQ** (*Forbes*, April 18, 2005).

2005). On the right page of the ad (Figure 5.7), we see the left bracket at the upper right of the page and lower down, the right bracket. These brackets enclose a calendar page showing April 15 on the top, under which is written "Intuit," and a tea bag underneath, under which is written "Whole Foods Market." There is a substantial amount of text, both on this page but more on the opposing left page of the ad, which is not shown in Figure 5.7. What is interesting here is the nonverbal iconic signs for the date that tax returns are due and the tea bag, with some type of Chinese character on the end of the tea bag string. Choosing Intuit and Whole Foods as the sample company names for QQQ draws the reader to think—perhaps differently than she or he usually thinks about investments. The left page of the ad also verbally invites the reader to "Expand your IRA retirement portfolio with QQQ >"—using the forward pointing arrow discussed earlier in this chapter to lead the reader toward the rest of the ad. This ad exploits several different sign systems (technology, investment, income tax refund checks, Chinese lifestyle) in juxtaposition to lead the reader to explore what might be inside the brackets for his or her future retirement years.

Short programming commands, terminal punctuation, and dots

Computer programming and computer-mediated communication applications have developed unique formats for the linguistic structure of statements. As artificial languages, computer languages have syntactic and semantic rules that govern the formation of statements and commands. These rules differ from English as a natural language (and from other natural languages) because precision is the key element involved. Although we might think that we are always striving to be precise in our use of human language, what we produce is often incomplete, vague, indirect, ambiguous, wordy, and confusing. As humans, we can be creative with language, choose in a given situation how to formulate something we wish to say or write, and decide whether or not to communicate and how much to say or write. If computer languages were as open as natural languages, there would be great difficulty in getting anything accomplished; word processing systems can be programmed to correct common spelling errors, but a misspelling in a library search will yield no results or odd results. Computer languages function through systematic command statements (and in today's software, many of these commands are available with toolbars and clicks from choices on a menu). The commands are specific statements telling the computer's operating system what to do, e.g. recognize my password and let me into my e-mail account, capitalize the letters, show me my files that I organized in a Job Search folder.

Computer-mediated communication systems (e-mail, chatting, and instant messaging) also have distinctive, patterned ways of forming sentences and expressing information, thoughts, and emotions; some of these patterns exist because of the possibilities and constraints of software, and others because communities of practice naturally develop their own rules for language use. E-mail, on-line chatting, and instant messaging all share the attribute of being relatively informal (in most cases) and quick modes of communication in comparison to phone conversations, letters, and even face-to-face interactions in which there are often demands for additional time or preparation.

The particular types of ellipsis employed in advertising, and especially the premium placed on economy of words, make some of the formats and patterns of computer commands and computer-mediated communication suitable for modeling in advertising discourse. Advertising also often uses single words or short phrases to create a verbal image of a product: "advanced"; "rapture"; "style"; "indulge yourself"; "think fresh"; "pure luxury"; and so forth.

Advertising in recent years speaks to the potential consumer using a language style suggestive of the formats and patterns found in computing and computer-mediated communication. The proliferation of short command statements typical in technology formats and the use of the now-familiar "dots" abound in advertising.

Command syntax

The simple syntax of the command is familiar in famous advertising tags like Volkswagen's "Drivers wanted" and Nike's "Just Do It." Each gives a command—a simple statement yet complex command that relies on the reader retrieving something from the text that was omitted through ellipsis. It's not just that drivers are wanted. "Drivers" mean "buyers" in this case, but it would be too crass to say, "Buyers wanted." And they are wanted for the VWs that are for sale (initially for the reissue of the VW Beetle), not for any car on any lot by any maker. The "It" in "Just Do It" invites the reader to imagine and to transport him- or herself into the action steps required to take risks, fulfill your dreams, do what you have been reluctant to do—whatever that might be; and Nike would like the interpretation to involve their shoes, either because the shoes fit "it" or because the message inspires the consumer, who then remembers that Nike led to the inspiration.

Examples of simple command syntax followed by terminal punctuation with a period abound in advertising. The Hennessy Cognac ad campaign in 2000 pictured different combinations of attractive people with contrasting characteristics or motives labeled in text boxes; each ad included the tag that reads: "mix accordingly." (the tag includes the period). Keds 2005 style is tagged, "be cool." The QVC shopping channel advertised a special shopping evening with "speak gold." Kool cigarettes' recent campaign uses two quick commands, "BE BOLD." and "BE TRUE."

Some ads also use simplified syntactic ellipsis followed by the terminal period to stress attributes of the products being promoted or emphasize characteristics of people associated with the products and their cultural practices. The Toyota Avalon is "ALL SCIENCE. NO FICTION." (*New Yorker*, June 19, 2006). The Hennessy Cognac campaign already mentioned includes one ad showing two well-dressed Black men, one labeled "teddy bear" (he's wearing a business suit, with a dress shirt and tie) and the other "corporate shark" (he appears more casual in a blazer, turtleneck, and braids). Another shows a man and woman together, with the text box above the man saying "wants a commitment" and the one above the woman saying "wants a crème brulée." An ad for Rain·X Bug and Tar Remover announces in the middle of the page that "DEBRIS HAPPENS." Kenneth Cole's men's fragrance with the name "Reaction" uses the tag, "Get Reaction."

"Dot" punctuation

Some ads use the period mark in a manner suggesting that the "period" be interpreted as "dot." Because the "dot" is now commonplace in reciting web addresses and referring to on-line businesses as "dot coms," it has moved into the broader lexicon and may even be interpreted as something different from the period. Examples of such formatting in advertising abound. Especially noteworthy is the absence of spaces in most of the ads between the dots/periods. Some of these are in advertisements for technology products such as mobile phones and PDAs (including the ad for the Blackberry described in the section on Highlighting):

- Sony's VAIO [Voice Audio Integrated Operation] laptop in five different colors is advertised with no spaces between the elements as: "like.no.other™" (*Shape*, December 2005).
- Verizon wireless advertises its phone with V Cast using a large picture of American rhythm and blues singer Jaheim (Hoagland), a picture of a mobile phone with a music download on the screen, and the statement, with no spaces:

  "DOWNLOADSONGS.INFULL" (*Sports Illustrated*, January 23, 2006).

- The LG audio-visual mobile phone is presented in an ad with two large words separated by the dot: "MUSIC.VIDEO" (*Blender*, December 2005).
- An ad layout for T-Mobile's Blackberry shows a swimmer in blue-green water with her towel, Blackberry, and sandals on the dock. The center of the ad places the following text superimposed on the water:

"OUT.BROUGHT TO YOU BY T-MOBILE" (*Forbes*, November 15, 2004).

- The Canon EOS Rebel camera advertises with a picture of Andre Aggassi, the tennis player, and the caption: "Fast. Stylish. Precise" (*Newsweek*, June 14, 2004).

Even more interesting are the ads that use the dot/period to divide very simple verbal elements—single words or very short phrases:

- An ad for Quaker Oatmeal Breakfast Squares, which is shown in Figure 5.8, shows how clearly the "dot" has invaded advertising (*Parade*, August 1, 2004). "Oatmeal" is conventionally one word, with the possibility of an unconventional representation as two words because each morpheme can stand alone, as in "oat" and "meal." Presenting it as "Oat.Meal" associates a completely non-technology product with a convention drawn from technology.
- Mitsubishi presents an ad for one of its cars with the textual display of: "GALANT. PROTECTION." (*Newsweek*, November 8, 2004). The descriptive text below this display notes "frontal crash safety" and a "comprehensive protection package."
- Playing with words both to describe the product size and its anticipation, a Mercedes-Benz ad for the R-Class Grand Sports Tourer proclaims: "Long. Awaited." with the second word positioned beneath the first word (*Boston Magazine*, October 2005).
- One ad in the Coca-Cola "Real" campaign shows roommates settling into their apartment, and the tag line describes the scene as: "first home.second family." (*Essence*, December 2004).
- More text with the dot punctuation occurs in an Estée Lauder ad for eye cream called "Idealist" which includes four lines of introductory text prior to the longer, smaller font size description (*Vogue*, September 2005). The dot punctuation is used as a lead-up to the product name:

> **Your ideal eyes.**
> **Unlined. Smoothed. Revitalized.**
> **New. Idealist**
> **Refinishing Eye Serum**

- The headline on an ad for Appearex, a nail strengthener, boasts: "Healthy nails. Inside and out." (*Ladies Home Journal*, April 2005).
- In keeping with the increasing fattening of America, M&M released a new mega-sized candy targeted at adults in August 2005 (M&M's get

Figure 5.8 **Quaker Oatmeal Breakfast Squares** (*Parade*, August 1, 2004).

mega-sized, 2005). The ad shows four pieces of candy, each larger than the next, all aligned on a horizontal plane. Under the candy the labels use the dot punctuation: "Perfect. Spoils dinner. Is dinner. Eats you for dinner." (*Sports Illustrated*, January 16, 2006).

Television advertising also makes use of the dot punctuation. Typically, we see separate elements appear on the screen one after the other, sometimes following a voice-over articulation of the same element and sometimes as shorthand for what the voice-over is saying. Four examples are presented here:

- A promo for "Late Night with David Letterman" ends with two successive dot punctuated words: "Read." followed by "Funny." (CBS, January 22, 2006). Similarly, a commercial for Tylenol P.M. ends with the dot-punctuated word "Stop." followed by "Think." (CBS, June 27, 2006).
- Like the Letterman and Tylenol ads, a television commercial for Harvey Windows pops "Home. Improved." at the viewer, but this time the words appear along with a voice-over saying the same words (NBC, May 10, 2006).
- Target department stores aired a commercial with a hip-hop style that ends with a quick succession with a rap rhythm voice-over of: "Want it. Need it. Get it." (NBC, June 7, 2006).
- The slogan "Not A. The." was emblazoned on billboards for the Range Rover SUV in major cities in late 2003.

All of these formats present a bare bones casual style that in its repetition across ads begins to appear formulaic. The impression is a hybrid between web addresses and the shortened, quick sentence structure of much IM communication. The consumer who is more familiar with navigating the web, Internet communication, and the dot-com world may see these reflected more readily than others. As such, the use of the simple commands, punctuation, and dots may be legitimized through advertising discourse.

Font as technographic paralanguage

When we speak, we give meaning to our utterances not only through linguistic features such as syntax and phonology but also through pitch, stress patterns and intonation. These vocal elements are known as *paralanguage*, and they provide important communicative information. When we urge someone to "speak up" or "tone it down," we are often referring to paralanguage. When we hear a person as having a terrific "radio voice," we are responding to paralinguistic features of speech. In print, there is also more to text than the words chosen and the syntax. The paralanguage of written text consists of font style, font size, placement of the font on the page and so forth.

One particular aspect of advertising's use of paralanguage that *en...* technological meanings is the use of font style. If an ad uses:

a script with rounded, forward-leaning letters

or

a script that appears child-like

or

a script that is aptly named Papyrus

we are not likely to think of technology. Conversely, scripts that look like stereotypic computer-generated text may engage a semantic association with technology. For example, using dot matrix script, even though it is rarely used in the types of communication most of us engage in over the Internet, carries— because of its heavy use in early computer printing—an association with technology. The American Civil Liberties Union, for example, uses dot matrix capital letters in an ad seeking membership enrollment. The ad features a picture of actor and director Tim Robbins (who is identified as part of the "Scrapbook for Freedom Series"), with a first-person statement of belief, stating in part:

I AM AN AMERICAN WHO BELIEVES IN QUESTIONING OUR LEADERS . . . I SUPPORT THE ACLU BECAUSE WE SHARE THE BELIEF THAT THE RIGHT TO DISAGREE AND EXPRESS DISSENT IS FUNDAMENTAL TO FREEDOM & DEMOCRACY

(*New Yorker*, April 19 and 26, 2004)

The CitiCard "Live richly" advertising campaign addresses the consumer using a font in all of the ads that appears unembellished and somewhat reminiscent of dot-matrix format. The many ads in this campaign—beginning with billboards in New York in 2001 and broadening to magazines, television, the Internet and languages other than English—offer advice and also refer to information available on the web, all designed to make the consumer comfortable with credit cards and borrowing money. The font appears very similar to "Microsoft Sans Serif" font—with examples from ads shown here:

A credit card is a powerful tool. By all means have fun, just don't go overboard.

(*Time*, September 2003)

Citi Premier Pass card, the only credit card that earns you Thank You rewards points. . . .

(*New Yorker*, November 1, 2004)

Font styles that evoke technological associations often look like simple typeface draft style. Reebok, for example, uses this in an ad for their NFL Thorpe Mid D shoe. Figure 5.9 shows the top part of an ad featuring a picture of high school quarterback Donovan McNabb from Chicago (*Sports Illustrated*, August 1, 2005).

Advertising discourse presented in technology templates

In recent years, an interesting change in magazine ads that appears to be linked to technology has emerged in relation to the format or template for the visual presentation of text. One example of this is in layouts that look like web pages—some more directly than others. Other ads are presented with the orthography commonly used in Instant Messaging.

Web page layout style

Internet users have become accustomed to navigating through web pages by following links that can be clicked, thus carrying the web user from one page to the next. The architecture of the layout for these pages varies, but one standard format provides the categories for what can be linked to on the left side of the page, which is separated from content for a particular page or category that occupies the space slightly left of center moving right to the edge of the page. In this style, the area of the page placed vertically contains what is called the "navigation bar." In these layouts, the eye moves left to right, but with a juncture between the navigation bar and the more elaborated content elements. It is almost as though the navigation bar is outside the left margin.

The vertically placed navigation bar format seems to have inspired page layout schemes now commonly used in magazine advertising. Most of these layouts appear over two facing pages, with the left page containing a column on the far left occupying one-third of the page, which is separated from two columns of something unrelated to the ad—table of contents for the magazine and text for an article being the most common. The ad resumes on the right-facing page as a full page presentation of the product being advertised. Although less common, one-page ads using this layout format do exist. An early example is an ad for State Farm Insurance that appeared in the August/

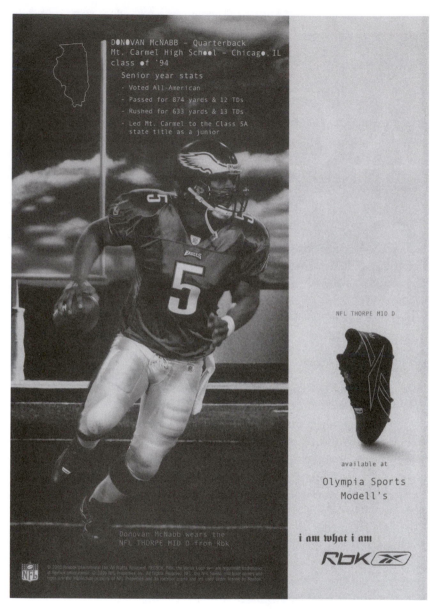

Figure 5.9 **Reebok NFL Thorpe Mid D** (*Sports Illustrated*, August 1, 2005).

September 2000 issue of *aMagazine: Inside Asian America*. This one-page ad places single words vertically on the left side of the page that correspond to the types of products—auto, home, life, health and financial services. A picture of three Asian-looking toddlers is placed to the right of this vertical listing, along

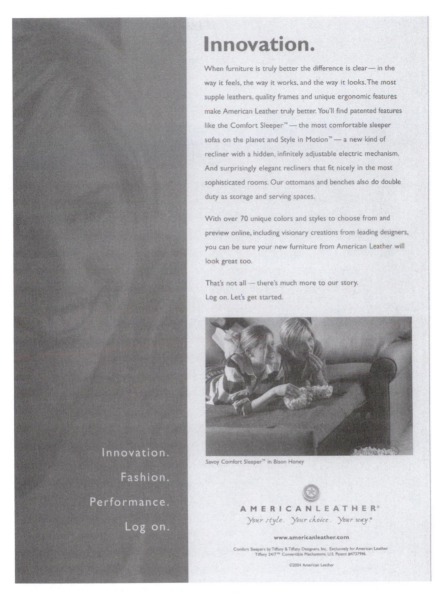

Figure 5.10 **American Leather** (*Architecture Digest*, June 2004).

with text about the insurance company. Similarly, an ad for American Leather, which is shown in Figure 5.10, displays four verbal elements set in a rust-colored panel on the left side of the page, the last of which actually invites the reader to log on to their web site: "Innovation. Fashion. Performance. Log on." (*Architecture Digest*, June 2004). The first element, Innovation, is picked up at the top of the next and wider vertical panel, which is titled "Innovation."

BROOKS, THE MAYOR of North College Hill, thinks about that kind of stuff all the time. Sitting in his office, he unrolls architectural drawings that illustrate his grand vision for the town. A few blocks from the school, Brooks wants to erect a $13 million community center with pools and gyms, offices and classrooms. "Imagine how people would feel having something like that in their town," he says. He has raised $100,000 and hopes that the presence of O.J. and Bill will attract more money. "Reebok and Nike, we plan on hitting them up," Brooks says. "If they want to put their name on it, that is fine with us."

Brooks isn't the only one eyeing bigger things. Nickel called the athletic director at St. Vincent–St. Mary, LeBron James's former school, for tips on how to handle the offers pouring in. During James's senior season, 2002–03, the basketball team reportedly made $400,000. The school got appearance fees upward of $10,000 for games in Philadelphia, Los Angeles, North Carolina and New Jersey. Two games were televised on ESPN2.

Following that season, the Ohio High School Athletic Association passed the LeBron Rule, which limits schools to one game per season beyond the five states bordering Ohio. Still, Nickel persuaded the members of the Miami Valley Conference—a collection of small schools now greatly overmatched—to allow NCH to reduce its status to associate member. This will enable the Trojans, whose season opens on Friday, to play 12 nonconference games, some in arenas at the University of Cincinnati and Xavier. The team will play two games in Huntington and one in Charleston, W.Va. Its one big trip will be to Southern California. Nickel estimates the team will net $75,000 this season and, if all goes well, $100,000 during the boys' senior year, when some games could be nationally televised. "If we manage the money right, we are set for a decade," he says.

But the boys' most lasting legacy, Brooks believes, will be as a unifying force within the town. To illustrate this, he tells a story about a middle-aged white woman upset with her young black neighbors. They played their music too loud, she told the mayor, and borrowed her lawn chairs without asking. Brooks says the young family and the woman are now the sort of friendly multiracial neighbors that he

envisions filling every tree-lined street in North College Hill. "When we had a ceremony to give the team the keys to the city, that woman put her arms around Bill and O.J. and said. 'Don't you ever leave North College Hill.' "

It is a tale so corny, so allegorical, that one can't help but believe it's the concoction of a small-town politico. "But that kind of stuff happens to us all the time around here," Mayo says. "Sometimes you get tired of it."

BACK IN the SUV, returning to North College Hill, O.J. and Bill recall the highlights from the game and scan the new text messages on their phones. Walker calls a friend to get the score of that night's Huntington High football game.

Mayo occasionally returns to Huntington to see his mother, Alisha, and other relatives, but he still misses the place, as does Walker. "Sometimes you just want to be around people like you," Mayo explains.

The SUV approaches Mayo's apartment, from which O.J. and Bill can see the football field, its stands full. The two teens leap from the car, cross a swath of grass and pass through the stadium's chain-link gate.

Their schoolmates are standing in front of the snack bar, on the dirt track that rings the field. The oval will soon be replaced by rubberized asphalt, thanks to revenue brought in by the basketball team. Walker wades into the crowd. He teases a cheerleader, then talks to his English teacher. She mentions a slam poem he wrote for her class titled Please Understand, about a former girlfriend. "It was really good," the teacher says, and Walker blushes.

Mayo is all over the place, talking to parents and teachers in the stands and students on the track. He even goes onto the field to slap hands with the football players as they return from the locker room for the second half.

"It's a big difference," Mayo says when asked how this compares with his visit to the West End. "People treat you differently here." He then spots a group of kids he wants to greet. Before he moves toward them in his speedskater walk, he pauses. "But this is a good place. A good place. And we like it here." He smiles, showing off those cavernous dimples.

Then he adds, with unintended irony, "The people here, you know, they do a lot for us."

Figure 5.11 **Wrangler Jeans Co** (*Sports Illustrated*, December 5, 2005).

Wrangler
JEANS Co™
ESTABLISHED 1947

A NEW GENERATION OF WRANGLER

TEST DRIVE A PAIR TODAY

Wrangler®

OFFICIAL JEANS OF DALE EARNHARDT JR.

NEW FITS · NEW COMFORT · NEW STYLES

CALL 1-888-784-8571 FOR A STORE NEAR YOU OR VISIT WWW.WRANGLER.COM

One of the early entrants into the web page style layout was Bacardi rum. In 2000, many ads appeared in magazines such as *Maxim* and *Details* that used the split page, with the Bat logo placed on the left accompanied by some text that would link to the full page layout on the right; the remainder of the left page contains unrelated information, for example, an article on how to organize a clothes closet. A more detailed illustration of this discourse presentation is found in an ad for Wrangler Jeans, which is shown in Figure 5.11 (*Sports Illustrated*, December 5, 2005). Here the left panel/left page includes the company name, a picture of a pair of jeans, and three product attributes set out vertically. One can imagine clicking on one of the attributes—and visually, they are shown in the right-facing page.

Other examples of using this format to list attributes on the left page/left panel include:

- an ad for Nabisco/Planters "100 Calorie Packs" (*InStyle*, November 2005) where seven varieties are listed on the left page and a specific variety on the right page;
- an ad for Raymond James financial advisors (*Forbes*, May 23, 2005), which shows four faces on the one-third page panel, each with different financial needs (saving for college, opening a coffee house, etc.), and a full page featuring one face as an example (the intervening material is part of a feature article on entrepreneurs);
- Canon's ad for its PowerShot SD450 camera (*Sports Illustrated*, October 10, 2005) with three separate attributes listed on the left page panel (photo printer price, cost per print, and retractable USB cable) leading to a full right page featuring a picture of tennis star Maria Sharapova and information about the camera (with left page intervening text containing a Q&A about Dallas Cowboys' Troy Aikman); and
- Unlimited Access (*Stuff*, August 2006) pictures a torso shot of a man embracing a sexually posed, seemingly naked woman in the left page panel (the rest of the left page is the monthly editor's column titled "We're Kung-Fu Awesome"), leading to a full right page with full body, sexually explicit mirror images of the man and woman (yes, the woman is naked except for a possible g-string).

Some of the ads using this web page format make use of the left page panel for more text intensive material and the full page to the right for less text and more visual image. Patrón Tequila advertises a recipe for a cosmopolitan in the left page panel (*Spin*, August 2005); one of the many "got milk?" ads—this one for milk as an ingredient in weight loss—offers the "recipe" for how to drink 24 ounces of milk each day on the left panel and a picture of Kelly Preston and her personal statement on the right page, with the tag, "Lighten Up"; Crestor prescription cholesterol medication is advertised (*Newsweek*, July 12, 2004) with a promotion on the left page panel for the Crestor Charity Challenge Golf Tournament, part of the PGA Tour, and information about the drug on the full right page (in this case, a third page follows with the information in small print that is required by the Food and Drug Administration); and an advertisement for Nice 'n Easy hair color (*More*, March 2004) includes a left panel with information about a weekly giveaway contest for a beauty basket.

These ad formats move the eye in particular ways—certainly left to right, but also with a boundary between what is on the left and what is on the right, with there being a relationship but not a complete continuity of text. They also invite some thought about how to move from one part of the text to the other, perhaps to think about choices, or to look at one part and disregard the other. A reader could, in fact, completely miss seeing the left column on the left side page—just as you can navigate in a web site to a particular page without going first to the home page. We've become accustomed to seeing multiple displays on the television screen, divided up in various ways—moving news running across the bottom of a news broadcast, inserted blocks of different but related activity within the visual field. These are related textual/discourse structures to what we are seeing in advertising.

Mimicking IM and Text Message language

We're all familiar with vernacular language appearing in advertising. Throwing in today's hippest, coolest, *au courant* words gives currency and cachet to the product—often by stressing its attachment to urban trends and youthfulness. The hip-hop magazine *XXL* ran an ad in 2004 for Diadora shoes with the tag line, "datswhussup." The GMC Yukon Denali is headlined "Get a grip." (*Money*, September 2004). The Hummer H2 sport utility truck is described in an ad (*Vanity Fair*, February 2005) as "wookie sized" (which could mean lots of things—you figure it out using urbandictionary.com). In all of these examples, the equation is essentially *vernacular* + *product* = *pace-setter*.

The variety of language use common in Instant Messaging (IM) and in Text Messaging (TM) alike is in itself a vernacular code. The many abbreviations and emoticons used in IM—although often expressing conventional phrases—signify the discourse of a special community of practice. Like other aspects of technology that have seeped into advertising, the conventions of this new vernacular need to be sufficiently recognizable to the reader for the ad to be comprehensible. TM takes what can be imported from IM and uses it as the code for communication; the reduced spelling conventions are the basis for TM. That IM/TM language appears in ads attests to this level of recognizability.

At the same time, using this language in ads gives stability and greater public exposure to this new language variety. Because IM language is graphic and visual, its manifestation in advertising is well suited to magazines and Internet promotions. Like the cross over of other vernaculars into wider usage, only a subset of elements from IM/TM language appear in advertising, but we should expect more elements to appear in the future as usage broadens.

As early as 2001, hair products by "b-intense" were advertised in magazines like *Spin* with the risqué pun in the tag line, "we give good head." IM language showed up in the text for the ad as "professional hairstuff 4U @ stores wherever." In this case, not only is "4U" taken from IM language but the ad also uses the @ symbol to underscore the technological signification, all wrapped up in sexual signification. An ad for CIT Commercial Equipment Financing and International Steel Group (*Forbes*, November 1, 2004) uses an Instant Messaging presentation which is also a play on the company's name: "c it rise." With an image of a heavily muscled male construction worker holding a girder, the ad plays with the company's name, IM/TM language, and phallic sexual innuendo. A line of hair products by Schwarzkopf is named "göt2b"—here playing with both IM/TM language and the veneer of foreign quality signified by using the umlaut over the "o" (*Cosmo Girl*, June/July 2006).

Mobile phones are the most obvious products to advertise with IM/TM language conventions because a large part of what is now being sold—especially to younger consumers—is the text messaging function:

- Sprint advertises to teens (*Cosmo Girl*, March 2005) with the assurance that "with Instant Messaging from Sprint, you can take your chat on the road." The ad visually represents a short exchange between two girls:

    VG: what up
    lady?
    CM: we're
    @ skyler's.
    VG: chillin?
    CM: j.cn.u? [just chillin and you?]
    VG: hmwrk!
    CM: oh. 18tr! [later]

- Motorola has named its phones with enhanced features MOTOSLVR, MOTORAZR, and MOTOPEBL—the first hyped for its "huge color screen, Bluetooth technology, quad band, video capture and iTunes" (*Sports Illustrated*, February 22, 2006); the second for "high speed V CAST downloads on-the-go . . . weather, sports and prime-time TV in the palm of your hand" (*Newsweek*, January 9, 2006); and the third for small size and multiple colors (*Cosmo Girl*, June/July 2006) and for "21st century technology" (*People*, November 28, 2005).

One of the ads in the Grand Marnier series, which is dubbed "The conversation is waiting," blatantly makes fun of the spelling conventions and the extensive ellipsis of IM and TM. This ad proclaims that "Its tme to spk in rl wrds agn." (*New Yorker*, January 9, 2006).

IM and the TM that has grown in its wake have developed forms of ellipsis that are now so stable that they occasionally appear in student papers (probably through carelessness in editing, as when one of my students wrote, "If you hear a dialect that is associated with the south, u [sic] might also have certain ideas about the speaker." Several times in conferences with students, I've asked to see lecture notes to check on what they thought were the important points. I've noticed many of the IM conventions for spelling and an occasional emoticon scribbled on the page as well.

When spelling conventions are violated and new spelling used, understanding the discourse meaning is more than a matter of filling in the missing letters. It also involves engaging a meaning system, in this case the background of Instant Messaging—its use in daily life, association with immediacy in communication, and marked trendiness. When IM and TM conventions appear in advertising, *semantic ellipsis* is at work. McShane (2005) explains this type of ellipsis as "the nonexpression of information that, although syntactically not required, is necessary for a full semantic representation of the sentence . . . and directly establish[es] a link to a real-world referent" (p. 25). At the final stages of revising this chapter, I saw TM language represented in oral style in a television commercial for AT&T mobile phone services. The commercial shows a mother and daughter arguing over the daughter's text messaging bill. The daughter is speaking in TM language, and the mother doesn't understand what she's saying. Yet, by the end of the commercial, the mother too uses some of the TM lingo. Moral: It's an ever-changing world of public discourse, with yesterday's vernacular becoming today's commonly understood speech.

Conclusions and implications

Why is any of this of interest? What does the presence of technographic language and discourse formats in ads tell us about advertising and its role in culture?

Let me first return to the notion of the discourse image. The idea of the discourse image foregrounds the ways in which verbal elements of advertising engage broader cultural discourses, and not just the persuasive function of ads; the term is also intended to highlight the important role of language in a culture that is most often characterized as visual and anti-language, and conceptions of image-based culture as synonymous with culture dominated by visual representation. Discourse, broadly conceived of, is of course both verbal and visual, with each element bearing reciprocally on the other. When a mass culture medium as prominent as advertising carries new codes of language, repeating these over and over, we can be sure that patterns of text are being modeled and perhaps taken up by their interpreters. The idea that technology can be an image circulated through verbal symbols—or in keeping with Williamson (1978), can be technology without technology performed, is not far removed from ideas about everyday metaphor structured into language, such as described by Lakoff and Johnson (1980–2003) in *Metaphors We Live By* (1980) when they trace the elements of war throughout US English usage.

But does advertising really have an influence on culture, on cultural practice, and the communities of practice that arise in new cultural circumstances? This is one of the most heated questions among scholars who study advertising beyond its specific function to sell something to someone by saying very little. Guy Cook (2001) contends that: "In many ways, ads are parasitic upon their surroundings and other genres. Just as the substance of an ad is often stuck to some other significant substance, so its discourse both occurs within other discourse and also implicates it" (pp. 33–4). Others such as Sut Jhally (2003) and Jean Kilbourne (2000) contend that advertising poses dangers through its message system of consumption, the way in which it contributes to the circulation of appearance as the sine qua non of identity, and the methods used to interpellate viewers and listeners.

Perhaps there is some truth to both perspectives. In partial support of Cook (although writing before him), Williamson (1978) characterized the situation this way: "advertisements cannot create or invent referent systems, but . . . they can shake the meaning out of them and insert their own" (p. 137). Commenting more broadly on mass media, Stuart Hall, who deals mainly with the role of media in circulating certain representation systems, offers the view that, "how things are represented and the 'machineries' and regimes of representation in a culture do play a constitutive, and not merely a reflexive, after-the-event, role" (quoted in Wetherell and Potter, 1992, p. 63).

Representation in advertising, then, likely plays a constitutive role. When technology is implicated through the discourse used to advertise products, the issue is not so much whether or not the product itself resulted from some advanced technology or the degree to which something made possible by technology is now on the market. For advertising, the issue is always with the image that the ad is trying to present to the potential consumer for a particular product. For broader cultural meaning, what is of interest is in the patterns running through advertising and how they play into the continuing movement of cultural practices. In the case of technology appearing in advertising, the issue is, thus, always image: the image of technology and what that represents in the semiotic system at play at a particular time and in relation to cultural practices and communities of practice. No ad describes the ways in which technology made a lipstick or a shoe or a mobile phone or car wax possible. But the ad does attach the cachet of technology to the product by bringing technology as metaphor into the discourse devised to help sell the product.

The rise of technological applications and the maturation of the first computer generation are significant cultural moments. As enacted through practices of web surfing, mobile phone usage and text messaging, on-line shopping and services, e-mail, instant messaging and the blogosphere, cultural practices now include for many people an active daily dose of contact with technology. The younger the age cohort, the more this is true. The appearance of technological discourse codes in advertising shows the confluence of these everyday practices and the discourses surrounding them. Indeed, advertising is parasitic on culture—just as Cook observes. Yet, advertising because of its prominence in daily life and its key role in the culture of consumption, cements and normalizes cultural practices evident elsewhere. As more and more people are able to "read" the technology codes in the discourse of advertising—or even not notice them because they are so obvious—those codes will indicate more than ephemeral shifts in mode of expression.

Advertising is but one part of the cultural environment, one part of a complex discourse environment, a perpetual ellipsis of narrative. Language takes from every possible source and changes over time in every aspect from lexicon to syntax to style. Language surely influences perception and cognition. Today's advertising, I believe from the evidence, surely plays a role in the ever-changing codes of language and in the possibilities for cognitive reorientations formatted by language change. One part of that role appears to be in the circulation of technological codes through technographic language. It's new, technology-infused language appearing in advertising and is a link to selling culture's newest wares and to cultural practices more broadly.

Chapter 6

From Barbie to BudTV

Advertising in the Fifth Frame

The Internet is the medium of our time. Although not everyone has access, use of the Internet for a myriad of purposes is now commonplace. Survey data from 2006 established that 73 percent of adults (approximately 147 million) were using the Internet, and over 40 percent of the adults surveyed reported having broadband connections in their homes (Madden, 2006). Internet communication has transformed political campaigns, facilitated the sharing of important research, and assisted millions of people in finding answers to questions. From specific sites such as WebMD to general inquiry tools such as "Ask Jeeves," those with access to the Internet have a wealth of information and viewpoints available to them day and night—"24/7" in Internet lingo. Along with these resources and potentials come the problems of unregulated Internet communication. The biggest plagues facing many Internet users are pornography and advertising—both of which have proliferated because they are successful in this new cyberspace venue. Pornography claims about 13 percent of the Internet activity, making it the largest part of web traffic (Gerson, 2007), and Internet advertising is "in your face" just about every time you log on. Software to control pop-ups helps those who want fewer advertising distractions and interruptions, and Spam blockers can keep out unwanted messages that carry advertising. Yet, as a new frontier, the Internet demands that advertisers continuously develop innovations in both format and style to try to keep the potential consumer's attention. Reports from the Interactive Advertising Bureau and PricewaterhouseCoopers announced 2006 Internet advertising revenues at $16.8 billion, an increase of 32 percent from 2005 (Interactive Advertising Bureau, 2007). Simply stated, in aggregate, those companies who produce Internet advertising are seeing dramatic revenue growth pointing to the speed with which the Internet craze is reshaping advertising.

Most of us think of Internet advertising as those pesky little pop-ups that appear when we're trying to navigate our way to some site or toward the information we want at a particular time, or as the web site we can consult when we're interested in a particular product or service. Yet, there is another more expansive form of Internet advertising that occurs in Internet sites, and it's not always as explicitly formatted as conventional advertising. These are the sites sponsored by particular companies and products that provide "places to go to" and "experiences" in the form of narratives for the Internet user. The experience provided might be clearly tied to the product, tangentially tied to the product, or in some cases not clearly tied to the product at all. With the Internet unquestionably the new frontier of advertising, the sponsored site experience is at the cutting edge of advertising innovations and brand promotion. This chapter is devoted to an analysis of the ideological implications of these extended Internet-based advertising experiences—their stress on the individual either as an isolated entity or as virtually identified with others, and their anti-civic character. Although the destinations for these advertising extensions suggest that the individual is free to choose what she or he desires and to fashion the experience in multiple ways, the agency of the Internet traveler here is very limited—essentially amounting to a ploy to bring the potential or already captured consumer into an individualistic relationship with the product/brand/corporate entity that is highly channeled.

The chapter is organized into three sections. The first section provides an overview of the conceptual foundations for one type of Internet narrative available for exploitation by advertisers. Two conceptual ideas are introduced: (1) the ideology of self-absorption and (2) what has been called the "Fifth Frame" of advertising and marketing strategy. The second section focuses on narratives as a discourse modality for bringing consumers into closer contact with brands and products through the Internet. Narratives are brought into the Fifth Frame both as pre-set content that is available in narrative form and as something that the viewer can construct for her/himself based on what is suggested by the content that is available. The third section is an analysis of four varied examples of how Internet advertising develops narratives that rely on self-absorption through characteristics of the Fifth Frame. The examples are for *Infiniti in Black*, *Brawny Man*, *Barbie*, and *BudTV*. The chapter concludes with an assessment of the personal and political implications of these more recent trends in advertising.

Conceptual foundations

In sharpening the focus on what I will call *Internet Brand Extension* (IBE), two conceptual ideas will be central. One of these is the *ideology of self-absorption*, which refers to the way in which current trends in American society that place emphasis on satisfying personal desires become the driving force behind much Internet use. The second is what is termed the *Fifth Frame* in advertising. This period of advertising, according to Leiss et al. (2005), stresses fluidity, limitless possibilities, and self-definition of the situation.

The ideology of self-absorption

The *ideology of self-absorption* grows from the importance on individualism in the history of US culture, but it differs in fundamental value. While individualism stresses the right to pursue individual interests, think for oneself, and make decisions for which one is then held personally accountable, self-absorption can be associated with social isolation, narcissism, hedonism, and sometimes even a disregard for others. To the extent that self-absorption can be political at all, its politics are a politics for the self and in the interest of causes and political positions that coincide with personal priorities. As such, the ideology of self-absorption is the opposite of altruism and the antithesis to genuine community identity. As a cultural orientation, this ideology drives practices that make up what Jib Fowles (1996) terms "The Project of the Self." Key to the notion of self-as-project is the idea that self-identity has come to be the locus of social control, replacing the strong role of more stationary and culturally grounded identity categories that reside in institutions such as religion, marriage, family as well as in social categories ascribed with relatively fixed qualities within a specific cultural context (race, heritage group, social class, gender). The more stationary categories of identity at a given time in a given society often provide foundations for the project of the self, but in this project, the individual entity and not the group takes center stage. Fowles (1996) argues that "the creation and maintenance of the self becomes not just a leading personal concern of these times but the paramount one" (p. 198). He further sees gender as "the keel of self-identity" (p. 199), with the most important influence on gender identity development resting in real-world experiences, with media, including advertising, playing a secondary role. Writing over a decade ago, Fowles did not formulate his ideas in the context of the vast product proliferations and advertising that have occurred in the span of just a few years or, even more significantly, of the substantial role of the Internet in shaping lifestyle choices and interpersonal communication. In many ways the project of the self that Fowles wrote about has broadened and deepened. More media environments are available. More products with small differentiations can be bought to change and stylize one's personal identity (ethnic foods, endless beverage varieties, snack food options both healthy and unhealthy, cell phone after cell phone with slight variations in functionality but accentuated variations in appearance, personal care products to deal with every possible "flaw," hair products labeled for different textures and colors, colognes and perfumes presented with a vast array of connotations in their names, on and on). The notion of body surface in recent years has moved into a less fixed and more malleable space that is a site for self-absorption. Not long ago, bodies were considered to be relatively fixed material entities belonging to the realm of biology. In this conceptualization, society intervened with practices for how to put something on the body such as clothing, make-up, accessories, and so forth. More recently, the body is becoming a process open to alteration and to a broad range of discursive renderings. As Judith Butler (1993) notes, the materiality of the body and discourse are not separate "for language both is and refers to that which is material, and what is material never fully escapes from the process by which it is signified" (p. 68). With the body now more elastic and pliable, there are endless images of experiences and lifestyles to be culti-vated in association with products—what to say and where to say it, where to be and how to appear in spaces charged with identity-forming potential, what visual images to capture in what ways through language. In the project of the self, the underlying philosophical idea of *tabula rasa* informs the basic prop-osition that through various arrangements of products and social practices, a self can be created—and changed when the winds of whim blow in another direction.

Advertisers cultivate this cultural environment of self-absorption in differ-ent ways to accelerate the opportunities now available in consumer culture to market and advertise products. The first and most recognized way to sell something in the context of the cultural preoccupation with self, self-discovery, and self-design is for advertisers to directly hail the potential con-sumer; such strategies position the consumer as an object to be brought into the discourse of the product through interpellation: "Hey you—this is for/ could be you" is the basic formulation. The visual and verbal images used in advertising are important both for drawing the person to recognize that the ad is for them and for enticing the person who is attending to the ad to make the connections between him- or herself and the product, idea, or image being advertised. Some ads beckon directly by speaking to the viewer to come into the ad and then discover the product. Olay's "Love the skin you're in" tagline is a good example of this. In this case, the linguistic function of the second-person "you" in "you're" is potentially both the collective you (every woman who attends to the ad) and the individual you (the specific person being called into the ad). Windows' "Calling all music lovers," and Gillette's "Feel the power of the world's best shave" are also examples of this type of direct hailing. In the Windows ad, the appeal is for the spectator who loves music to identify him- or herself as being called because this is exactly what the ad says. In the Gillette ad, the second person "you" is implied and left to the spectator of the ad to fill in as a missing ellipsis element: "[*you* can] feel the power of the world's best shave."

Other ads use more extensive ellipsis but still hail the consumer directly, as in these examples. A Lexus ad pairs a picture of a sleek silver car against a light gray-white background with the words "Unexpectedly Fast." In this instance, we must assume that the advertiser works with the proposition that the Lexus automobile is not readily identified with speed, rapid acceleration, or high performance. Here the desired potential consumer must fill in a number of missing elements, in the formulation of: "[You probably do not identify the Lexus as a fast car/You probably think of Lexus as a luxury car, but the Lexus is] unexpectedly fast [so you should not dismiss it as a choice if you want a fast car in the luxury category]." An ad for Covergirl mascara demonstrates another example of direct hailing through reliance on ellipsis. The ad pictures a close-up shot of a young woman's face. Chin raised, she is looking upward. The lighting on her face is controlled to make her blue eyes shine and lashes stand out. The visual image is paired with the single verbal element "dramateyes"— an invented advertising word that functions as a verbal image to suggest that *you* too can have dramatic eyes like the women pictured if *you* use the Covergirl product.

The second way to bring the consumer into the aura of the product or brand is more indirect and involves some effort or action on the part of the consumer beyond filling in the elements left missing through ellipsis. The simplest illustration of this is when a television or print ad provides a web address or 800-number to call. If the person wants either more information or simply to find out what is provided at the web site or phone number, that person has to do something—first, have the ad at hand, write down or remember the address and then actually go to the web site or make the call. The most indirect connection between something we would call an ad and the potential consumer occurs when the individual actively seeks out what the product or brand has to offer. In today's advertising environment, where branding reigns as the most important overall strategic issue, much more than that a specific product can be purchased is put out there for the potential consumer. In a 2007 interview broadcast on National Public Radio, David Lubars, chair and chief creative officer of BBDO North American, explained the challenge to advertisers: "So it is our job to create content that is engaging . . . that instead of us coming to you, and you have to take it, you come voluntarily . . . It [the product] is so great that you seek it out" (Neary, 2007). Lubars' signature is boldly present in advertising because of his innovation move in Internet advertising when he worked at the Fallon agency. While at Fallon, Lubars initiated the idea behind the BMW Films series. Launched in 2001, this series of eight short films (ranging from nine to 12 minutes each) brought acclaimed directors such an Ang Lee, John Woo, and Alejandro González Iñárrita to the project of making engaging, highly artful films in which the BMW could be seen in high performance mode (Carter, 2004; Howe, 2002). The idea was to gain critical acclaim for the films, *qua* films, early in the process as a way of drawing people to the Internet site. The release of the site drew an estimated 100,000 hits in the first two days (Clark, 2001), and the series was enhanced by including a player application through which directors' commentaries could be viewed. The whole first series on DVD was inserted into an issue of *Vanity Fair*. This high-end style of advertising looks like underwriting with the twist of product placement. The series aimed for and achieved critical success as a way of underscoring the quality of the BMW branding. Among the accolades were the Cannes 2002 International Advertising Festival's Cyber Lion Grand Prix prize, induction into the film collection at the New York Museum of Modern Art (MoMA), and the Los Angeles International Short Film Festival's "Best Action Short" for John Woo's "Hostage" ("BMW Hire Films end," 2005). Most significant for our purposes is the fact that BMW Films is recognized as the innovator of online films.

The concept of interpellation, or hailing, is precisely about the idea of drawing the potential consumer into the discourse of the ad. Advertisers through their discourse of self-enhancement/self-development/self-awareness/even selfishness seek to bring the consumer into a relationship with the products that are for sale and the lifestyles associated with those products. To be hailed is to be "ad-tacked"—meaning that the advertising images attempt essentially to tack their signifiers onto the consumer. This brings us to the second conceptual idea that I believe helps illuminate the discourse of Internet Brand Extension.

The "Fifth Frame"

The Fifth Frame follows from a succession of earlier frames in advertising, where frame means essentially the discursive blueprint and borders through which advertisements are presented. Leiss et al. (2005) describe the history of frames in advertising as a cumulative succession of five different approaches to positioning goods in relation to consumers through marketing and advertising. They specify the prevailing advertising medium and strategy for each frame and provide names for the cultural priority featured in each frame. Beginning with early advertising strategies at the end of the nineteenth and early in the twentieth centuries that stressed rational appeals (First Frame), newspaper and magazine advertisements emphasized *utility* of the product through a cultural priority that these authors label "idolatry." The era of radio advertising through the 1940s presented products as carrying *symbolic attributes* (Second Frame), with the cultural priority placed on "iconology." The diffusion of television in the 1950s and 1960s saw advertisers stress *personal attributes* of products as vehicles for interpersonal advancement (Third Frame) by giving priority to "narcissism." As television matured during the 1970s and 1980s, advertisers stressed *lifestyles* (Fourth Frame) and the cultural value of "totemism" and the role of products in identifying individuals with culturally desirable social groupings. These authors stress that the emergence of a new frame in advertising does not displace preceding frames but, rather, builds upon them. The succession of frames demonstrates, then, both an accumulation and a series of disjunctive innovations.

The idea of the Fifth Frame as developed by Leiss et al. arises from the emergence in the 1990s of advertising strategies that focus on "demassifying" and the cultural frame for goods as "Mise-en-Scène" style whereby elements of a scene or situation can be arranged and rearranged in creative ways through mixed media to suit local and individual purposes. Whereas the Fourth Frame stressed "fixed representation of 'approved' social distinctions . . . [and] enduring forms of social differentiation," (p. 567) the Fifth Frame shifts emphasis to fit a culture where acts of consumption, social uniqueness, and the cultivation of "coolness" have permeated every age cohort, social identity category, and economic class. Several characteristics, according to Leiss et al., mark the Fifth Frame as a distinctive context for promoting products and their more significant brand signatures. Some of the main elements of the Fifth Frame are listed here:

- provides "limitless possibilities for fast-paced rearrangements of the setting" (p. 567);
- emphasizes fluidity and is "relentlessly active" (p. 567);
- places individuals in the role as "directors" of scenes where the products are "props in the service of a virtually unlimited set of creations and re-creations of value and shared meanings" (p. 568);
- presents life "as a script-writing exercise" (p. 568);
- stresses "maintaining identity and individuality in relation to the group" (p. 570);
- draws on technological possibilities of all kinds for editing, animation, and—in short—"an entire electronic universe" (p. 568); and
- offers "resources, ideas, or moments of pleasure" (p. 570).

Well into the first decade of the twenty-first century, the Internet offers endless opportunities as a Fifth Frame advertising context, especially in relation to the ideology of self-absorption. A visitor to a web site can move quickly through links to start, stop, restart and replay content, to make choices about what is to be exposed to among various options, to engage content when convenient or desirable, and in many cases, to create the content from specified choices and options that are presented. The Fifth Frame offers agency, but it is an *oxymoronic agency* because the agency offered by the advertiser is already constrained by the content that is available and the cultural priorities that place value on certain ideas deeply lodged in the ideological codes of consumption. In some cases, the agency or director role is one of seeking out what is offered. In some cases, agency is about actively choosing what content to be passively exposed to but always with the possibility of choosing something else. In some cases, agency is provided through highly interactive selection processes.

An example of clearly identifiable Fifth Frame advertising through IBE would be the BecomeAnMM.com website for M&M's candies, where the visitor to the site can spend quite a lot of time first creating characters and then playing games, putting the character in the "Movie Studio" where choices for the type of narrative and music are provided, playing games in the "Arcade" with the character, and of course shopping at the "Emporium" where purchases can be made of a variety of M&M's-related items with your personalized character on them. You can register and save your character, send your photo to the site to be matched with your character, and watch M&M's television commercials—including the popular Addams Family narrative introducing M&M dark chocolate. The verbal message is that "There's an M&M in everyone. Find yours." If you like M&M's at all, this immersion into M&M fantasy will make your mouth water for those colorful little candies! This commercial strategy includes all of the attributes of the Fifth Frame approach that are described by Leiss et al. in a seemingly innocent, fanciful, no-harm-done web site activity. Yet, it is no accident that this web site corresponds in time to the proliferation of M&M candy varieties—extended advertising all there for the price of playing on the Internet. The M&M's Fifth Frame strategy is pure *advertainment*—advertising thinly veiled as entertainment

A clear print advertising example of Fifth Frame strategy is the Gap campaign that began in 2006, which was designed to brand gap clothing as suitable for any mood, any type of person, any occasion. Many of the magazine ads are multi-page and printed on stiff stock and with a dull finish. The hooded sweatshirt series, for instance, featured 12 pages, each with a different famous person and verbal image. The imaging in this advertising spread features models, actors and directors, and music icons of different genders, races and ages. Each page pairs a picture of the model wearing a different version of the Gap hoodie with a verbal image. Claudia Schiffer (German supermodel and actress) is paired with "shine in your hood"; Maria Bello (American actress) with "imagine in your hood"; Deepak Chopra (Southeast Asia Indian MD known for his writing on spirituality and mind–body connections) and son Gotham pictured nose-to-nose with "reflect in your hood"; Helen Mirren (British actress) and Taylor Hackford (producer and Mirren's husband) with "celebrate in your hood"; Jefferson Hack (fanzine publisher and partner to supermodels) and Anouck Lepere (supermodel) with "hang in your hood"; Max Minghella

(British actor) with "think in your hood"; Diane Kruper (German actor) and godchild Luna with "hug in your hood"; Raquel Zimmerman (Brazilian model) with "shine in your [cashmere] hood"; Aaron Eckhart (actor and producer) with "reveal in your hood" (hairy chest showing); Stephanie Seymour (super-model) and her sons with "relate in your hood"; Bow Wow (rap artist) with "remember in your hood" (he's looking at the name Teresa tattooed on his hand); and Seal (British soul singer and songwriter) and dog with "holiday in your hood." The whole campaign includes different themes for clothing, each of which is then illustrated as an item or attribute (e.g. the color red as part of the campaign to fight AIDS in Africa) open to broad uses and occasions. Gap's idea in this campaign was to stress diversity in both the *who* of their target markets and the *what* of their product lines. The Fifth Frame fits especially well for Gap, which is making an effort through the ad campaign "to appeal to a diverse range of customers at a time when specialty stores targeting increasingly specific age groups are the order or the day" (Birchall, 2007).

The Fifth Frame, then, is a phase in the accumulative, chronological movement of advertising strategies and modalities over time. Through this frame, individuals become the center of experience. We can think of this approach as selling a lifestyle but on an individual basis rather than as a lifestyle dictated by a crowd mentality. Yet, if Fifth Frame ads are examined carefully, in most of them there is always a crowd lifestyle present, especially in this era of celebrity worship. The Fourth Frame provides the sediment for the discourse of the Fifth Frame. The Fifth Frame works at its best through Internet web sites that can be easily changed and updated and where consumers can be drawn back again and again either because they have not finished their exploration and experience or because the sites themselves are designed to release new elements one at a time, or to replace older material with newer material at dates provided for the consumer. Through this frame, individuals are positioned to create personal narratives stressing the appearance of choice, freedom, and hyper-individualism. Fifth Frame experiences also have the potential to move their participants into apolitical priorities—a point to which I will return later. The narratives available for consumption and the narratives that can be constructed in Fifth Frame advertising work particularly well as strategic tools for Internet Brand Extension. We turn next to a consideration of narrative as an approach to advertising text and as an ideal discourse style for Fifth Frame strategy.

Narratives as advertising text

Narratives are a vast cultural resource for meaning creation and transfer. Scholars of narrative have construed the notion of the narrative pattern in several different ways: as a way of thinking, as the means for creating shared meaning with others through connected discourse, and as a vehicle for cultural transmission. Jerome Bruner (1991), one of the major figures associated with narrative as a mode of thinking, argued that the narrative mode of thought engages experience in the form of stories, and that thinking narratively is just as common, if not more so, than the more conventionally recognized rational mode of thought. In explaining how narrative functions as an instrument of mind, Bruner had this to say:

> [W]e organize our experience and our memory of human happenings mainly in the form of narrative—stories, excuses, myths, reasons for doing and not doing, and so on. Narrative is . . . transmitted culturally and constrained by each individual's level of mastery and by his [sic] conglomerate of prosthetic devices, colleagues, and mentors. . . . Narratives, then, are a version of reality whose acceptability is governed by convention and "narrative necessity" rather than by empirical verification and logical requiredness. (p. 4)

Bruner distinguishes narrative thinking from the telling of narratives, but he admits that these two narrative modes blur together into indistinguishable sequences. Our thought processes often move in narrative directions as we sort out how experiences and sensations fit together and what makes sense at an intra-personal level. Narratives also are the mode through which we share experiences interpersonally, as in the telling of stories, giving of accounts and explanations for things that have happened. When we tell stories, we create what is designated "reality" through discourse. Reality in this sense can be said to be achieved through "interactional activity" (Mehan and Wood, 1997). Narratives as temporally grounded can be about the past, present or future. In telling others (and even oneself) of the past, the range of perceptions we have already experienced are selected and organized into newly formed experiences that form a story. Some of these stories are about the self and some about other people, things or events. We can all recognize our tellings of what happened in the past: "Hey, I have to tell you what happened today when I was driving to the mall . . ."; "Don't get mad about me being late. I was doing fine and then . . ."; "My girlfriend went to this new club last weekend, and . . ."; "Dan is such a jerk. We had this group project, and he was in our group, and he said he knew how to get these great visuals, but then . . ." Narratives are often prompted by someone asking for an account or a story: "How was your day?" "How did the two of you meet?" "How did you select Clark University?" "What happened to the $100 I gave you last week?" "Why did you change your mind about . . .?" We also tell others about ongoing events that are still unfolding (". . . and we just couldn't agree on how to proceed, so we left and said we'd talk about it again tomorrow"), and about projected narratives for the future ("After I finish my degree, I'm going to try to get a job in another part of the country, maybe for five years, and then . . .").

Narratives, according to Bruner (1991), are accrued, that is, they build up to "eventually create something variously called a 'culture' or a 'history' or, more loosely, a 'tradition' " (p. 18). In the larger cultural context, accrued narratives shape what is normative and expected. Stories about heterosexual couples falling in love and getting married are standard fare in the US, as are stories about career paths, child rearing, the consequences of crime and drug use, youthful (but not mature) indiscretions, and so forth. *Accrued narratives* guide people in their living by providing templates and story lines—often about how to behave, what is right and wrong, what paths are available in advancing through life, family, citizenship, labor and profession, how the social order fits together, what is just and unjust, and so forth. Accrued narratives can also be disrupted and changed. Social movements have disrupted narratives of race and gender. Advances in information technology and the advent of "24/7" have disrupted narratives related to time and the sequencing of time.

In their structure, narratives—whether interior or communicated to and constructed with others—typically have *settings*, *characters* and at least loose *plot lines* organized into a *temporal sequence* with a beginning, middle and end (or some recognizable terminal punctuation point in time even if that punctuation is like a comma to signify that something is yet to be added). In communicating with others, we regularly narrate our experiences by telling stories, and we also suggest narrative sequences to be followed in the future (sometimes labeled goals, plans, intentions, and so forth). Advertisers craft stories with settings, characters, plot lines and temporal sequences to draw upon our familiarity with narrative as a way of knowing about the world and pursuing possibilities and priorities highlighted in mass culture. Two examples illustrate how the narrative formatting works in advertising: an ad for the Toyota Highlander and an extensive advertising campaign for Jim Beam Bourbon.

The ad for the Toyota Highlander shown in Figure 6.1 ran in many magazines during 2005 and 2006, with especially high saturation in late summer and early fall. The ad presents a narrative with all the standard elements, some of which the spectator must infer. The *setting* is a college scene, which we know because of two verbal elements in the picture (the word "college" and the word "freshmen"), plus the story that unfolds. There are two *characters* in this narrative. The first character is a male, first-year college student (we infer that he is just starting college because of the "Welcome Freshmen" sign on the building) who is prominently pictured in the front left of the page amid all his belongings for college sitting on the lawn (suitcases, television, fan, skateboard, crate filled with personal items, free weights). The second character is the implied

Figure 6.1 **Toyota Highlander** (*Newsweek*, September 12, 2005).

driver of the Toyota Highlander who has just brought the boy to college. The "parent brings son/daughter to college with all their stuff at the beginning of the school year" narrative is familiar enough for the ad's spectator to easily infer that the Toyota Highlander pictured belongs to a parent of the boy, likely the boy's mother. Reading the character as the boy's mother is likely because part of the accrued gender narrative in US society is that mothers have time or make time to do things like drive their kids to college, and that it is mothers more than fathers who would celebrate freedom (from meal preparation, laundry, errands and so forth) once their children went to college. The plot line is simple and laid out in the chronological time stamps at the upper left of the ad:

5:15 pm. Dropping the kid off at college.
5:17 pm. What kid?

This is an instance of an accrued narrative in which a parent drives the child to college in the fall and then has freedom to do what she (he) wants. The yellow leaves on the green grass, tree branches, and roadway clearly place the scene as taking place in early fall. We also can read the scene as early fall because many of the tree leaves are still green. The text beneath the Toyota logo indicates that "*You* have your whole life ahead of you." The spectator can infer that *you* in this sentence is not the young man but, rather, the driver of the car—the parent. This inference is likely because this is an ad for the Toyota Highlander, which is not represented as linked to the college freshman. The narrative projects the parent into the future, now that the child is off to college and more time will be available to "make the most of it [whole life] with the Highlander's available V6, smooth ride and incredible versatility." The slightly odd element in this narrative example is that the parent apparently just dropped the son and his stuff at the side of the road and two minutes later, was gone. This element gives the narrative a fantasy quality that helps boost the spectator's fantasies about driving a Highlander.

The second illustration is taken from a print campaign for Jim Beam that ran from 1999 to 2003. The ads all centered on male friendship, with the branding tagline "Real Friends. Real Bourbon." The basic story line in these ads has to do with scenes of male friendship free of the demands and constraints of women. Tyson Smith (2005) has characterized this ad campaign as a post-feminist ironic narrative that provides an "updated script for young heterosexual males." The characters in the ads are young, White heterosexual men who are just being themselves—uncivilized, bad boys who drink "brown liquor" rather than "chick drinks," hang out," and are pretty slovenly. The layout of all the ads has a bold red background and an inserted black-and-white photo-type representation of three or four guys shown in a scene of male bonding. A verbal message, usually placed around the photo, reinforces and explains the photo in simple terms that often explicitly signify the polarity between men and women. The bottom of the page shows the tagline in white lettering on black background, and a bottle of Jim Beam is shown prominently in the bottom right of the page. The photo grounds each ad in a setting, and the main verbal element is

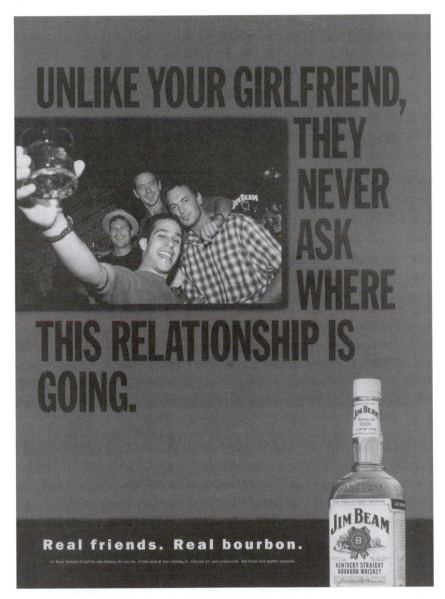

Figure 6.2 **Jim Beam** Real Friends (*Maxim*, November 1999).

linguistically structured as a declarative statement about male relationships. The example in Figure 6.2 (*Maxim*, November 1999) shows four happy-looking young men in what appears to be a bar scene. The man in the foreground holds a raised glass (of presumably Jim Beam) pushed straight out toward the camera. The photo is positioned in a manner to represent carefree photography in which a quick picture was taken without regard for framing the shot, yielding a frame that is just a little sideways.

The verbal text to accompany the photo reads: "Unlike your girlfriend, they never ask where this relationship is going." Here, the word "your" referentially points to both the men in the photo and to the male spectator of the ad, with the message that we guys are different than "they [the women]" are. The entire campaign, running for five years, extended the narrative around a theme in which an older accrued narrative of masculinity and male camaraderie was resuscitated to embolden men to, well, "be men." Each ad repeats clearly delineated characters and scenes in vignettes of male bonding that have been captured in a temporal moment through a photo. We might call this not just narrative accrual, but narrative reaccrual. This is old style male bonding over booze, represented in the image of black-and-white photography.

In his discussion of narrative accrual, Bruner (1991) points to the build-up of stories that come together as cultural knowledge and cultural lessons. In past eras, the major storytellers in society were the family and religion. The late George Gerbner, who studied television and its social impact during his long research career, saw television as the modern-day replacement for more traditional forms of story telling (Gerbner, 2003). He was specifically concerned with what he called the "mean world syndrome" in television stories and with the privileging of stories about White people to the exclusion of people of color. Gerbner came to see television as a major part of the cultural environment for everyone and as the most important part of that environment for many people. His massive list of research studies of television programming over a number of decades and with many colleagues led him to see this medium as "the monopolizing storyteller for an entire culture. Gerbner wanted to know whose story was being told and who was doing the telling" (Andersen, 2006). Gerbner might well have said that television is the focal point for what Bruner termed narrative accrual.

Gerbner and those he inspired were focused mainly on television programming, but the idea of the mediated storyteller is equally appropriate for advertising, especially in the era of brand extensions. Ads often tell stories using characters. For example, a mother has to clean up a mess in her kitchen that was made by her small child, and she is saved by "Mr Clean" or the "Swiffer Sweeper." Even today, this accrued narrative repeats in television and print advertising over and over like a broken record. Sometimes ads directly invite viewers and readers to enter into a story made possible by a particular product; for example, "You can earn an IT degree in just 6 months from IT Tech Center"; "Prom coming up? No problem. Zap that zit with . . ."; "If you can imagine it, we can get you there," which American Express used for advertising its Membership Rewards Program. Hailing the spectator is all about drawing him or her into some kind of story where the product or image being featured will bring relief, satisfaction, pleasure, entertainment, escape, efficiency, and so forth.

Combining the ideology of self-absorption, the Fifth Frame in advertising, and the possibilities of narrative yields an analytical perspective for understanding how many newer forms of Internet Brand Extension work. With advertising playing a significant role as storyteller, and the Internet providing a new frontier for story telling, the ideology of self-absorption can be played out through the Fifth Frame perspective. Four extended examples are analyzed next to show how this works.

Self-absorption and the Fifth Frame meet the Internet

In this section, four examples will be presented to demonstrate how the Fifth Frame works in Internet advertising to promote self-absorption. I have chosen examples aimed at different audiences as a way of emphasizing the flexibility and elasticity highlighting the type of narrative advertising that is emphasized in this chapter: (1) the Infiniti Black campaign addressed to middle class, adult African Americans; (2) the Brawny Man web site, which seems to have a broad appeal to both men and women of various ages because of its comedic aspects; (3) the Barbie web page addressed to young girls; and (4) BudTV, which is a new IBE of Budweiser that is directed at men. In all of these examples, the participant can engage for a considerable amount of time in the offerings of the web site—some directly keyed to the product and others only loosely associated with the product. The branding involved in these "experiences" on the web is, thus, more about the symbolic associations of the product with other experiences than with more direct product promotion.

Infiniti in Black

An advertising campaign directed at African Americans for the Infiniti luxury automobile was unveiled in November 2004. The first period in the campaign featured five Black innovators and five Infiniti models, all presented with the theme of showcasing current Black creativity. The innovators were artist Kehinde Wiley, musician Paul Miller (DJ Spooky), filmmaker Euzhan Palcy, designer Stephen Burks, and choreographer Deirdre Dawkins, each coupled with a particular model of the Infiniti. The entire first period of the campaign included print advertising, live events, billboards, illuminated street displays, television programming, and a web site (which will be the focus in the analysis that follows). Scott Fessenden, director of marketing for Infiniti, described the campaign focus this way:

Infiniti values the African American community as an important customer. With the "Infiniti in black" campaign, we hope to showcase significant achievements the African American community has made to the arts . . . The Infiniti brand represents bold personality, creative design and individuality that reflect the artistic creativity of "Infiniti in black."

(quoted in Infiniti launches phrase II, 2006)

The first print ads that I saw in this campaign were published in *Black Enterprise*, which bills itself as "the premier business, investing and wealth-building resource for African Americans, . . . the definitive source of information for and about African American business markets and leaders, and the authority on Black business news and trends." Each release of a newly featured innovator was advertised in a three-page spread: the first page provided a wall of words in the process of being painted against an urban landscape with distinctive representation of the sky. Figure 6.3 shows the first page of the February 2005 ad featuring musician Paul Miller (DJ Spooky) and the Infiniti FX45 (which is a sport utility model). The white writing on the black wall reads, "Black notes move through black rooms, reinventing notion. Break-beating, double-timing, freestyling, recreating classics, never stopping, moving forward through the darkness, enlightening the world, t//hrough a fusion of motion, style and form in black" (the // mark indicates the point in the visual image to which the painting of the words has progressed and after which we see letters stenciled but not filled in with white paint). The second page introduces the artist who is shown playing with his group in front of the black wall. The artist's name is positioned at the top left of the wall, and the web site address to "Hear a score in black" is given here. The third page shows the car in front of the same black wall. The web site at this stage of the campaign included a statement by the innovator—essentially a personal narrative—about his or her work, and an opportunity to see and/or hear the innovator's creation; the featured artists never mentioned Infiniti. The last segment of the web site presentation introduced the featured Infiniti model. The web site viewer was also informed of the date for the next installment of Infiniti in Black. The website visitor would have to come back for more—but on Infiniti's calendar.

For the next stage of this campaign, Infiniti bought program time on Black Entertainment Television (BET) for its original production titled ". . . in Black" (Infiniti drives new pitch, 2006). The 30-minute program premiered on February 9, 2006, during Black History Month. Directed by Otis Sallid (chorographer for *Malcolm* X, *Do the Right Thing, Summer of Sam* among others, sequence director for *Sister Act II*) and hosted by Elvis Mitchell (film critic who until recently wrote for the *New York Times*), this program included all five innovators spotlighted in the magazine ads and on the web site. The style of the

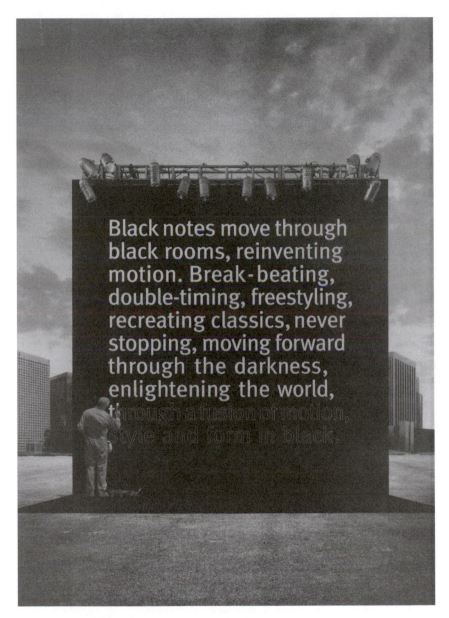

Figure 6.3 **Infiniti** Black (*Black Enterprise*, February, 2005).

visual presentation mirrored the web site by (1) using white text on a black background to communicate philosophical ideas and (2) placing the creative innovators in front of the black wall. The program included a panel discussion as well as individual profiles of the innovators. The openness of the program concept, and by inference of Black identity, was captured in the closing verbal display: "We move out of black at the speed of light traveling through black pupils, influencing how we concept it, script it, shoot it, edit it, premier it." This is followed by a sequence of white lettered verbal images on the black screen, each presented separately: "Making it drama. Making it action. Making it fantasy. Making it reality."

The third stage of the "Infiniti in Black" campaign began to unfold in mid-2006, with completely new web page content. The home page for the web site relates Infiniti the automobile with the infinite possibilities for creativity. The text is positioned in tiered format:

> Inspired by Infiniti and brought to life by three artists,
> "In Black" speaks to a place of pending brilliance
> and the infinite void where all creative spirit is born.

Like the first iteration, the series unfolds over time, with a succession of segments arriving at roughly two-month intervals. The three installments, cumulatively added to the web site, feature: Mike Thompson, urban illustrator; Shirley Jo Finney, stage and film director; and Orbert Davis, jazz artist and director of the Chicago Jazz Philharmonic. This time, the creative individuals who are featured are directly linked in the presentations to various models of the Infiniti because they have been commissioned to create something (a large urban illustration, a screenplay and performance, a jazz orchestra composition) based on the inspiration of the Infiniti. Although each artist tells her/his personal story about the creation they achieved through Infiniti's inspiration, the individual uniqueness of each is accentuated, and the web site visitor chooses what content to view. The stories—called "films"—are all in three acts: The Introduction, The Process and The Presentation. Yet, even though the creations are tied to specific Infiniti models, the theme of "infinite possibilities" runs through the narrative and textual displays. Unlike the first period of "Infiniti in Black," this second period features cars of various colors—none of them black. Also unlike the first sequence, the print advertisements, although distinctly African American in their presentation of the artists, nowhere provide the specific web site address to reach "Infiniti in Black."

At first glance, the "Infiniti in Black" advertising campaign appears as straightforward thematic Fourth Frame advertising in which products signify group-oriented consumption and the images used define "social norms (gender relations, limited ethnic mixing, socio-economic class distinctions, and a hierarchy of cultural activities)" (Leiss et al., 2005, p. 567). The campaign seeks to brand Infiniti as suitable for the aspirations of a culturally-minded affluent Black cohort (we see no people in the ads that are represented as other than

Black). Strategically, the campaign builds on Nissan Altima's standing as the car model most often purchased by African Americans and may also be oriented to drawing African Americans who buy luxury cars away from the Mercedes E-class ("Who's winning," 2005). But there is much more to the campaign that makes it a blend of Fourth and Fifth Frames. The web site in particular demonstrates all of the basic Fifth Frame characteristics. The approach is definitely "demassification" of the car-buying audience and even the Black audience. The theme of innovations and creativity in the profiles is not simply a theme of achievement but a special theme that can serve as a metaphor to arouse the spirit of creativity in the affluent Black audience. Infiniti did not chose to profile just any series of Black high achievement (surgeons, engineers, CEOs) but, rather, honed in on the group that would have potential to open the possibilities for creative thought. Fantasy is clearly invited—and it's Black fantasy accelerated by the fusion of the Infiniti models and the models of innovation and creativity that are profiled on the web site series. The way the campaign is structured also conveys a sense of individuality: eight artists to date with eight specialties and with diverse models of Infiniti.

What Infiniti offers "in Black" is narrative on a couple of levels. The first is the set of narratives about the innovators. The visitor to the web site is introduced to their stories—what they value, how they do their work, what their priorities are for expressing the Black experience. In the second period of web site stories, the story line is organized into a clear beginning, middle, and end, with the "film" for each innovator organized into three acts. The second level of narrative involves the story that the visitor to the web site can create for him- or herself. Here there is the potential for the fantasy to engage more of the qualities that Maines (1999) attributes to narrative as cultural paradigm than as story telling. The cultural narrative in question taps into upward mobility, growing affluence and the possibility that Blacks in America can have access to products associated with upward mobility even while maintaining their own values related to some nebulous Black experience that the innovators reference in a variety of different ways. For a White visitor to the site, the narrative might be perceived as more universally applicable, as in Watts and Orbe's (2002) analysis of the "Whassup" Budweiser ad campaign. Within the context of this narrative potential, the visitor has the option to build a particular story that engages any combination of innovators and Infiniti models that are displayed on the web site. In this sense, the site has high potential for self-absorption. The Fifth Frame "individual as director" role guides the web site visitor with the Infiniti as a central prop.

Finding and navigating the web site is also very Fifth Frame. Unless the person has seen a print ad for "Infiniti in Black" or the BET segment where the web site address is listed (www.infiniti.com/black), finding the site will not necessarily be possible with one URL. This is because the main Infiniti home page does not have a direct link. In the search box, the home page can be found if "Infiniti in Black" is typed. The would-be visitor to the site has to do a little work to get there. Once there, the site offers many choices: choices of which innovator to follow, which car to look at, whether or not to play the entire length of the segments or to stop the player or possibly replay an entire segment. The web site can also be construed as educational and entertainment-rich. If the visitor does not want to look at the cars closely, that is not required—even in the second version of the on-line series of innovators (in this case, the visitor can skip over most of the material directly related to the car that is featured). The production values are high, and the profiled innovators are visually attractive and engaging in their verbal expression. The timing of the productions seems unrushed and relaxed—which is another way of stimu-lating the fantasies that are suggested by the artists who metaphorically move the web experience along for the viewer.

"Infiniti in Black" is a retreat from the masses and a place to celebrate personal success, creativity, dreams, or any of these separately or together. With this campaign, Infiniti is extending its branding to the value of Black creative arts and to Black achievement and disposable income. These cars, after all, carry price tags ranging from the mid-$30,000 to above $50,000. As a celebration of the potential of affluent Blacks who might decide to channel their affluence toward the purchase of an Infiniti, the branding is clear. At the same time, the viewer is not required to have any real interest in buying an Infiniti to enjoy navigating the web site. The creations of the featured innov-ators are themselves interesting, and the aesthetics of the production alone can keep one's attention. The campaign does attempt to capitalize on Black images and the value of Black expression as a way to link these ideas to Infiniti's brand recognition, but in so doing, the political implications are quite limited because of the demographic profile of the market segment for whom the web site is suit-able and potentially attractive. Yet, with expenditures upwards to $10 million on the campaign (McMains, 2006), Infiniti was banking on some payoff not only in sales but in broader recognition of Black achievement, defined here as artistic achievement. The campaign, however, is sheltered from the White audience, which minimizes its message of support for Black artists and innov-ation. What if Nissan (the parent company) or Infiniti had celebrated Black arts and expression on its main website? The political implications would have been more far-reaching but also more risky for the company.

A new Fifth Frame "Brawny Man"

Moving from high culture to a more popular form of cultural entertainment and promotion, I next examine the case of the new Fifth Frame version of

Brawny Man—the icon of Brawny towels. The Brawny Man has been around since the 1970s, seen mainly in television commercials played during daytime programming. He has undergone some changes over the years, but 2004 was the big makeover year (Atkinson, 2004). Brawny Man's hair was changed from blond to brown, his strong body made more visible, and his denim shirt traded in for a plaid flannel version under which he wears a white t-shirt. In 2006, the new Brawny Man came to life in the web site named Brawny Academy. The web site (brawnyman.com) was advertised in print and television spots prior to its opening.

Brawny Man Academy is a mock-serious parody of the makeover of eight men who have been sent by the women in their lives to camp in the woods so that Brawny Man can clean up their acts and they can become "better men" (we learn in one of the episodes that two of the men are shills for the Brawny Man and have been sent to the camp to help the process of developing these men). The web site was host to eight 9–13 minute installments of the camp experience, told in a narrative structure with a clear temporal sequence. The first episode was released on June 12, 2006, and the other seven followed at two-week intervals. At the opening of the first episode, the Brawny Man is listening to birds singing in the woods, which reminds him, as he says it, of "what's important, [pause in his speech] like being a dependable, strong yet caring man."

Each episode has a theme and a lesson to be learned, and by the end of the seventh installment, the men are ready to host the women in their lives, who will arrive at the camp and be shocked by the lovely arrangements of furniture and decorations in the cabins. Along the way to this finale, we see the men learn to fix a nasty plumbing repair, run with boulders in their arms to build their strength, but also write down a bad habit on a piece of paper, read it aloud to the others, and then burn it. In one episode, they are visited by a female sex therapist, who has a frank discussion with each of them. In the last installment, the Brawny Man is host to a cotillion complete with the men in tuxedos and the women in evening dresses. It is here that the men display their gentlemanly manners, poise, as well as the fruits of their cooking skills. Every episode opens and closes with a twangy, western-style theme song. The narrative series is created for laughs, and every now and then, here and there, a paper towel is used to deal with a mess or some other need.

The narrative of the overall Brawny Man Academy stories is about hetero-sexual relationships and the desire of women for their male partners to be more caring, helpful, and revealing of their feelings. As advertising for Brawny towels, this is clearly in the realm of Internet Brand Extension, where the extension associates the product with lighthearted domesticity and entertain-ment with a message. In line with this, John Bowman, brand manager for Brawny, is quoted as saying, "Our approach hasn't been to focus on the technical attributes. It's to drive better brand affinity by making a more emotional connection" (quoted in Neff, 2006). There's nothing very radical about the scenarios; in fact, the idea of "civilizing" the male beast seems old-hat. It's the parody that makes the series entertaining. The viewer can take it seriously, laugh at it, talk about it, or pass it on to a friend or to the man in her life (the series is likely intended for women, although the men in my classes have found it very entertaining, and Brawny Man also has connotations that give it appeal as a version of gay male masculinity).

The Fifth Frame aspects of brawnyman.com involve choices that the visitor to the web site can make—take it or leave it. As the series unfolded, the viewer had to wait for the next episode, but once they had all been added to the web site, the viewer could pick and choose, watch in any order, replay episodes they enjoy, and watch particular parts of episodes using the player functions. The web site also includes a questionnaire called the Brawny Academy Quiz—"Is your man like the Brawny Man?" Once the multiple choice questionnaire has been completed (the answer options include realistic things a man might do plus more outrageous options), a profile is displayed (presumably based on the answers) followed by advice given to the woman telling her which episode of Brawny Academy she should encourage her man to watch. As the viewer engages the web site, she (or he) may get that Fifth Frame sense of life "as a script-writing exercise" (Leiss et al., 2005, p. 568).

Barbie in Internet land

This next example of Fifth Frame self-absorption begins with Barbie, whose life is now approaching three decades. What we have today, however, is a revitalized Barbie who is the gateway through Barbie.com to a wide range of ways to pass the time of day on the Internet. I selected the Barbie website for focus because it is aimed at tweens and early teens and, thus, demonstrates the ways in which the Fifth Frame works to its fullest with younger consumer culturalists who are accustomed to surfing the Internet and maneuvering links.

The best metaphor I can think of for the Barbie.com site is hyperactive. After Barbie.com has been typed in, the site that appears with the URL Barbie.everythinggirl.com is filled with choices, making it the perfect place for seemingly "limitless possibilities for fast paced rearrangements of the setting" and "relentlessly active" experiences (Leiss et al., 2005, p. 567). The Barbie icon on the home page immediately greets the visitor with a chatty, "Hey, I'm Barbie. I'm so glad you're here." On that page are various choices: decorate the page and make it your home page; check out the Barbie advertisements that have been on TV; link to "Chat Divas"; find out what's at "Fashion Fever"; go to "B-TV"; look at what's next on "Magic of the Rainbow"; or engage in "Fun and Games." Links across the top of the page are for Parents, Collectors, Global Barbie (which provides choices for eight different languages plus UK and US English), and Shop with Barbie. Even farther up on the top of the home page are rolling links to Polly Pocket, Teen Trends, Pixel Chix, and MyScene. Each of these, in turn, offers a range of options for the visitor's choice.

Several examples will suffice to provide some orientation to what is available through this web site. From the Barbie.com homepage, the visitor can link to Polly Pocket and from there can link to "My Scene." Here there are games (including "Shop 'til you Drop" and makeovers), "My Freebies" hyped with the invitation that "You can be a downloadin' diva too"; buddy icons; "sassy mani-cure"; and "stylin' bedroom" activities. From the "Teen Trends" link on My Scene, the visitor is invited to "Meet the Girls." There are four of them, named Kianna (dark haired but ethnically unclear), Deondra (likely intended to be perceived as Latina), Courtney and Gabby (both of whom are White). Kianna says she's "edgy, independent, rocker chic." Deondra says, "My vibe is dance, fashion & bling, baby" (rather stereotypic for the Latina-appearing representa-tion). Courtney's "faves" are "soccer, horses & hitting the beach" (which sounds very suburban upper-middle class White girl). Gabby loves "being a girly girl!" and says that "pink is my #1 color!" The visitor can also answer some questions to find out which of these girls she is most like. Kianna, for example, speaks to the visitor in a stylized, teenage girl's voice to say a few things about herself and her room: "*This is my slammin' room. I'm into writing, going to rock concerts and experimenting with fashion. Move over my stuff [on the web page] to find out more.*" As the cursor moves across the page and lands on various items in the room, the items are labeled on screen and vocal descriptions are activated. For example when the cursor lands on a guitar, the label is "My too-cool guitar." The Kianna representation then speaks—presumably to the visitor, saying, "Wanna be a rocker? Me too."

This web site with all its options appears almost endless. The visitor chooses what she wants to do, how she would like to fashion her identity, whom she will emulate, and what she will leave behind. Self-absorption is high level. In this generation of advertising through IBE, Barbie has become the portal to a host of fun activities and personally constructed narratives, made possible by the pre-fabricated, vapid narratives placed on the site. The young girl navigat-ing the site will most certainly be unaware that all of the products and char-acters featured through the links are Mattel products. Because everything on the site is so cutesy and girlie-girl, the political slant is very conservative—in fact reactionary. The Fifth Frame approach makes it appear that the visitor has a broad range of possibilities to create her personal narrative that are just a click away. The choices, in fact, are quite limited by the ideological slant of the gender scripts that define the characters on the site and delimit what is available for creating personal stories for the visitor.

Mattel also owns Tyco, maker of Hot Wheels and Matchbox Cars. The websites for these products are clear evidence of the gender polarization that exists in the toy and entertainment industry for youth. The Hot Wheels home page blasts aggressive, loud music as background for the many choices that are available for games, shopping, various downloads, and what is termed "cool stuff" to create the verbal image of trendy, guy-friendly interests. The narrative offered for the boys exploits themes of the wild, reckless, adventuresome, out-of-control kid who can fashion an identity through the choices offered on the homepage. If the Barbie web site is metaphorically hyperactive, then the Hot Wheel site is XL-hyperactive.

The Fifth Frame for Mattel thus relies on the Fourth Frame to structure gender identities in a segmented manner. Having chosen the appropriate gender category, the visitor to the web site is offered an extravaganza of choices to meet personal preferences within the constraints of what Mattel has to offer girls and boys in its highly gender-stereotyped display of verbal and visual images. This gender-polarizing approach is entirely consistent with how toys have been marketed and advertised for years (Johnson and Young, 2002; Larson, 2001). The difference is that there now exists the illusion of choice and individualization through Fifth Frame web strategy.

BudTV

Budweiser beer is well known for its creative, engaging advertising. Millions of people in the US and elsewhere watch the "Superbowl" each January in anticipation of entertaining and highly creative ads, but there is always special expectation for Budweiser. Budweiser has for years worked with themes that function essentially as narrative episodes: the frogs in various vignettes croaking out "Bud—why—zer" and the "Whassup" guys doing guy things are widely recognized for their narrative formats. Now Budweiser is into something entirely different—something very Fifth Frame-oriented and steeped in multiple narrative possibilities.

BudTV debuted in February 2007 as a web site carrying video programming, games, comedy segments, and other features. Reports estimate that Anheuser-Busch spent approximately $30 million on this new venture in the first year as part of its annual advertising budget of over $1 billion (Deagon, 2007). When I reviewed BudTV in March, just one month after it opened, I found a range of options. Kevin Spacey provided the welcome to BudTV along with a plug for his web site, TriggerStreet.com, which he characterized as "a site that serves as a showcase for those interested in pursuing their passion in making movies."

Spacey tells the visitor to BudTV that he (she) will be able to see movies from his Trigger Street venture, which is supported by Anheuser-Busch. The home page for the Trigger Street site clearly announces Budweiser Select sponsorship (Select is a Budweiser label introduced in 2005 that is designed, according to the Budweiser web site, to be "a new kind of beer brewed for a crisp taste that finishes clean.") In later weeks, the home page opens with a humorous mini-movie advertisement for Budweiser. Other contents displayed on the home page were:

- an episode of a comedy series, set in the backseat of a taxi, titled "Joe Buck Show," which the viewer can rate, share, download, or add to "faves";
- "Do You Want to Break Into Hollywood" which asks the visitor to enter a contest called "FINISH OUR MOVIE" by writing the *middle* section for an incomplete movie (the winner gets to write, direct, and edit something for BudTV);
- a video of the 2007 *Sports Illustrated* Swimsuit Edition party;
- a NASCAR video feature on Dale Earnhardt, Jr.;
- a comedy news program called "Hardly News";
- something called "Spring Jam—a Kardboard Derby Race";
- an episode of "Sebastian," who is a stand-up comedian;
- a feature on the NBA playoffs; and
- "Truly Famous—Orlando Hotel Fake," which is a short video about star imposters who scam a hotel.

All totaled, quite a lot of time can be spent with the site, and there are various options to pursue after a site visit. There are plenty of opportunities to follow up, for example, the next episode of "The Joe Buck Show" or the latest additions of short films.

Like the other web sites I have described, BudTV is firmly anchored in an identity category. This is primarily a male site steeped in hyper-masculinity and the "manly man." Connell and Messerschmidt (2005), in their analysis of changes in the concept of hegemonic masculinity, describe its foundation "as a [normative] pattern of practice (i.e. things done, not just a set of role expectations or an identity) that allowed men's dominance over women to continue" (p. 832). As challenges to this type of brute masculinity evolved over the past several decades, the concept of the more sensitive man emerged, as did the style called "metrosexual." The "manly man" idea appears to be a response to these developments by moving back to old forms of masculinity that embrace what Mark Simpson (2003) was first to characterize as "retrosexual." BudTV embraces the conventional interests of men (sports, women in bathing suits, swearing, farting jokes), making it "retro-" to older mores of masculinity.

Yet, it's not a replica of these older forms, which would not have embraced filmmaking and some of the spoofs that can be seen through links on this web site. It is precisely this tension between conventional masculinity and the breaks from it that give BudTV its Fifth Frame-ness. The narratives offered through the links, as well as the narratives that the visitor can fashion for himself (including the possibilities of telling stories of BudTV to others), are not as rigid as the older forms of hegemonic masculinity. To navigate this site requires self-indulgence, which is signified at every turn by the unexpected appearance of a Budweiser somewhere in the scene. The retro quality makes it not a copy of previous masculinities but, rather, a stylized pick-and-choose set of masculinities that exists in opposition to femininities. The old branding of "This Bud's for you" applies to BudTV in an interesting way. The web site essentially "speaks" to its visitor by saying that Budweiser is giving you, a guy (manly man), this place/site for retreat from the barrage of social expectations for you to be a kinder, gentler, new-style man.

Conclusions and implications

In this chapter, I have considered a particular type of Internet Brand Extension that has proliferated in recent years. This IBE encourages self-absorption through what has been called the Fifth Frame strategy for advertising—the strategy that positions the consumer in a seemingly active role as creator of his/her own script through which to make use of the products and images that are circulated through advertising.

Furthermore, I have emphasized the ways in which narrative as a discourse form is especially well suited to Fifth Frame IBEs catering to self-absorption. Certainly not all IBE strategies make use of the Fifth Frame, nor do all IBE campaigns cater to an ideology of self-absorption. Yet, when companies are interested in creatively approaching the potential consumer, using the flexibility of the Fifth Frame to position the consumer in a seemingly active role relative to the product provides a good match with practices of Internet exploration. Internet users have become accustomed to finding their own way, to choosing what to attend to, and to taking side routes through links that they encounter. Unlike the print ad, which is either seen or not seen, attended to or passed by, the IBE developed with Fifth Frame strategy and narrative structures offers options within the advertising, making it more a continuum of attention than an either–or phenomenon. The IBEs that are closely examined in this chapter take the form of multiple-choice web sites—lots of fixed choices, but in the end, openness with distinct boundaries and limitations. Spending time with these sites and others like them is one form of web indulgence that functions as a retreat into personal interests. As cultural texts that are shaping practices for Internet use, IBEs in this case raise questions about agency, the relationship of the individual to the process of branding, and about what retreat into Fifth Frame narratives might mean in a broader socio-political context.

In the analysis of the Barbie website, I called attention to the limitations of the type of agency that advertising offers to its viewers and potential consumers, labeling it oxymoronic agency—an agency coupled with constraints. The Fifth Frame approach makes it appear as though the consumer has choice, especially in Internet environments where links are optional and plentiful. Yet, there are many constraints on choices because the choices are always provided for a particular anticipated market. Agency is a more superficial illusion than actual empowerment. This type of oxymoronic agency may heighten a web site visitor's sense of choice and freedom, but IBE will always be about *brand* in some way, with all the choice possible in the service of the branding strategy. The Brawny Man, regardless of how humorous his Brawny Academy persona and students may be, is associated with Brawny towels, which are associated mainly with female domesticity. A web site visitor can choose which of the segments to watch and laugh out loud at the humor, but the visitor is still in the cultural corral of strained gender relations. The stories in the various episodes are part of the pile of narratives concerning the battle of the sexes, and Fifth Frame choice channels agency into a limited number of scripts.

A second question raised by the type of advertising dealt with in this chapter concerns the relationship of the individual to branding. How and to what extent is the individual branded through IBEs involving Fifth Frame strategy? Although there is no definitive answer to this question, we can speculate about what it means to be engaged in extended Internet activity that exploits various Fifth Frame elements with branding always lurking in the background either explicitly or implicitly. "Infiniti in Black" is about brand up front, but each segment begins not with the car, but with the Black innovator. Corporate image lies behind every aspect of the advertising campaign, and the attempt here is clearly to associate Infiniti with respect and admiration for the accomplishments of creative Black innovators. The Black person who visits the web site (or watches the BET program) is being asked to respect Infiniti (and Nissan) for respecting them. The discourse of respect in this case stays at the margins in several ways. First, the discourse hails the middle class and affluent Black person by drawing them into a place where they might be branded with a commodity image that has not yet been theirs—probably because Infiniti made no earlier effort to draw this group into its branding strategy. Second, the innovators used to hail the Black spectator are polished, carefully directed, and above all else, creative. What are African Americans praised for in addition to sports? Music, art, dance, a flare for design—in short, expression. Third, the location of the advertising itself is marginalized. If you cannot find the web site easily, those who are featured within it and those who are hailed to visit it are diminished and once again marginalized. To be in the center of the advertising campaign but at the same time to be marginalized within the broader discourse of the parent company is another type of oxymoron. This time it is oxymoronic centering, where the centering is contradicted by the larger discourse in which it exists.

Like the Infiniti campaign, each of the other three examples relies on cultural conceptions of fixed identity. Whereas Infiniti depends on polarized race, the others depend on polarized and polarizing gender. Brawny works only if gender polarization is stressed. Barbie.com works only if gender polarization is stressed. BudTV works only if gender polarization is stressed. These applications of the Fifth Frame strategy use narratives to create personal stories, but the personal stories and choices available all place the consumer neatly into an identity box. The illusion of choice and freedom in navigating the websites may even retard recognition of how rigidly the IBE sponsors use deeply implanted cultural codes for identity to advance their branding and product promotions.

The third question pertains to self-absorption in web sites that allow the individual to linger for the benefit of a corporate sponsor. What are the implications for democracy of dalliance in IBE productions steeped in narrative possibilities? Explicit voting in frivolous contests is now standard fare on the Internet. More indirect voting by deciding what link to follow on the web site for Brawny or BudTV is still voting in the guise of self-empowerment. To the extent that consumers choose to spend time with Internet sites produced as advertising, they are not spending time on other endeavors or with people. The Internet offers many valuable options for those who have access to it, but when advertising takes its stories to the Internet, the potential for escalated self-absorption is high. When part of IBEs, narratives are about drawing the individual into a world of self-orientation through a semblance of self-design. When products become portals to a particular world of stories, we need to be concerned about the role of advertising in influencing the directions of cultural change. Do these developments in the Internet "create a fragmented culture in which individuals pursue narrow personal agendas at the expense of larger social concerns?" (Campbell et al., 2007, p. 223) The expansive prompts for creating personal narrative fantasies that populate many advertising websites and the many options for advertainment on others easily isolate real, living people from one another. Sut Jhally's (2000) statement about values in relation to advertising is a sobering warning. Advertising, warns Jhally, "addresses us not as members of society talking about collective issues, but as individuals . . . The market appeals to the worst in us (greed, selfishness) and discourages what is best about us (compassion, caring, and generosity)" (p. 33). The threats in advertising's address to the individual became more serious with the advent of Internet Brand Extension in the Fifth Frame. The Internet is like a vortex, drawing more and more time from more and more alternatives into its center. As the Internet becomes increasingly used by advertisers for brand extension programming, a society already preoccupied with self-orientation and "me-me-me" moves a little farther away from productive, collective activity.

References

Abelson, J. (2005, August 7). Gillette tries to capture a whiff of teen market. *Boston Globe*. Retrieved January 3, 2007 from http://www.boston.com/business/articles/2005/08/07/gillette_tries_to_capture_a_whiff_of_teen_market/

Acne. (2006). Acne Encyclopedia article. Retrieved September 8, 2006 from http://www.bookrags.com

Acne Vulgaris. (2005). A–Z health guide from WebMD: Health Topics. Retrieved May 17, 2006 from http://www.webmd.com

Acne, zits and pimples. (2006). Retrieved September 1, 2006 from http://parentingteens.about.com/cs/acne/a/acne.htm

Althusser, L. (1970). *For Marx* (B. Brewster, Trans.). New York: Vintage.

Althusser, Louis. (1971/2001). *Lenin and philosophy and other essays* (B. Brewster, trans.). New York: Monthly Review Press. (Original work published 1971.)

American Academy of Dermatology. (2005). Frequently Asked Questions about Acne. Acne net. Retrieved September 1, 2006 from http://www.skincarephysicians.com/acnenet/FAQ.html

American Academy of Dermatology. (n.d.) Acne. Retrieved September 7, 2006 from http://www.aad.org/public/Publications/pamphlets/Acne.htm

American Cancer Society. (2004). Questions about smoking, tobacco, and health. Retrieved January 28, 2005 from http://www.cancer.org/docroot/PED/content/PED_10_2x_Questions_About_Smoking_Tobacco_and_Health.asp?sitearea=PED

American Lung Association. (2003). Fact sheet: African Americans and tobacco, June 2002. http://www.lungusa.org/tobacco/african_factsheet99.html

American Lung Association. (2004, November). Smoking and African Americans fact sheet. Retrieved January 19, 2005 from http://www.lungusa.org/site/pp.asp?c+dvLUK9O0E&b=3598

Andersen, R. (2006, March/April). George Gerbner, 1919–2005—From anti-fascist fighter to cultural environmentalist. *Fairness and Accuracy in Reporting*. Retrieved December 3, 2006 from http://www.fair.org/index.php?page=2881

Arnette, J. J. (2001). Adolescents' responses to cigarette advertisements for five "youth brands" and one "adult brand". *Journal of Research on Adolescence*, *11*, 425–43.

Arnould, E. J. & Thompson, C. J. (2005). Consumer culture theory (CTT): Twenty years of research [Electronic version]. *Journal of Consumer Research*, *31*, 868–82.

Atkinson, C. (2004, February 16). $20 million makeover: Brawny man now a metrosexual. *Advertising Age*, 75 (7), p. 8.

Audit Bureau of Circulations. (2006). eCirc for Consumer Magazines. Retrieved March 2007 from http://abcas3.accessabccom/ecirc/index.htm/

Bailey, B. (2001). The language of multiple identities among Dominican Americans. *Journal of Linguistic Anthropology*, 10, 190–223.

Baker, C. N. (2005). Images of women's sexuality in advertisements: A content analysis of Black- and White-oriented women's and men's magazines. *Sex Roles*, 52, 13–27.

Balbach, E. D., Gasior, R. J. & Barbeau, E. M. (2003). R. J. Reynolds' targeting of African Americans: 1988–2000. *American Journal of Public Health*, 93, 822–7.

Bang, H.-K. & Reece, B. R. (2003). Minorities in children's television commercials: New, improved, and stereotyped. *Journal of Consumer Affairs*, 37, 42–67.

Binns, C. (2006). Zit myths cleared up. Special to LiveScience. Retrieved September 12, 2006 from http://www.livescience.com/humanbiology/060904_zits_myth.html

Birchall, J. (2007, January 10). Size matters in challenges to turn round Gap's fortunes. *Financial Times* (London). Retrieved March 2, 2007 from Lexis-Nexis database.

BMW Hire Films end. (2005). Retrieved May 20, 2007 from http://www.duncans.tv/2005/bmw-short-films

Bollier, D. (2005). *Brand name bullies: The quest to own and control culture*. Hoboken, NJ: John Wiley.

Borio, G. (1997). The history of tobacco Part IV. The History Net. Retrieved March 20, 2005 from http://www.historian.org/bysubject/tobacco4.htm

Botox Product and Service Market. (2006, June). *Feed-back.com E-zine*, 9 (2). Retrieved April 2, 2007 from http://www.feed-back.com/jun06ezine.htm

Bristor, J. M., Lee, R. G. & Hunt, M. R. (1995). Race and ideology: African American images in television advertising. *Journal of Public Policy and Marketing*, 14, 48–59.

Bruner, J. (1991). The narrative construction of reality. *Critical Inquiry*, 18, 1–21.

Butler, J. (1993). *Bodies that matter: On the discursive limits of "sex"*. New York: Routledge.

Butler, J. (1999/original 1990). *Gender Trouble: Feminism and the subversion of identity*, 10th anniversary edition. New York: Routledge.

Campbell, R., Martin, C. R. & Fabos, B. (2007). *Media and Culture*, 5th edn. Boston: Bedford/St Martin's.

Carter, M. (2004, March 22). Media: New Media: drivetime on the web? *Guardian* (London). Retrieved March 18, 2006 from Lexis-Nexis database.

Center for the Digital Future. (2005). Fifth study of the internet by the Digital Future Project finds major new trends in online use for political campaigns. Los Angeles: USC Annenberg School for Communications. Retrieved May 13, 2006 from http://digitalcenter.org

Centers for Disease Control and Prevention. (2003). African Americans and tobacco. Retrieved February 3, 2004 from http://www.cdc.gov/tobacco/sgr/sgr_1998/sgr-min-fs-afr.htm

Centers for Disease Control and Prevention. (2004). Percentage of adults who were current, former, or never smokers, overall and by sex, race, Hispanic origin, age, education, and poverty status. National Health Interview Surveys, Selected Years—United States, 1965–2004. Retrieved August 20, 2007, from http://www.cdc.gov/tobacco/data_statistics/tables/adult/table_2.htm

Centers for Disease Control and Prevention. (2006a). Smoking and tobacco use—Fact sheet, Youth and tobacco use: current estimates. Retrieved May 8, 2007 from http://www.cdc.gov/tobacco/data_statistics?Factsheets/youth_tobacco.htm

Centers for Disease Control and Prevention. (2006b). Smoking and tobacco use—Fact sheet, Health Effects of cigarette smoking. Retrieved May 8, 2007 from http://cdc.gov/tobacco/data_statistics/Factsheets/health_effects.htm

Centers for Disease Control and Prevention. (2006c). Tobacco use among adults— United States, 2005. Retrieved May 8, 2007 from http://www.cdc.gov/mmwr/preview/mmwrhtml/mm5542a1.htm

Centers for Disease Control and Prevention. Office of Women's Health. (1996). Tobacco use. Retrieved November 8, 1999 from http://www.cdc.gov/od/owh/whtob.htm

Chouliaraki, L. & Fairclough, N. (1999). *Discourse in Late Modernity: Rethinking critical discourse analysis*. Edinburgh: Edinburgh University Press.

Clark, J. (2001). All the access money can buy. *A List Apart* #15. Retrieved May 10, 2007 from http://alistapart.com/articles/alltheaccess/

clear. (n.d.). *Merriam-Webster's Medical Dictionary*. Retrieved September 14, 2006 from Dictionary.com website: http://dictionary.reference.com/search?q=clear

Collins, P. H. (2004). *Black Sexual Politics*. New York: Routledge.

Connell, R. W. & Messerschmidt, J. W. (2005). Hegemonic masculinity: Rethinking the concept. *Gender and Society*, *19*, 829–59.

Cook, G. (2001). *The Discourses of Advertising* (2nd edn). London: Routledge.

Cortese, A. J. (2004). *Provocateur: Images of women and minorities in advertising* (2nd edn). Lanthan, MD: Rowan and Littlefield.

Cullen, L. T. (2002, July 29). Changing faces. *Time Magazine*. Retrieved June 19, 2006 from http://www.time.com.printout/0,8816,501020805-332097,00.html

Cummings, K. M. Giovino, G. & Mendicino, A. J. (1987). Cigarette advertising and black–white differences in brand preference. *Public Health Reports*, *102*, 698–701.

Damsky, L. (1999). Beauty secrets. In O. Edut (ed.), *Young women write about body image and identity* (pp. 133–143). Seattle: Seal Press.

Daniels, C. (2007). *Ghettonation*. New York: Doubleday.

Das, A. (2007, January 21). The search for beautiful. *Boston Globe Magazine*, 23–4, 33–5.

Deagon, B. (2007, February 28). With Budweiser's Web TV push, this channel's for you. *Investor's Business Daily*. Retrieved May 2, 2007 from Lexis-Nexis database.

Degrassi: The Next Generation. Retrieved February 2, 2007 from http://www.tv.com/degrassi-the-next-generation/show/6810/summary.html

DiFranza, J. R., Richards, J. W., Paulman, P. M., Wolf-Gillispie, N., Fletcher, C., Jaffee, R. D. & Murray, D. (1991). RJR Nabisco's cartoon camel promotes Camel cigarettes to children. *Journal of the American Medical Association*, *22*, 3,149–3,153.

Dyer, R. (1993). *The Matter of Images: Essays on representation*. London: Routledge.

Eckert, P. & McConnell-Ginet, S. (1999). New generalizations and explanations in language and gender research. *Language in Society*, *28*, 185–201.

Fairclough, G. (2000, June 12). Philip Morris removes slogan from ads in second attempt responding to critics. *Wall Street Journal*. Retrieved May 14, 2007 from Lexis-Nexis database.

Fairclough, N. (1995). *Media Discourse*. London: Arnold.

Federal Trade Commission. (2001). Cigarette report for 1999. Retrieved from: http://www.ftc.gov/opa/2001/03/cigarette/htm

Federal Trade Commission. (2007). Cigarette report for 2004–2005. Retrieved from: http://www.ftc.gov/reports/tobacco/2007cigarette2004–2005.pdf

Ferguson, R. (1998). *Representing Race: Ideology, identity and the media*. New York: Arnold.

Fischer, P. M., Schwartz, M. P., Richards, J. W. Jr., Goldstein, A. O. & Rojas, T. H. (1991). Brand logo recognition by children aged 3 to 6 years. Mickey Mouse and Old Joe the Camel. *Journal of the American Medical Association*, *22*, 3,145–3,148.

Fowles, Jib. (1996). *Advertising and Popular Culture*. Thousand Oaks, CA: Sage Publications.

Fox, S. (2004, March 25). Older Americans and the Internet. Washington, DC: Pew Research Center. Retrieved June 6, 2006 from http://www.pewinternet.org/PPF/r/117/report_display.asp

Frith, K. T. (1997). Undressing the ad: Reading culture in advertising. In K. T. Frith (ed.), *Undressing the ad* (pp. 1–17). New York: Peter Lang.

Gardiner, P. S. (2004, February). The African Americanization of menthol cigarette use in the United States. *Nicotine and Tobacco Research*, *6*, Suppl 1: S55–65.

Gee, J. P. (1992). *The Social Mind: Language, ideology, and social practice*. New York: Bergin and Garvey.

Geis, M. (1982). *The Language of Television Advertising*. New York: Academic Press.

Gerbner, G. (2003). Television violence—At a time of turmoil and terror. In G. Dines & J. M. Humez (eds), *Gender, race and class in media: A text reader* (2nd edn, pp. 547–57). Thousand Oaks, CA: Sage.

Gerson, J. (2007, April 23). Social networking rivals porn on Web. *Toronto Star*. Retrieved April 29, 2007 from Lexis-Nexis database.

Goffman, E. (1974). *Frame analysis*. New York: Harper Colophon.

Goldman, R. (1992). *Reading ads socially*. London: Routledge.

Goldman, R. & Papson, S. (1996). *Sign Wars—The cluttered landscape of advertising*. New York: Guilford Press.

Greenberg, B. S. & Brand, J. E. (1993). Cultural diversity on Saturday morning television. In G. L. Berry & J. K. Asamen (eds), *Children and television: Images in a changing sociocultural world* (pp. 133–42). Newbury Park, CA: Sage Publications.

Grossberg, L., Wartella, E. & Whitney, D. C. (1998). *Mediamaking: Mass media in a popular culture*. Thousand Oaks, CA: Sage Publications.

Hall, S. (1981). The whites of their eyes: Racist ideologies and the media. In G. Bridges & R. Brunt (eds), *Silver linings* (pp, 28–52). London: Lawrence and Wishart.

Hall, S. (ed.). (1997). *Representation: Cultural representations and signifying practices*. Thousand Oaks, CA: Sage Publications.

Hay, A. (2006, September 13). Outrage over fashion skinny model ban. Reuters. Retrieved   March   4,   2005   from   http://www.news.com.au/story/0,23599,20403593-13762,00.html

Health disparities experienced by Black or African Americans—United States [Electronic version]. (2005). *Morbidity and Mortality Weekly Report*, *54*, 1–3.

Hecht, M. L., Collier, M. J. & Ribeau, S. A. (1993). *African American communication: Ethnic identity and cultural interpretation*. Thousand Oaks, CA: Sage Publications.

Herman, E. (2004, October 2004). Cigarette maker cuts hip-hop ads. *Chicago Sun-Times*. Retrieved June 12, 2006 from Lexis-Nexis database.

Hoefer, M., Rytina, N. & Campbell, C. (2006, August). Estimates of the unauthorized immigrant population residing in the United States: January 2005. *Population*

Estimates. Washington, DC: Department of Homeland Security Office of Immigration Statistics.

Howe, D. (2002, November 8). A fresh batch of BMW films. *Washington Post*. Retrieved March 18, 2006 from Lexis-Nexis database.

Ignelzi, R. J. (2004, August 17). Face-saving; Marketing to men, cosmetic companies take the stigma out of styling products. *San Diego Union-Tribune*, p. E1. Retrieved July 18, 2006 from Lexis-Nexis database.

Infiniti drives new pitch with original TV program. (2006, January 2). *Brandweek*, p. 3. Retrieved February 20, 2006 from Lexis-Nexis database.

Infiniti launches Phase II of "Infiniti black" campaign. (2006, January 18). *Business Wire*. Retrieved May 8, 2007 from Lexis-Nexis database.

Interactive Advertising Bureau. (2007, March 7). Internet advertising revenues estimated at $16.8 billion for full year 2006. Retrieved May 2, 2007 from http://www.iab.net/news/pr_2007_03_07.asp

International Communications Research. (2005). Girl power: Teen girls spend more than boys. Retrieved September 7, 2005 from http://www.icrsurvey.com/Study.aspx?f=Teen_Survey_0805.html

Jhally, S. (2000). Advertising at the edge of the apocalypse. In R. Anderson & L. Strate (eds), *Critical studies in media commercialism* (pp. 27–39). Oxford, UK: Oxford University Press.

Jhally, S. (2003). Image-based culture—Advertising and popular culture. In G. Dines & J. M. Humez (eds), *Gender, race and class in media: A text reader* (2nd edn, pp. 249–57). Thousand Oaks, CA: Sage.

Johnson, F. L. & Young, K. (2002). Gendered voices in children's television advertising. *Critical Studies in Media Communication, 19*, 461–80.

Johnson, L. & Learned, A. (2004). *Don't think pink: What really makes women buy—and how to increase your share of this crucial market*. New York: AMACOM American Management Association.

Jones, V. E. (2007, April 25). The ghetto culture machine—What goes wrong when stereotypes become part of the mainstream. *Boston Globe*. Retrieved April 26, 2007 from Lexis-Nexis database.

Kantrowitz, B. & Wingert, P. (1999, October 18). The truth about tweens. *Newsweek*, 62.

Kilbourne, J. (1999). *Can't buy my love: How advertising changes the way we think and feel*. New York: Simon and Schuster.

Kilbourne, J. (2000). *Killing Us Softly 3* [video]. Northampton, MA: Media Education Foundation.

Kimmel, M. (1994). Masculinity as homophobia. In H. Brod & M. Kaufman (eds), *Theorizing masculinities*, pp. 119–41. Thousand Oaks, CA: Sage Publications.

LaGuardia, C. (ed.). (2005). *Magazines for libraries* (14th edn). New Providence, NJ: Bowker.

Lakoff, G. & Johnson, M. (1980; 2003). *Metaphors we live by*. Chicago: University of Chicago Press.

Larson, M. S. (2001). Interactions, activities and gender in children's television commercials: A content analysis. *Journal of Broadcasting and Electronic Media, 45*, 41–56.

Leigh, J. H. (1994). The use of figures of speech in print ad headlines. *Journal of Advertising, 23* (2), 17–33.

Leiss, W., Kline, S., Jhally, S. & Botterill, J. (2005). *Social communication in advertising: Consumption in the mediated marketplace* (3rd edn). New York: Routledge.

Lenhart, A., Madden, M. & Hitlin, P. (2005, July 27). *Teens and technology: Youth are leading the transition to a fully wired and mobile nation*. Washington, DC: Pew Internet & American Life Project. Retrieved June 1, 2006 from http://www.pewinternet.org/pdfs/PIP_Teens_Tech_July2005web.pdf

Linn, S. (2004). *Consuming Kids: The hostile takeover of childhood*. New York: New Press.

Lippi-Green, R. (1997). *English with an accent*. New York: Routledge.

Li-Vollmer, M. (2002). Race representation in child-targeted television commercials. *Mass Communication and Society*, 5, 207–28.

Louis, B. (2005, June 28). R. J. Reynolds launches new ad campaign for Kool cigarettes. *Winston–Salem Journal*. Retrieved November 7, 2005 from Lexis-Nexis database.

M&M's get mega-sized. (2005, August 4). CNNMoney.com. Retrieved June 27, 2006 from http://money.cnn.com/2005/08/04/news/funny/m_and_ms/index.htm

Macdonald, M. (2003). *Exploring media discourse*. London: Arnold.

Machin, D. & Thornborrow, J. (2003). Branding and discourse: The case of *Cosmopolitan. Discourse and Society*, 14, 453–71.

Madden, M. (2006). Internet penetration and impact. PEW Internet & American Life Project. Retrieved June 1, 2006, from http://www.pewinternet.org/pdfs/PIP_Internet_Impact.pdf

Maines, D. R. (1999). Information pools and racialized narrative structures. *Sociological Quarterly*, 40, 317–26.

Mamos, R. & Saw, N. (2002). Nissan's new SHIFT: Interview with Steve Wilhite-VP, Marketing Nissan NA. *Fresh Alloy*, interviews. Retrieved June 12, 2006 from http://www.freshalloy.com/site/feature/interviews.wilhite/001/home.shtml

Mastro, D. E. & Stern, S. R. (2003). Representations of race in television commercials: A content analysis of prime-time advertising. *Journal of Broadcasting and Electronic Media*, 47, 638–47.

Mazzarella, W. (2003). Critical publicity/public criticism: Reflections on fieldwork in the Bombay ad world. In T. D. Malefyt & B. Moeran (eds), *Advertising cultures*, pp. 55–74. Oxford/New York: Berg.

McGrath, C. (2005, June 8). In fiction, a long history of fixation on the social gap. *New York Times*. Retrieved December 12, 2006 from Lexis-Nexis database.

McMains, A. (2006, January 3). Infiniti's 30-minute spot. *ADWEEK Online*. Retrieved May 8, 2007 from Thomson Gale, Clark University.

McQuarrie, E. F. & Mick, D. G. (1996). Figures of rhetoric in advertising language. *Journal of Consumer Research*, 22, 424–38.

McQuarrie, E. F. & Mick, D. G. (1999). Visual rhetoric in advertising: Text-interpretive, experimental, and reader-response analyses. *Journal of Consumer Research*, 26, 37–54.

McQuarrie, E. F. & Mick, D. G. (2003). Visual and verbal rhetorical figures under directed processing versus incidental exposure to advertising. *Journal of Consumer Research*, 29, 579–87.

McShane, M. J. (2005). *A theory of ellipsis*. New York: Oxford University Press.

Mead, R. (2000, 13 November). You've got blog. *New Yorker*, 76 (34), pp. 102ff.

Mehan, H. & Wood, H. (1997). Five features of reality. In J. O'Brien & P. Kollock (eds), *The production of reality* 2nd edn, pp. 379–95. Thousand Oaks, CA: Pine Forge Press.

Milkie, M. A. (1999). Social comparison, reflected appraisals, and mass media: The impact of pervasive beauty images on Black and White girls' self-concepts. *Social Psychology Quarterly*, 62, 190–210.

Mintel. (2006, April 12). Teen spending estimated to top $190 billion by 2006. Retrieved February 9, 2007 from http://www.marketresearchworld.net

Morrison. T. (1992). *Playing in the dark*. Cambridge, MA: Harvard University Press.

MSNBC. (2007, January 30). US Savings rate hits lowest level since 1933. Retrieved February 3, 2007 from http://www.msnbc.msn.com/id/11098797/

Murfin, R. & Ray, S. M. (2003). *Bedford glossary of critical and literary terms* (2nd edn). Boston: Bedford/St Martin's.

National Household Survey on Drug Abuse. (2003). Cigarette brand preferences. Retrieved January 28, 2005 from http://www.drugabusestatistics.samhsa.gov/2k3/cigBrands/cigBrands.htm

Neary, L. (2007, May 8). On Madison Avenue, old players learn a new game. *All Things Considered* (radio broadcast). National Public Radio. Retrieved audio and print version, May 9, 2007 from http://www.npr.org/templates/story/story.php?storyId=10061997

Neff, J. (2006, May 29). Move over Trump, here comes the Brawny Man. *Advertising Age*, 77 *(22)*, p. 3. Retrieved May 2, 2007 from Lexis-Nexis database.

Nissan takes "Shift" campaign wireless. (September 15, 2003). *iMedia Connection*. Retrieved June 21, 2006 from http://imediaconnection.com

Paek, H. J. & Shah, H. (2003). Racial ideology, model minorities, and the "not-so-silent partner": Stereotyping of Asian Americans in US magazine advertising. *Howard Journal of Communications*, *14*, 225–43.

Palmer's. (n.d.) Skin Success FAQ. Palmer's Skin Care. Retrieved November 29, 2006 from http://www.etbrowne.com/about/skinsuccess_faq.aspx

Peiss, K. L. (1998). *Hope in a Jar: The making of America's beauty culture*. New York: Henry Holt.

Pierce, J. P. & Gilpin, E. A. (2004). How did the Master Settlement Agreement change tobacco industry expenditures for cigarette advertising and promotions? [Electronic version]. *Health Promotion Practice*, *5*, 84–90.

Polito, J. R. (2005, June 15). The New Jazz Philosophy Tour 2005. Retrieved November 7, 2005 from http://whyquit.com/pr/061505.html

Pollay, R. W., Lee, J. S. & Carter-Whitney, D. C. (1992). Separate, but not equal: Racial segmentation in cigarette advertising. *Journal of Advertising*, *21*, 45–57.

Pots of promise—The beauty business. (2003, May 24). *The Economist*, 367.8325. Retrieved August 5, 2006 from Expanded Academic ASAP.

Preston, E. & White, C. (2004). Commodifying kids: Branded identities and the selling of adspace on kids' networks. *Communication Quarterly*, *52*, 115–28.

Rainie, L. (2006, March 23). Life online: Teens and technology and the world to come. Speech to annual conference of Public Library Association, Boston, Massachusetts. Retrieved June 1, 2006 from http://www.pewinternet.org/ppt/Teens%20and%20technology.pdf

Rainie, L. & Horrigan, J. (2005). A decade of adoption: How the internet has woven itself into American life. In *Trends 2005* pp. 56–69. Washington, DC: Pew Research Center Project. Retrieved June 8, 2006 from http://www.pewinternet.org/PPF/r/148/report_display.asp

Rainie, L. & Keeter, S. (2006, April). Pew Internet Project Data Memo on Cell phone use. Retrieved June 7, 2006 from http://www.pewinternet.org/PPF/r/179/report_display.asp

Reed. J. (2006, September). The HD face. *Vogue*, 587–8, 746–7.

Reynolds American Ind. (n.d.) Retrieved February 18, 2005 from http://www.reynoldsamerican.com/Who/whoweare_cover.asp

Richards, B., MacRury, I. & Botterill, J. (2000). *The dynamics of advertising*. Newark, NJ: Harwood Academic Publishers.

Rickford, J. R. & Rickford, R. J. (2000). *Spoken soul: The story of Black English*. New York: John Wiley and Sons.

Rideout, V., Roberts, D. F. & Foehr, U. G. (2005, March). Generation M: Media in the lives of 8–18 year-olds. Kaiser Family Foundation. Retrieved June 7, 2006 from http://www.kff.org/entmedia/entmedia030905pkg.cfm

Rodriquez, J. (2006). Color-blind ideology and the cultural appropriation of hip-hop. *Journal of Contemporary Ethnography*, *35*, 645–68.

Salem launches "Stir the Senses" campaign [Electronic version]. (2003, August). *Tobacco Retailer*, *6 (4)*, 16.

Schillinger, L. (2005, December 22). Smart enough to understand your moisturizer? *New York Times*, p. G3. Retrieved July 18, 2006 from Lexis-Nexis database.

Schwartz, R. A. (2006). Cosmeceuticals. *eMedicine*. Retrieved July 17, 2006 from http://www.emedicine.com/derm/topic509.htm

Scott, L. M. & Batra, R. (eds). (2003). *Persuasive imagery: A consumer response perspective*. Thousand Oaks, CA: Sage.

Seiter, E. (1990). Different children, different dreams: Racial representation in advertising. *Journal of Communication Inquiry*, *14*, 31–47.

Simpson, M. (2003, June 28). Beckham, the virus. *Salon.com*. Retrieved May 18, 2007 from http://archive.salon.com/mwt/feature/2003/06/28/beckham/print.html

Slade, J. (1999). Trust? No—verify [Electronic version]. *Tobacco Control*, *8*, 240–1.

Smith, S. (2007, January 18). Nicotine boost was deliberate, study says. *Boston Globe*, p. 1A.

Smith, T. (2005). Pumping irony: The construction of masculinity in a post-feminist advertising campaign. *Advertising and Society Review*, *6 (3)*, article E-ISSN 1154–7311. Retrieved August 25, 2006 from Project MUSE.

Smitherman, G. (1994). *Black talk: Words and phrases from the Hood to the Amen Corner*. Boston: Houghton Mifflin.

Solman, G. (2006, June 15). Nissan "Shifts" perspective. *AdWeek.com*. Retrieved June 21, 2006 from http://adweek.com/aw/creative/article_display.jsp?vnu –content –id =1002689052

State cigarette excise tax rates and rankings. (2004, November 3). Campaign for Tobacco-Free Kids. Retrieved February 18, 2005 from www.tobaccofreekids.org/research/factsheets/pdf/0097/pdf

Stern, B. B. (1991). Who talks advertising? Literary theory and narrative "point of view." [Electronic version.] *Journal of Advertising*, *20*, 9–23.

Sutton, C. D. & Robinson, R. G. (2004). The marketing of menthol cigarettes in the United States: Populations, messages, and channels. *Nicotine and Tobacco Research*, *6 (Supplement 1)*, S83–S91.

Sutton, D. H. (2004). *Globalizing Modern Beauty: The Women's Editorial Department at the J. Walter Thompson Advertising Company, 1910–1945*. Unpublished doctoral dissertation, Clark University.

Taylor, C. & Stern, B. (1997). Asian-Americans: Television advertising and the "model minority" stereotype. *Journal of Advertising*, *26*, 47–61.

Taylor, S. C. (2003). *Brown skin*. New York: Amistad.

Taylor, S. C. (2004). WedMD. Skin, hair care for women of color. Retrieved

January 2, 2007 from http://onhealth.webmd.com/script/main/art.asp?articlekey =56867

Tucker, L. (1998). The framing of Calvin Klein: A Frame analysis of media discourse about the August 1995 Calvin Klein jeans advertising campaign. *Critical Studies in Mass Communication*, *15*, 141–57.

Twitchell, J. B. (2003). Adcult and gender. In T. Reichert and L. Lambaise (eds), *Sex in Advertising: Perspectives on the erotic appeal* (pp. 181–93). Mahwah, NJ: Lawrence Erlbaum.

Underscore: Facts and details from Encyclopedia Topic. (n.d.) Retrieved June 12, 2006 from http://www.absoluteastronomy.com/u/underscore

Urban Legends Reference Pages. (2000, October 2). Retrieved August 1, 2006 from http://www.snopes.com/movies/actors/mmdress.htm

US Census Bureau. (2001). Race alone or in combination, for states, Puerto Rico, and places of 100,000 or more population: 2000. Retrieved March 7, 2005 from http://www.census.gov/population/cen2000/phc-t6/table06.xls

US Census Bureau. (2003). State population estimates-characteristics July 1, 2002. Retrieved September 28, 2003 from http://eire.census.gov/popest/data/states/ST-EST2002-ASRO-04.php

US Census Bureau. (2006). National sex, age, race and Hispanic origin. Retrieved February 6, 2006 from http://www.census.gov/popest/national/asrh/NC-EST2005-asrh.html

US Census Bureau News. (2006, August 29). Income climbs, poverty stabilizes, uninsured rates increase. Retrieved May 19, 2007 from http://www.census.gov/Press-Release/www/releases/archives/income_wealth/007419.html

Watts, E. K. (1997). An exploration of spectacular consumption: Gangsta rap as cultural commodity. *Communication Studies*, *48*, 42–58.

Watts, E. K. & Orbe, M. P. (2002). The spectacular consumption of "true" African American culture: "Whassup" with the Budweiser guys? *Critical Studies in Media Communication*, *19*, 1–20.

Webster's New Millennium Dictionary of English. (2003–2005). Lexico Publishing Group.

Wetherell, M. & Potter, J. (1992). *Mapping the language of racism: Discourse and the legitimation of exploitation*. New York: Harvester Wheatsheaf.

West, C. & Fenstermaker, S. (1995). Doing difference. *Gender and Society*, *9*, 8–37.

West, C. & Zimmerman, D. (1987). Doing gender. *Gender and Society*, *1*, 125–51.

Who's winning among African American consumers?, asks strategic vision. (2005, December 19). *Business Wire*, Thompson Gale Doc. No. A140454796. Retrieved May 8, 2007 from http://findarticles.com/p/articles/mi_m0EIN/is_2005_Dec_19/ai_n15953932

Wilke, M. (2005, March 31). Cosmetic companies compete for gay shelves. *Commercial Closet*. Retrieved August 2, 2006 from http://www.thegully.com/essays/gay_mundo2/wilke/050330_gay_ads_cosmetics.html

Williamson, J. (1978). *Decoding advertisements: Ideology and meaning in advertising*. New York: Marion Boyars.

Wilson, J. J. (1999, March). Summary of the attorneys general master tobacco settlement agreement. National Conference of State Legislators. Retrieved January 2005 from http://academic.udayton.edu/health/syllabi/tobacco/summary.htm

Wolf, N. (1991). *The beauty myth*. New York: Anchor Books.

Yousman, B. (2003). Blackophilia and blackophobia: White youth, the consumption of rap music, and white supremacy. *Communication Theory*, *13*, 366–91.

Index